The Sense of Community
in French Caribbean Fiction

T0312570

Contemporary French and Francophone Cultures 10

Contemporary French and Francophone Cultures

Series Editors

EDMUND SMYTH
Manchester Metropolitan University

CHARLES FORSDICK
University of Liverpool

Editorial Board

LYNN A. HIGGINS
Dartmouth College

MIREILLE ROSELLO
University of Amsterdam

MICHAEL SHERINGHAM
University of Oxford

DAVID WALKER
University of Sheffield

This series aims to provide a forum for new research on modern and contemporary French and francophone cultures and writing. The books published in *Contemporary French and Francophone Cultures* reflect a wide variety of critical practices and theoretical approaches, in harmony with the intellectual, cultural and social developments which have taken place over the past few decades. All manifestations of contemporary French and francophone culture and expression are considered, including literature, cinema, popular culture, theory. The volumes in the series will participate in the wider debate on key aspects of contemporary culture.

CELIA BRITTON

The Sense of Community in French Caribbean Fiction

LIVERPOOL UNIVERSITY PRESS

First published 2008 by
Liverpool University Press
4 Cambridge Street
Liverpool L69 7ZU

This paperback edition published 2010

British Library Cataloguing-in-Publication data
A British Library CIP record is available

ISBN 978-1-84631-137-6 cased
978-1-84631-500-8 limp

Typeset by XL Publishing Services, Tiverton
Printed and bound in the UK by Marston Digital

Contents

Acknowledgements

A shorter version of Chapter 1 of this book originally appeared in 2006 as an article in *Research in African Literatures*, and I am most grateful to the editors for granting me permission to reuse it here. I would also like to express my gratitude to the British Academy for funding a research visit to the Bobst Library at New York University.

I would especially like to thank Charles Forsdick, Leslie Hill, Nick Nesbitt and Mervyn Poley for their extremely helpful suggestions and comments on the manuscript; Anthony Cond for being such an efficient and encouraging editor; and Lyle Conquest for providing moral support throughout.

Abbreviations

Works by Jean-Luc Nancy are referred to using the following abbreviations (full publication details are given in the Bibliography):

BSP   *Being Singular Plural*
IC   *The Inoperative Community*
SW   *The Sense of the World*

Introduction

The Caribbean's history of transportation, slavery and migration has created a situation in which the question of community becomes particularly urgent. The islands' societies are the pure product of colonization, which eliminated most of their indigenous inhabitants and transported millions of Africans to work on the plantations in conditions that obliterated most of their traditional social structures and practices. In these violently dislocated populations, there could be no 'natural' sense of community evolving peacefully over the years; rather, the *problem* of community, conceived both in terms of collective practices and institutions and on the subjective level of collective identity, generates a deep-seated anxiety in the French Caribbean.[1] This book will examine representations of community in seven novels from the region: one from Haiti, three from Martinique and three from Guadeloupe. My project is to interrogate the *sense* of community expressed in these novels – in the double 'sense' of both a *feeling* of belonging to a community and the various *meanings* that the concept of community acquires.

The confrontations between colonizers and colonized have meant that race has been from the start a basic structuring principle of Caribbean society; black communities fought to assert themselves in the face of white racism, and therefore came to define themselves also along these lines. But the situation was complicated by two factors. In the first place, the economic and cultural dominance of the European colonial powers, and later also the United States, created a countervailing desire to become part of, rather than oppose, white society. This was particularly true of France, whose policy of 'assimilation' ('une des formes les plus pernicieuses de colonisation'[2]) was designed to ensure the replication and internalization of French cultural norms throughout its colonies – and even more true of those French ex-colonies such as Martinique and Guadeloupe whose status since 1946 as 'Départements d'Outre Mer' (DOMs) has, at least in theory, incorporated them more closely into France itself – resulting in the psychological denials and splitting that Fanon analyses in *Peau noire, masques blancs*.[3] The more recent massive growth of tourism in Martinique and Guadeloupe has introduced a different kind of relationship with white people, although it often produces similar tensions; and the establishment of large communities of Antilleans in metropolitan France (so much so that Paris is now sometimes referred to as the 'troisième île') has made the question of defining 'the French Caribbean community' far more problematic.[4] The situation of Haiti is very different: an independent republic since 1804, it has been much less influenced by France, and its successive occupations by the United States have produced a far more unambiguous hostility than French assimilationism in the DOMs. Nevertheless there was considerable cultural contact between Haiti and both metropolitan France and the DOMs before the Duvalier regimes from the 1950s to the 1980s; and migration from Haiti, in the form of political exiles as well as economic migrants, has had a comparable effect to that in Martinique and Guadeloupe.

Secondly, the islands' populations were never simply made up of two opposed racial groups: those of European and of African descent. There were always some surviving Native Americans, and the mulattoes became a distinct and powerful group as early as the eighteenth century. From the abolition of slavery onwards, large groups of indentured labourers from India and traders from the Middle East settled in Martinique and Guadeloupe, and the question of whether these different ethnicities each form their own community within the island, or whether they have merged together into a common Martinican or Guadeloupean community, has complicated the debate. Broadly speaking, earlier representations promote the importance of black unity in the struggle against colonialism and racism, whereas more recent ones emphasize and celebrate the islands' multiracial diversity. (The concept of diversity in itself of course attacks racism, but with different implications for the community's representation of itself.)

But, beyond these different emphases, it has generally been assumed that community cannot be taken for granted; it must be consciously constructed as a political act or consciously preserved and protected from the homogenizing forces of globalization. In this perspective, the subjective dimension – the importance attached to *feeling* that one belongs to a community – is very prominent. For instance, Edouard Glissant, in his article 'Structures et tensions de groupe' (*Discours*, pp. 86–93), argues that all political and economic progress in Martinique depends upon its people developing a stronger sense of relatedness to their surroundings and, hence, a consciousness of themselves as a community:

> Ce caractère ambigu, double et trouble, de la conscience collective explique comment les structures ne sont souvent contestées qu'avec passivité, dans le traumatisme et le déséquilibre. La non-responsabilité, qui entraîne ici à l'ir-

responsabilité; l'absence du sentiment de solidarité sociale [...]; la propension, d'ailleurs encouragée, à la mendicité sociale organisée: ce sont là quelques-uns des accompagnements négatifs du refus de vivre la structure sociale comme une donnée pertinente. (p. 90)

Glissant stresses here his conviction that 'l'indispensable équipement du pays resterait lettre morte s'il n'était pensé d'abord par la communauté s'arrachant de son traumatisme et *naissant à sa propre conscience*' (p. 93, my italics). One could argue that this is in fact the major task that French Caribbean intellectuals have set themselves. The main cultural and political movements that have brought together writers, artists and politicians since the Second World War have all revolved around the issue of consciously creating a sense of community, and, while Glissant himself is cautious in this regard, this has often been interpreted in *identitarian* terms. The negritude movement, led in Martinique by Aimé Césaire, sought to create a common identity of 'blackness' in which Caribbeans would unite with Africans; Glissant's 'antillanité' aimed to overcome language barriers to foster a sense of unity between all the islands of the Caribbean; and the 'créolité' movement led by Patrick Chamoiseau, Raphaël Confiant and Jean Bernabé articulated a collective identity based on multiracialism and emblematized in the 'mixité' of the creole language.[5]

Literature plays a particularly important role in this creation of community; all the authors discussed in this book feel that it is their duty *as writers* to contribute to the process. Maryse Condé, for instance, argues that 'la littérature antillaise s'est toujours voulue l'expression d'une communauté. Ecrire se veut un acte collectif'; and sees it as the duty of Antillean writers to help the people recover their own capacity to express themselves.[6] Simone Schwarz-Bart describes her motives for writing *Pluie et vent sur Télumée Miracle* as: 'pour moi, le fait d'avoir écrit ça, c'était déjà un acte politique. Il fallait [...] que nous nous retrouvions... Il fallait quelque chose qui ferait que chacun se retrouve au lieu de faire des dissensions'.[7] Glissant writes: 'La parole de l'artiste antillais ne provient donc pas de l'obsession de chanter son être intime; cet intime est inséparable du devenir de la communauté' (*Discours*, p. 439). For Daniel Maximin, the writer's link to the community involves preserving and incorporating its oral culture: 'le désir principal est de retrouver le "nous", de retrouver des paroles antérieures qui ont déjà été dites, et pas seulement par des écrivains. J'essaie de rechercher ce que les peuples ont pu exprimer dans l'oralité'.[8] Jacques Roumain and Vincent Placoly saw their writing as inseparable from their political activity; and Chamoiseau reinvents the figure of the writer as a mere scribe recording and preserving the words of the community.[9]

* * *

Community is thus a central and problematic issue in French Caribbean literature. The concept of community, however, is itself problematic. Its connotations are usually conservative; it is used as an apolitical alternative to other terms such as 'class', 'interest group' or 'movement'. It often acquires moralistic overtones ('service to the community', 'a pillar of the community', etc.). It is contrasted with 'society' in so far as the latter is seen as impersonal and alienated, whereas 'community' implies a lack of alienation, a group bonded by the relationships between its individual members and which generates a feeling of togetherness and belonging: the individual members of the community *identify* with it and with each other. The disadvantage of this is that it is necessarily based on a defensive attitude towards whatever is perceived as outside its boundaries: the 'local community' is summoned into existence when it is a question of opposing some external threat, whether this is the building of a new motorway or providing housing for asylum seekers, for instance. Community, in other words, is founded on exclusion and always requires a certain homogeneity of its members. It is not a purely neutral designation of groups of people who happen to live in the same place or have something else in common, but rather an ideological construct which signifies a rejection of large-scale industrial society, a nostalgia for social units that are small and stable enough for everyone in them to know each other, a virtuous sense of mutual responsibility, an ideal of homogeneous identity and a negative attitude towards social difference.

Nevertheless, we do *need* a term for 'people who happen to live in the same place or have something else in common'; the relationships we have within these groups are important, and different both from those that connect us to society as a whole and from those we have with close family and friends. And there is no obvious substitute for 'community'. Rather than reject the term altogether, therefore, we need to rework it in a way which resists its traditional connotations of homogeneity and closure; which recognizes that the equation of community with collective identity is neither the only nor necessarily the best way to conceive of it; and which focuses simply on the diverse ways in which we are actually implicated in our day-to-day relations with the people with whom we come into contact.

Fictional representations of community, however, involve more than simple description of such supposedly empirical relations. With varying degrees of explicitness, novels propose their own *models* of community;

and while some of these are fairly traditional, others offer a radically different conception. The chapters of this book are ordered chronologically, from Jacques Roumain's *Gouverneurs de la rosée* in 1946 to Maryse Condé's *Desirada* in 1997, and to some extent this progression enacts a move away from the 'closed' towards a newer sense of an 'open' community.[10] This can be seen as reflecting the historical shift over this fifty-year period from anti-colonial struggle to more recent concerns with ethnic diversity and migration. Up until the 1960s, the question of community in Caribbean societies was mainly seen in the context of political campaigns for national independence – or, in the case of Haiti, for equality for the black population and resistance to American domination. Therefore, *unity* was a central goal, and communities defined themselves in opposition to their enemies: they needed to have boundaries and conscious common aims. Equally, both individuals and communities needed to think of themselves as autonomous, sovereign subjects capable of uniting in political action. This overtly political conception of unity is significantly different from the conservative, taken-for-granted homogeneity associated with the traditional sense of community in Europe and North America; it is a militant and strategic response to a situation of oppression which can only be overturned by organized collective action, which in turn is predicated on a strong sense of unity and solidarity. To disapprove of such a 'closed' community would be in effect to condemn it to continued oppression. At the same time, however, it is not the only possible way of conceiving of political resistance in all situations, as a comparison of, for instance, *Gouverneurs de la rosée* or Glissant's *Le Quatrième Siècle* with Placoly's *L'Eau-de-mort guildive* demonstrates.[11] In general terms, the type of community represented or envisaged in these texts moves from the anti-colonial imperative of building a cohesive national identity towards the more recent, less militant view of community as a looser, more open-ended grouping of diverse people. But it is far from being a consistent progression: *L'Eau-de-mort guildive* (1973) is, I argue, less freighted with concern for identity and origin than Chamoiseau's *Texaco* (1992).[12]

It would also be an over-simplification to suggest that these communities can simply be evaluated on a scale going from closed to open, because the question of community is also inseparable from a range of other issues. For instance, the question of political agency and the possibility of bringing about social change through collective action is bound up with the concept of leadership: whether or not the community is led by an individual who motivates and organizes its actions determines the type of resistance that is possible. Leadership is in turn just one of the possible relationships between individual and community; more generally, the way in which individual subjectivity is characterized depends to a significant degree on the extent to which, and the way in which, the community regards itself as a collective subject (and vice versa).

The conceptualization of community also, however, has an important *temporal* dimension. The emphasis on the active construction of community might lead one to expect a parallel stress on the future – that these newly formed communities would be defined in terms of their goals rather than their antecedents. In fact, however, the *past* often seems to be more dominant. In a general sense this is explicable simply in terms of the extremes of historical oppression to which the Caribbean has been subjected: history still weighs heavily on the present. But different conceptions of community also make different use of the past. For some, it signifies Africa and the attempt to preserve or recover the original cultural traditions of the transported Africans as a means of countering colonial domination: as for instance the 'coumbite' in Roumain's *Gouverneurs de la rosée*, the figure of the 'quimboiseur' in Glissant's *Le Quatrième Siècle* and that of the 'Mentô' in Chamoiseau's *Texaco*. Alternatively, the desire to recover the past is sometimes a response to the scarcity of available historical information concerning the period of slavery, in which the slaves' lives went largely unrecorded; this is another major theme in Glissant's work.[13] Literature, in other words, can fill the gap left by historiography and so compensate for the feeling of rootlessness experienced by many of the slaves' descendants – also an important factor in Simone Schwarz-Bart's representation of ancestry in *Pluie et vent sur Télumée Miracle*. In a slightly different way, looking back to the past is also a defence against the gradual disappearance of a distinctive traditional French Caribbean culture, now eroded by increased contact with Europe and the United States and by the mass media and globalization in general; the appeal to folklore and the supernatural, the use of traditional creole proverbs, and so on, are prominent features here, as in *Texaco* and *Pluie et vent sur Télumée Miracle*, and to a lesser extent in Daniel Maximin's *L'Ile et une nuit*.[14]

And, finally, the literary representation of community also has repercussions on literary form itself. The seven novels that will be analysed here reveal a correlation between a tightly knit, purposeful community and a linear narrative that ends in definitive resolution, and, conversely, between a dispersed or heterogeneous community and a narrative structure that avoids linearity and closure. Equally, narrative point of view can be assigned to one individual throughout, or the community's diversity can be foregrounded by the use of multiple points of view; and the writer's relationship to the community, to which he or she may or may not belong fully, is also embodied in the narrative perspective. The use of imagery can link the human community to the natural world or express its alienation; the incorporation of creole words and phrases into dialogue and/or narrative discourse signifies a particular stance in relation to the specificity of Antillean culture; and dialogue can be used didactically to convey a political message, or to characterize individuals, or to illustrate the oral fluency of creole culture.

* * *

In discussing these seven novels I shall be drawing on the writings of the French philosopher Jean-Luc Nancy. Nancy is one of a number of contemporary figures working on the question of community; he can be situated in the phenomenological, anti-metaphysical strand of French philosophy and is greatly influenced by Jacques Derrida.[15] Heidegger is an important point of reference in his work, as is Rousseau and, in more antagonistic fashion, Lacan; and his writing also engages with Georges Bataille and Maurice Blanchot. What emerges from all these philosophical dialogues is a radical re-thinking of the notion of community. Its frame of reference is largely European, with the long historical time-scale that that implies; but I hope to demonstrate that, potentially, it has much to offer for an understanding of the much newer postcolonial societies of the Caribbean. Despite the historical specificity of these societies, founded on the violence of transportation and slavery, the problems of migration, racism, hybridity and globalization that have come to be perhaps their dominant characteristics are, after all, very significant in present-day Europe too; and Marxism and Christianity, which are central concerns in Nancy's work, have played an equally major if somewhat different role in the cultural and political history of the Caribbean. In the final section of this introduction, therefore, I shall give a brief outline of the main ideas in Nancy's theorization of community that I shall be referring to in connection with particular novels in subsequent chapters.

Nancy's starting point is the widespread contemporary perception that we have lost our 'sense of community' and are left only with individual existences, atomistic and alienated, in an impersonal, conflict-ridden society. But rather than simply lament this condition, or attempt to re-create the kind of community and community feeling that we believe existed in the past, Nancy argues that we need to find a new way of thinking about 'community' that accounts for the ways in which we do in fact still co-exist and relate to each other:

> At this end point [of community], this limit where we are, there remains in spite of everything – and it shows therefore – that *we* are there. The era of the limit abandons us together on the limit, for if not, it would not be an 'era' or a 'limit', and 'we' would not be there. If we suppose that there was before (or elsewhere) something else, we can say that there remains this remainder of community that we are *in* common.[16]

The notion of *being-in-common* is the basis for this reconceptualization of community, and Nancy's first claim for it is that it is indeed basic. That is, the error underlying our conventional idea of community is that we tend to think of it as a secondary attribute of individual being – in other words, individuals exist, and they may or may not form a community. The individual subject has always been the basis of Western philosophy: in his introduction to a collection of essays on Nancy's work entitled *Community at Loose Ends*, Georges van den Abbeele argues that our intellectual disciplines have 'attempted to explain the world by extrapolating its existences outward from the inner workings of a subject' (p. ix). If this 'self-generating' (p. ix) individual subject is taken as the primary form of existence, then community is indeed something that it could have 'lost'. But Nancy's insight is to reverse the terms of the relation, and to argue that our fundamental condition is to exist *in common*: 'the existence of being-in-common [...] gives rise to the existence of being-self'.[17] He goes on:

> This presupposes that we are brought into the world, each and every one of us, according to a dimension of 'in-common' that is in no way 'added onto' the dimension of 'being-self', but that is rather co-originary and coextensive with it. But this does not mean that the 'common' is a substance uniformly laid out 'under' supposed individuals, nor is it uniformly shared out among everyone like a particular ingredient. No: this means that the mode of existence and appropriation of a 'self' (which is not necessarily, nor exclusively, an individual) is the mode of an exposition in common and to the in-common, and that this exposition exposes the self even in its 'in itself', in its 'ipseity', and in its own distinctiveness, in its isolation or in its solitude. Only a being-in-common can make possible a being-separated. (IC, p. xxxvii)

Being-in-common – or its variants, 'being-with' or 'being-with-one-another' – is thus not an attribute, a property or a possession, but the very matrix of our existence. It defines our relations with each other in terms of 'sharing', 'exposition' and 'compearance'. But, before exploring these concepts, it is important to emphasize the difference between being-in-common and the traditional notion of community that we feel we have 'lost', but which Nancy insists has never actually existed except in the form of political or religious ideologies and nostalgic fantasies.[18]

This traditional ideal of community is organic, homogeneous, self-conscious, and provides a strong collective identity for its members:

> Always it is a matter of a lost age in which community was woven of tight, harmonious, and infrangible bonds and in which above all it played back to itself, through its institutions, its rituals, and its symbols, the representation, indeed the living offering, of its own immanent unity, intimacy, and autonomy. [...] community is not only intimate communication between its members, but also its organic communion with its own essence [...] it is made up principally of the sharing, diffusion, or impregnation of an identity by a plurality wherein each member identifies himself only through the supplementary mediation of his identification with the living body of the community. (IC, p. 9)

It is, in other words, characterized by a fusional unity in which all its members identify with the community as collective subject, and this identification is continually reinforced by cultural forms which reflect back to the members images of their unity. Nancy often refers to it as 'immanent community': this is not simply to contrast immanence with transcendence, but to convey the sense of a reflective or closed immanence that, to quote B. C. Hutchens's helpful distinction, 'involves *closure* of the terms of any relation and *reduction* of the plural singularities of beings to a general or universal foundation' and 'creates *symbolic figures* of immanence (mythic, communal, political, etc.)'.[19] Nancy's other term for immanent community is *common being*, which he systematically contrasts with being-*in*-common. Unity implies closure – common being is 'a matter of a single community, of its essence, closure and sovereignty'[20] – and this is the opposite of the real nature of community as being-in-common, that is, as 'existence inasmuch as it is *in* common, but without letting itself be absorbed into a common substance. Being *in* common has nothing to do with communion, with fusion into a body, into a unique and ultimate identity' (IC, p. xxxviii).

Being-in-common 'excludes interior unity, subsistence, and presence in and for itself. Being with, being together and even being "united" are precisely not a matter of being "one"'(BSP, p. 154). Rather, the community of being-in-common consists in the *relations* between 'singular beings'. Just as being-in-common is defined in opposition to common being, so singular beings are fundamentally differentiated from 'individuals': the individual is a full, immanent, self-sufficient subject, whereas singular beings exist only through their relatedness to other singular beings: 'The concept of the singular implies its singularization and, therefore, its distinction from other singularities (which is different from any concept of the individual, since an immanent totality, without an other, would be a perfect individual' (BSP, p. 32). Therefore, the singular is necessarily also always plural; Nancy continues: 'The singular is primarily *each* one and, therefore, also *with* and *among* all the others. The singular is a plural' (BSP, p. 32). 'Being-singular-plural' thus reiterates the emphasis of being-in-common on a primary ontological plurality: 'essence itself' is 'in the hyphenation – "being-singular-plural" – which is a mark of union and also a mark of division' (BSP, p. 37). This plurality and relationality are quite different from the fusional unity of common being; what links the singular beings is not a common *identity*, but purely the open structure of singularity itself: 'The togetherness of singulars is singularity "itself". It "assembles" them insofar as it spaces them; they are "linked" insofar as they are not unified' (BSP, p. 33). They are not, in other words, linked by any common characteristics, interests or aims; unlike the conventional conception of community ('the Protestant community', 'the Asian community', 'the business community', etc.), being-in-common carries no presumption of homogeneity and involves no concern with identity. More specifically, the relations between singular beings take the form of a distribution and spacing which Nancy calls 'sharing' (*partage*), which involves separation as much as linking together; sharing happens

> between singular existences that are not subjects and whose relation – the sharing itself – is not a communion, nor the appropriation of an object, nor a self-recognition, nor even a communication as this is understood to exist between subjects. But these singular beings are themselves constituted by sharing, they are distributed and placed, or rather *spaced*, by the sharing that makes them *others*. (IC, p. 25)

Thus 'the modern experience of community' is 'space itself, and the spacing of the experience of the outside, of the outside-of-self' (IC, p. 19).

Sharing and spacing imply also that the singular being, unlike the individual, is not structured according to an opposition between 'inside' (equalling 'self') and 'outside' (equalling 'other'). Being is not a matter of interiority: it is to be *exposed* to the outside, and the singular being is aware of itself only through this 'exposition':

> 'To be exposed' means to be 'posed' in exteriority, according to an exteriority, having to do with an outside *in the very intimacy* of an inside [...] having access [...] to the proper of *one's own* existence, only through an 'expropriation' whose exemplary reality is that of 'my' face always exposed to others, always turned toward an other and faced by him or her, never facing myself. (IC, pp. xxxvii–xxxviii)

'Exposition' therefore annuls the distinction between 'outside' and 'inside': 'To be exposed is to be on the limit where, at the same time, there is both inside and outside, and neither inside nor outside'.[21] Thus whereas we are accustomed to think of our closest relationships as abolishing the 'outside' between two 'insides' through fusion or identification, exposition situates them as happening in the 'spaces' or on the 'surfaces' or 'limits' between people – but as nevertheless *constituting* the self: 'There is an extensive/intensive dynamic of the surfaces of exposition. These surfaces are the limits upon which the self declines *itself*. They partition and share being and existence.'[22]

But if, as singular plural beings, we have no option but to relate to one another, then clearly this very basic level of relatedness is far more general than that which we normally mean by 'a relationship'. In 'Of Being-in-Common', for instance, Nancy gives the example of people sitting in the same compartment of a train (p. 7). Elsewhere he defines it as the minimal level of 'curiosity' that singular beings inevitably arouse in each other, which 'falls short of a confrontation of subjects as well as of a communal idyll, falls short of both benevolence and malevolence. It can open up fear and desire, love and hate, pity or terror.'[23] He uses the term *comparution* (usually translated as 'compearance' or 'co-appearance': the French word means to 'appear' before a court) for this primary form of relationality which is both inevitable and contentless in its generality:

> Being *in* common means that singular beings are, present themselves, and appear only to the extent that they compear (*comparaissent*), to the extent that they are exposed, presented, or offered to one another. This compearance (*comparution*) is not something added on to their being; rather, their being comes into being in it. (IC, p. 58)

Compearance thus contests the classic (and also Lacanian) opposition between Self and Other as a fundamental structure of subjectivity, because 'Others "in general" are neither the Same nor the Other. They are one-another, or of-one-another, a primordial plurality that co-appears' (BSP, p. 67).

Nancy's earliest major work on community is entitled *La communauté désœuvrée*, translated as *The Inoperative Community*. But a better translation of 'désœuvrée' – a term which Nancy takes from Maurice Blanchot – would perhaps be 'workless' or 'unworked'. The notions of the work (*œuvre*, as in 'work of art', rather than labour) and of worklessness or unworking are central to this text's treatment of the distinction between common being and being-in-common. The traditional ideal of community, expressed for instance in political programmes or religious prescriptions, 'works' at being a community; communism, for example, is dominated by 'the goal of achieving a community of beings producing in essence their own essence as their work, and furthermore producing precisely this essence *as community*' (IC, p. 2). Community as a 'work' presupposes that it is the result of the actions of subjects that logically precede and control it, and also that it is a *project* with communal goals; it is willed into existence by subjects rather than being the condition of existence of singular beings – and this communal work of self-production necessarily results in common being rather than being-in-common.[24]

Being-in-common, conversely, is radically incompatible with 'work': 'One does not produce it, one experiences or one is constituted by it as the experience of finitude' (IC, p. 31).[25] Community as being-in-common takes place in 'désœuvrement' or 'unworking', 'which, no longer having to do either with production or with completion, encounters interruption, fragmentation, suspension' (IC, p. 31). The emphasis on the necessarily unfinished nature of community is important here: whereas a 'work' is orientated towards completion, being-in-common is rather the *endless* circulation and sharing of singular beings. 'Incompletion' is not a state of inadequacy but an active process , 'the activity of sharing [...] That is to say, once again, a workless and inoperative activity. It is not a matter of making, producing, or instituting a community [...] it is a matter of incompleting its sharing [...] For a complete sharing implies the disappearance of what is shared' (IC, p. 35).

Another of the important differences between common being and being-in-common concerns the significance of *death* to these types of community, and here Nancy is indebted to the formulation of this theme in Heidegger's *Being and Time*.[26] The singular being, as distinct from the subject, is characterized by *finitude* – by its limits – and this is manifested in exemplary fashion in the impossibility of experiencing one's own death (or one's own birth). No-one can die in my place: and yet 'my' death does not belong to me; the nearest I can get to experiencing it is to witness the death of others, and this can take place only within community. Thus 'Death is indissociable from community, for it is through death that the community reveals itself' (IC, p. 14). Community, in other words, 'is the presentation of the finitude and the irredeemable excess that make up finite being: its death, but also its birth, and only the community can present me my birth, and along with it the impossibility of my reliving it, as well as the impossibility of my crossing over into my death' (IC, p. 15). The notion of common being, on the other hand – the immanent community – requires a constant effort to sublate death into a meaningful, heroic element of its own self-production: as salvation, victory, sacrifice or martyrdom (Christ's crucifixion, Spartacus, the tomb of the Unknown Soldier, etc.). Death is recuperated, 'reabsorbed' into the community 'in an immortal communion in which [it], finally, loses the senseless meaning that it ought to have' (IC, pp. 13–14) – and this involves exactly the process of *work* that Nancy associates with common being. Ultimately, however, death remains resistant to any such work:

> Community no more makes a work out of death than it is itself a work. The death upon which community is calibrated does not *operate* the dead being's passage into some communal intimacy, nor does community, for its part, *operate* the transfiguration of its dead into some substance or subject – be these homeland, native soil or blood, nation […] (IC, p. 15)

The attempt to convert an individual's death into an edifying meaning that reinforces the immanent community can be seen as one example of the role of myth-making in common being. Myth in general is analysed by Nancy, in the section of *The Inoperative Community* entitled 'Myth Interrupted', as a central feature of common being. Myth ensures 'fusion': it 'represents multiple existences as immanent to its own unique fiction, which gathers them together and gives them their common figure in its speech and as this speech' (IC, p. 57).[27] This has to do with the importance of *foundation* in common being: the community defines its identity by reference back to its origin: 'Myth is of and from the origin, it relates back to a mythic foundation, and through this relation it founds itself (a consciousness, a people, a narrative)' (IC, p. 45). Conversely, origin itself in this sense is a myth; in *Being Singular Plural* Nancy develops the idea that since being is radically plural, it cannot have one single origin; and since there is nothing outside finite being, it cannot have an origin outside itself. 'Origin' thus becomes 'the indefinitely unfolding and variously multiplied intimacy of the world' (p. 12); '"Origin" does not signify that from which the world comes, but rather the coming of each presence of the world, each time singular' (p. 15).

Modern society can no longer believe wholeheartedly in myth because we now distinguish between truth and fiction and we are aware that myth is 'merely' fictional; we know, in Nancy's succinct formulation, that 'myth is a myth'. But this does not mean that we are now wholly unaffected by it; in an argument that seems to echo the Freudian concept of disavowal, *The Inoperative Community* claims that myth is 'not so much suppressed as suspended or interrupted' (p. 47). In other words, the two senses of myth juxtaposed in the sentence 'myth is a myth' remain inseparably connected, and this connection, precisely, produces a *disunion* at the heart of the concept itself: 'For this sentence contains, as well as two heterogeneous meanings for a single vocable, one mythic reality, one single idea of myth whose two meanings and whose infinitely ironic relation are engendered by a kind of internal disunion. This is the same myth that the tradition of myth conceived as foundation and as fiction' (p. 52). Myth thus embodies both the idea that 'foundation is a fiction' and that 'fiction is a foundation' (p. 55); and the combination of these two propositions means *both* that we can continue on some level to believe in, or at least be affected by, myth, *and* that the disjunction between the two meanings opens the concept up to the possibility of its 'interruption' (p. 55). Myth is never eliminated completely, but it is constantly *interrupted* by something else – something that resists it. This 'something else' takes two forms, but they are ultimately shown to be equivalent.

In the first place, since myth correlates with fusion – 'myth is always a myth of the reunion and the communion of community' (p. 58) – its interruption reveals instead the reality of being-in-common, of exposition and compearance: 'the interruption turns the community toward the outside instead of gathering it in toward a center [...] the interruption of community [...] is the very law of compearance' (pp. 60–61). When myth is interrupted, 'the community that resists completion and fusion [...] makes itself heard in a certain way' (p. 62). What interrupts myth, in other words, is the resistance of being-in-common reasserting itself.

Equally, however, the 'voice' of this interruption, Nancy goes on to argue, is *literature* (p. 63). He thus sets up an opposition between myth on the one hand and literature on the other, which depends upon a very specific interpretation of the term 'literature' – as, essentially, 'désœuvrée'. Myth is to do with totality, completion, *constructing* an identity; literature is to do with the fragmentary, the incomplete, the suspension rather than the institution of meanings.[28] Literature does not communicate *a* meaning, but 'unworks' meaning in general; and this involves also communicating meaning as circulation and as *sharing*: '"Literature", thought as the interruption of myth, merely communicates – in the sense that what it puts into play, sets to work, and destines to unworking, is nothing but communication itself, the passage from one to another, the sharing of one by another' (p. 65). That is, literature has all the characteristics of being-in-common; just as myth equates with common being, so 'being-in-common *is* literary' (p. 64), and conversely literature 'puts into play nothing other than being *in* common' (p. 65).[29] Literature's interruption of myth is not in addition to that of being-in-common, but because literature *is* being-in-common.[30]

As though to prevent the two concepts simply collapsing into one another, this notion is developed into what, in *The Inoperative*

Community, Nancy calls 'literary communism'.[31] 'Communism' emphasizes the idea that literature does not fundamentally consist in individual works, complete in themselves and separate from other works, but in the sharing that relates them – 'the sharing of community in and by its writing, its literature' (p. 65). Therefore the text 'recounts an unfinished story; it [...] interrupts itself at the point where it shares itself out – at every moment, to you, from him or her to you, to me, to them' (p. 65). One always writes for others (p. 66), not in the sense of desiring their admiration,[32] but because writing is a form of exposition , taking place on the limit between singular beings.[33] It does not create the fusion of myth or 'pass into a common space' but inscribes 'the sharing of places, their spacing' (p. 73).

In this way Nancy expands the meaning of 'literature' to include any form of expression or communication that reveals being-in-common; and conversely, not all works of literature in the conventional sense conform wholly to 'literature' in his sense. 'Myth' is equally given an expanded meaning, to include everything in literary or other works of art that inscribes common being, foundation, fusion, and so on. Thus Nancy sees the individual work as combining 'a share of myth and a share of literature or writing' (p. 63).[34] Thus one way of approaching a literary text would be to analyse its particular combination of myth and literature – the dynamic of the 'interruption' – and this is part of what I shall be doing in the following chapters of this book. Nancy's articulation, moreover, implies an antagonistic but necessary interdependence of myth and literature, through the inevitability of interruption: he goes on 'The latter interrupts the former, it "reveals" precisely through its interruption of the myth (through the incompletion of the story or the narrative) – and what literature or writing reveals is above all else its interruption' (p. 63). This, although Nancy does not make the point explicitly, would seem to differentiate the myth/literature opposition from that between common being and being-in-common, which are usually presented as far more independent of each other.

The starting point for Nancy's theorization of community and of myth is, as I have shown, a collective sense of *loss*: we have lost our community spirit, we have lost the ability to believe naïvely in myths. In the case of community, he questions whether we ever really had what we now think we have lost, and insists that the task facing us is to articulate this newly revealed form of community as being-in-common. He performs a similarly deconstructive move on the even more general question of *meaning* or 'sense'.[35] Nancy opens *The Sense of the World* with the claim that we can no longer even talk about a 'crisis of sense': 'Today, we are beyond this: all sense has been abandoned' (p. 2). But, even as we anxiously demand a meaning system that would provide 'security, identity, certainty, philosophy as distributor of values, worldviews, and – why not? – beliefs or myths' (p. 2), we also begin to recognize that we are already exposed to 'an unheard-of sense', that is different from our usual conception of discrete, linguistic meaning (which he calls 'signification').[36] The ideologies and belief systems that in the past enabled us to make sense of the world in terms of general, substantive concepts and values have disappeared – because, Nancy claims, they all relied on situating the world in relation to something transcendental, something outside itself. Now that we are faced with the reality of our finite existence in the world, we are in a position to realize that the world itself 'is' sense. The change is encapsulated in the distinction between 'having' and 'being' sense:

> For as long as the world was essentially in relation to some other (that is, another world or an author of the world) it could *have* a sense. But the end of the world is that there is no longer that essential relation, and that there is no longer essentially (that is, existentially) anything but the world 'itself'. Thus, the world *no longer has* a sense, but it *is* sense. (SW, p. 8)

Sense is no longer to be found in abstract concepts, but in 'the sense of the world as its very *concreteness*, that which our existence *touches* and by which it is *touched*, in all possible senses' (p. 10). It is not a question of interpreting particular phenomena by reference to general principles or truths (in fact, the very notion of reference arguably becomes untenable), but in recognizing that '[there] is something, there are some things, there is some there is – and that itself makes sense, and moreover nothing else does' (p. 55).

In other words, meaning becomes *singular*: 'Sense is the singularity of all the singular ones' (p. 68); it resides in the concrete distinctiveness, but also the *relationality* of singular beings.[37] This relationality is expressed in the notion of 'being-toward': singular beings are not closed entities, but exist 'toward' one another. Therefore, sense is nothing more or less than

> relation *to* or *being-toward*-something, this something evidently always being 'something *other*' or 'something *else*'. Thus, 'being-*toward*-the-world', if it takes place (and it does take place), is caught up in sense well before all signification. [...] If we are *toward* the world, if there is being-toward-the-world in general, that is, if there is world, there is sense. The *there is* makes sense by itself and as such.[38] (p. 7)

Being Singular Plural returns to the question of singular meaning, and relates it more explicitly to being-in-common. Its first section is entitled 'We are Meaning', and reiterates the distinction between 'having' and 'being' meaning, arguing that '"meaning", used in this absolute way, has become the bared [*dénudé*] name of our being-with-one-another. We do not "have" meaning anymore, because we ourselves are meaning – entirely, without reserve, infinitely, with no meaning other than "us"' (BSP, p. 1). Meaning is relationality and circulation (p. 3); therefore the equation between being and meaning is only possible if being is conceived of not as the monolithic fusion of common being but as the spacing of being-in-common, so that it can circulate between singular beings, inhabiting the spaces between them – that is, their sharing: '*meaning itself is the sharing of Being*', and '[meaning] begins where presence is not pure presence but where presence comes apart [*se disjoint*] in order to be itself *as* such. This "as" presupposes the distancing, spacing and division of presence' (p. 2).

Nancy's insistence on the finitude of being, the fact that there is nothing beyond our singular plural existence(s), seems to make it inevitable that almost everything he analyses ultimately turns out to be a manifestation or a form of being-in-common. Community is being-in-common, literature is being-in-common, meaning is being-in-common. And, finally, so is politics – or rather, 'the political'. In *Retreating the Political*, Nancy and Philippe Lacoue-Labarthe argue that 'politics', or established political practices and institutions, can no longer deal adequately with 'the political', that is, the basic issues of our co-existence in society and in the world.[39] As Nancy puts it in *Being Singular Plural*, 'the retreat of the political is the uncovering, the ontological laying-bare of being-with' (p. 37). The political, in other words, has 'retreated' from politics, and so has to be re-thought or 're-treated'. In the Preface to *The Inoperative Community*, Nancy places all his work on community in the context of the insistence that 'the political is the place where community as such is brought into play' (p. xxxvii). Accepting that '[the] political is the place of the in-common as such' (SW, p. 88) means elaborating a form of politics which is not concerned with domination,[40] and not based on the presupposition of an individual or collective subject. It requires, in other words, a move beyond 'the politics of self-sufficiency', as he explains in 'Politics II' in *The Sense of the World*. Rather than taking the social bond as something that has always already been 'tied', Nancy argues that 'a politics of nonselfsufficiency' must focus on the actual, infinitely repeated, act of tying the '(k)not', that is, the social bond, which he redefines as a kind of exposition of singularities – as 'that which involves neither interiority nor exteriority but which, in being tied, ceaselessly makes the inside pass outside, each into (or by way of) the other, the outside inside, turning endlessly back on itself without returning *to* itself' (SW, p. 111). Politics thus becomes 'an infinite tying up of sense from the one to the one [...] abandoning consequently all self-sufficiency of subject or city, allowing neither subject nor city to appropriate a sovereignty and a community that can only be those of this infinite tying' (p. 113).

Nancy's thinking on community branches out to engage with a range of other topics: worklessness, death, myth, origin, literature, meaning, politics. The above – necessarily schematic – presentation is simply an attempt to elucidate these and to show how they are linked together. I have deliberately avoided entering into the complexities of Nancy's similarities to and differences from other philosophers, or other theorists of community, because my aim is just to focus on those aspects of his thought that will, I believe, be illuminating for the discussion of the theme of community in the novels I have chosen to study. But this does not mean that I shall be using his work as a systematic framework for my analysis; it is not a question of trying to make a number of very diverse texts fit into one overarching schema. (Such a procedure would in any case run counter to his own emphasis on singularity.) Different aspects of Nancy's thought are relevant to different novels – and, indeed, to different degrees: I refer to him more extensively in some chapters than others, and always in conjunction with other more specifically postcolonial critics and theorists. Equally, and despite my sympathy with his views, I do not intend to suggest that the extent to which the novels conform to his ideals of being-in-common and worklessness is in itself a measure of their literary or ethical value. Roumain, Glissant, Schwarz-Bart, Placoly, Chamoiseau, Maximin and Condé are writing from different situations, with different aims and commitments; they all share, however, a concern with the problem of community, and in the chapters that follow I shall explore their texts in their singularity and their relatedness.

CHAPTER 1

Restoring Lost Unity in Jacques Roumain's *Gouverneurs de la rosée*

The theme of community is central to Jacques Roumain's *Gouverneurs de la rosée*. Manuel returns from a fifteen-year absence to find his village of Fonds-Rouge suffering from a life-threatening drought and split by a family feud which has divided the population into two camps; he resolves to find a new source of water and to reunite the people into the harmonious community that they used to be; and although (or because) he is murdered in the course of this, he succeeds on both counts. The community is thus placed throughout the narrative in relation to a leader who *saves* it: an archetypal hero, Manuel combines the roles of leader, saviour, and teacher, leading them from resignation and dissension to a new confidence in their ability to work collectively to change their lives for the better. Specifically, he teaches them not to rely fatalistically on the gods – either the Christian God or the vodou *loas* – but to take responsibility for their future; and to understand that they can only do this if they work together.

This double aim is symbolized in the 'coumbite': the traditional, originally African, practice of working collectively on each other's land. The novel opens with Bienaimé remembering the time before the drought and the feud: 'A l'époque, on vivait tous en bonne harmonie, unis comme les doigts de la main et le coumbite réunissait le voisinage pour la récolte ou le défrichage' (p. 13). There follows a long, vividly evoked memory of the 'coumbite' in which mastery of the land goes together with a sense of common purpose so powerful that individual identity is subsumed into 'un élan unanime' (p. 15); singing 'en une seule masse de voix' (p. 16), the men are fused into a single 'common being' galvanized by the rhythm of the drum: 'Une circulation rythmique s'établissait entre le cœur battant du tambour et les mouvements des hommes: le rythme était comme un flux puissant qui les pénétrait jusqu'au profond de leurs artères et nourrissait leurs muscles d'une vigueur renouvelée' (p. 17). *Gouverneurs de la rosée* is dedicated to the realization of this ideal: a community whose members are fused together into the harmonious, purposeful whole of Nancy's common being. Summed up in the symbol of the 'coumbite', it is presented as what has been lost, and what Manuel will enable the villagers to regain.

The novel has also been described as embodying an ideal of *organic* community, compatible with Nancy's common being and emphasizing in particular community as a living, natural being; Michael Dash identifies 'a particular phase in Caribbean modernism' characterized by 'the need for foundational myths, and the lure of the ideal of an organicist fantasy, outside of the contradictions of history' and situates Roumain's novel within it: '*Masters of the Dew* epitomizes the organicist longings of this phase of Caribbean modernism [...] What starts off as a dream of liberation from an oppressive Western system of knowledge ends up also asserting a new, closed, hegemonic system of values'.[1] The notion of the organic is in fact particularly appropriate to this novel in which the life-giving forces of nature are so prominent. The characters have always identified so closely with the land[2] – Manuel himself says 'Je suis ça: cette terre-là, et je l'ai dans le sang' (p. 69) – that damaging it (as in the deforestation that exacerbated the lack of rainfall) is the same thing as damaging themselves; and, conversely, working to make the land produce – the main concern and indeed the main moral value of the novel – is also, to use Nancy's terms, a work of production of themselves.[3] But until Manuel's return, the villagers' identification with the land which they work remained unself-conscious; and it is this lack of awareness that the novel holds responsible for their inability to overcome their divisions, and also for their political impotence on a wider scale. Manuel's first task is to remedy this; he reminds them repeatedly of what they are, defining and *naming* them as 'travailleurs de la terre'. With his intervention and through the eloquence of his rhetoric, the work of production of, inseparably, crops and themselves becomes a conscious immanence, a self-conscious community producing itself as essence:

> Et avec ça nous sommes pauvres, c'est vrai, nous sommes malheureux, c'est vrai, nous sommes misérables, c'est vrai. Mais sais-tu pourquoi, frère? A cause de notre ignorance: nous ne savons pas encore que nous sommes une force, une seule force: tous les habitants, tous les nègres des plaines et des mornes réunis. Un jour, quand nous aurons compris cette vérité, nous nous lèverons d'un point à l'autre du pays et nous ferons l'assemblée générale des gouverneurs de la rosée, le grand coumbite des travailleurs de la terre pour défricher la misère et planter la vie nouvelle. (p. 70)

The very deliberate metaphorical use of agricultural verbs applied to their social situation – 'défricher la misère et planter la vie nouvelle' – emphasizes both the organic and the productive nature of this community which 'grows' its own future. At times the text even suggests that the search for water is only the means towards the real end: that of transforming the villagers' attitudes so that they can once again live as a homogeneous fraternal community: 'Ces habitants de Fonds-Rouge, ces têtes dures, [...] il leur fallait cette eau *pour retrouver* l'amitié entre frères et *refaire la vie comme elle doit être*: un service de bonne volonté entre nègres pareils par la nécessité et la destinée' (p. 105, my italics).

The notion of common being is, for Nancy, a phantasy that is always situated in the past and that has always already been lost to dissension (IC, p. 10); and in *Gouverneurs de la rosée* the 'coumbite' appears at the beginning of the text as Bienaimé's memory of past unity and well-being, now seen as irrevocably lost: 'Mais tout ça c'était le passé. Il n'en restait qu'un goût amer. On était déjà mort dans cette poussière, cette cendre tiède qui recouvrait ce qui autrefois avait été la vie' (p. 22). When Manuel enters the novel in the following chapter, the contrast between memory and present reality is even sharper in so far as his return home from Cuba is presented as a return from exile and alienation. His descriptions of working on the Cuban plantations stress their inhumanity – their vast size, the impersonal cruelty of the bosses and the industrial-scale exploitation of the workers: 'Cuba, l'immensité, étendue d'un horizon à l'autre, des champs de canne, le batey de la Centrale sucrière, la baraque empuantée où le soir venue il couchait pêle-mêle avec ses camarades d'infortune' (p. 31). Fonds-Rouge, in contrast, is the community which he remembers as unified communion – but which no longer exists. The dissension which has ruined it stems from a quarrel over inheritance: the dividing up of the land leads to a division, also, of the villagers. As Bienaimé explains, 'On a fini par séparer la terre, avec l'aide du juge de paix. Mais on a partagé aussi la haine. Avant on ne faisait qu'une seule famille. C'est fini maintenant' (p. 56).

Manuel therefore decides to dedicate himself to restoring communal unity. His project is thus essentially nostalgic. The community he sets out to build will be a new, more self-conscious version of the original; it is not a question of creating something radically different, but of *re*-creating a lost intimacy and communion: as he says, 'Maintenant que l'eau va arroser la plaine [...] ce qui était ennemi *re*deviendra ami, ce qui était séparé va se *re*joindre et l'habitant ne sera plus un chien enragé pour l'habitant. Chaque nègre va *re*connaître son pareil, son semblable et son prochain' (p. 126, my italics). It is this unalienated transparency of relationships between individuals that defines his ideal as more than just a practical or even political unity; in order to succeed, he tells Annaïse, they have to be *fused* together: 'on est soudé en une seule ligne comme les épaules des montagnes' (p. 87).

Gouverneurs de la rosée is also dominated by the idea of death: the fear of death from starvation that opens it (Délira's 'Nous mourrons tous...'), the guilt of Dorisca's murder and, above all, Manuel's death. Nancy describes the way in which the immanent community recuperates the death of its members into the whole of common being: 'death, in such a community, is not the unmasterable excess of finitude, but the infinite fulfilment of an immanent life: it is death itself consigned to immanence' (IC, p. 13). The villagers' reverence for their ancestors, although it might be seen as a form of recuperation, is in fact derived from an African religious tradition whose transcendental dimension is somewhat different from Nancy's conception. Manuel's view of death, however, is precisely 'consigned to immanence'. His first expression of it conforms to the organic version of immanence: death is reabsorbed into the cyclical time of the natural universe with which the community identifies, as he tells them: 'même la mort n'est qu'un autre nom pour la vie. Le fruit pourrit dans la terre et nourrit l'espoir de l'arbre nouveau' (p. 34); but a second formulation later in the novel is both more communist and closer to Nancy's version, because here the death of the individual is subsumed into the community's collective *work*:

> Oh sûr, qu'un jour tout homme s'en va en terre, mais la vie elle-même, c'est un fil qui ne se casse pas, qui ne se perd pas tu sais pourquoi? Parce que, chaque nègre pendant son existence y fait un nœud: c'est le travail qu'il a accompli et c'est ça qui rend la vie vivante dans les siècles des siècles: l'utilité de l'homme sur cette terre. (p. 113)

Manuel's own death is seen in the same two ways: he lives on in the minds of the villagers as a source of guidance and inspiration to their continuing collective work, but also in the more biological, and hence organicist, form of his unborn son, the revelation of whose existence *negates* his death: placing Délira's hand on her pregnant belly, Annaïse closes the novel by saying 'Non [...] non, il n'est pas mort' (p. 192). Above all, however, the rhetoric of the text encourages us to see Manuel's death as a kind of martyrdom: he has given his life in the struggle to save the community from starvation and disunity.[4] As he says just before he dies, 'ce qui compte, c'est le sacrifice de l'homme. C'est le sang du nègre. Va trouver Larivoire. Dis-lui la volonté du sang qui a coulé: la réconciliation, la réconciliation pour que la vie recommence, pour que le jour se lève sur la rosée' (p. 160).

In fact, though, Manuel does not deliberately choose to risk his life for the community, as martyrdom in the strict sense requires; he is murdered by Gervilen, principally because he is the latter's rival for Annaïse. Nor is his death necessary on a practical level to the successful outcome of the irrigation project: the water has already been found, and it already looks, after his meeting with Larivoire's men, as though they are going to overcome their hostility and join in the 'coumbite' that will dig the canals. What his death does achieve, however, is the consecration of this new and fragile reconciliation by means of a secret pact: both sides agree to cover up the murder, in accordance with his dying wish, for the sake of harmonious relationships in the community. The fact that they all agree to this *proves* that unity has been restored. Manuel's death thus forms a symmetrical opposite to the murder of Dorisca that is the origin of the feud: the first murder breaks the community, the second heals and consecrates it, and in so doing is itself reabsorbed into its common being.

* * *

One of *Gouverneurs de la rosée*'s most important and most obvious features is simply its extraordinary success. It has had a greater impact on readers and other writers than any of the other novels studied here; the much earlier date of its publication is no doubt partly responsible for this, but in order to become the founding text of Caribbean literature that it is commonly said to be, it also had to exhibit exceptional qualities of eloquence, structural harmony and emotional force. Its influence extends far beyond the Caribbean: it has been translated into seventeen other languages, is very widely read in Africa and features on innumerable literature courses at school and university level.[5] The book's emotional power perhaps derives above all from Manuel's tragic death and the moving eloquence with which his mother and Annaïse respond to it; but this in turn is harnessed to Manuel's, and the novel's, ideal of the perfect community. In this sense the novel's power is intimately dependent upon its evocation of common being. More specifically, I want to argue that its ability to move us depends on the way the text *produces* the community by means of a very carefully orchestrated system of repeated and interconnected elements – and that this simultaneously provokes in the reader an undercurrent of unease, and even a slight feeling of being manipulated. In his study *Caraïbales* Jacques André describes the novel as a representation in which everything acquires a symbolic significance, and each element contributes harmoniously to the whole.[6] In this 'omniprésence de la signification' (p. 30) each detail of the natural landscape that is mentioned in the text (dust, drought, stagnant water, sinister black crows, and so on) serves to illustrate Manuel's words; and individual characters are merely stereotypes acting out the roles necessary to the drama: 'Cette cohérence totalitaire des significations dessine des personnes en tout point conformes à ce qu'ils *représentent*' (p. 31). (Gervilen, for example, is not only a jealous murderer: he is *also* ugly, in contrast to the beauty of Manuel and Annaïse, and he is a charcoal burner and therefore guilty of the deforestation which is the real cause of the drought.) In other words, the text builds up a complete, all-encompassing system of imagery in which each element is described in terms of another element in the system: human beings and the landscape, Annaïse and the spring, water and sunlight, water and blood, circulation versus stagnation, and so on.[7] It results in a representation that is wholly meaningful – literally *full* of meaning – in which there are no gaps or inconsistencies, and in which nothing is left ambiguous or indeterminate. The doves and the 'malanga' plants that Manuel sees while searching for the spring, for instance, are not there accidentally: they *mean* that water is near at hand (p. 104, p. 106); similarly, the beating of his heart as he approaches it echoes the 'pulsations précipitées et brûlantes' (p. 81) that he experienced before his first assignation with Annaïse, and makes him think 'On croirait que tu vas à une première rencontre avec une fille' (p. 105), thus explicitly linking the 'new life' offered by the spring with the 'new life' of Annaïse's pregnancy (springs are sexualized even more than the rest of the landscape: 'la source Fanchon' flowed 'des reins même du morne' (p. 50), 'la source de Mahotière' is 'dans l'entre-jambes du morne', p. 145).

There is also a strong proleptic dimension to this systematicity. Predictions are always fulfilled: Ogoun's high-profile warning during the vodou ceremony (p. 65), for instance, but also smaller hints of what is to come, such as Manuel's remark to himself, 'si tu tombes, tu seras semé pour une récolte invincible' (p. 36), or Délira's joyful relief that perhaps, after all, she will live to see her grandchildren (p. 97) – here, the irony of the outcome (she will see Manuel's child, but only after *his* death) makes the link all the more striking. The text is carefully structured to ensure that almost everything in it recalls or predicts its symmetrical counterpart, whether parallel or contrast: for instance, the idyllic coumbite evoked at the beginning of the novel was on the land belonging to Beaubrun and Rosanna, and it is they, ironically, who are first mentioned as belonging to the enemy camp (p. 55); not only that, but they are the parents of Annaïse, who together with Manuel will work to reunite them with the opposing camp. None of these coincidences is intrinsically unlikely, but their accumulation nevertheless creates an overall effect of 'meaningfulness' that seems a little too calculated.

In other words, the text seems to be *working* too hard to produce a completely and consistently meaningful representation of the community and its drama: and here one can make a further connection with Nancy's concepts of 'work' and 'unworking', on the level of the text itself. The phantasy of community as work implies a constant process of self-production and self-representation in which common being is 'objectifiable and producible (in sites, persons, buildings, discourses, institutions, symbols: in short, in subjects)' (IC, p. 31). In the case of *Gouverneurs de la rosée*, the literary work done by the text in its production of an immanent symbolic system is both a harmonious parallel to and an integral element of the represented community's self-production. In fact, the two levels are merged together even more seamlessly through Roumain's frequent use of free indirect discourse, so that the positioning of the narrative voice becomes indistinguishable from a 'voice' that seems to emanate from the community as a whole.[8]

The opposition between work and unworking is also relevant to the conflictual relationship that Nancy outlines between myth and literature. Literature suspends, or 'interrupts', the foundational and fusional meanings produced by myth, and so opens up a space in which being-in-common, as opposed to common being, can be revealed (IC, p. 62). But his claim that in any given literary work there is 'a share of myth and a share of literature or writing. The latter interrupts the former, it "reveals" precisely through its interruption of the myth' (p. 63) is not borne out by Roumain's novel: if incompletion, suspension, indeterminacy and other such attributes of unworking are what constitute the share of literature in the work, then *Gouverneurs de la rosée* would seem to be entirely mythical, because it creates a *complete* representation of the community based on a closed system of interconnected images and narrative elements. What André describes as 'cette cohérence totalitaire des significations' (see above) excludes any possibility of literary interruption or unworking. The fulcrum of the representation is of course Manuel, who is both represented as a hero and himself actively represents to the village its ideal form as community; he thus fits exactly Nancy's description of the mythic hero, who 'makes the community commune – and ultimately he always makes it commune in the communication that he himself effects between existence and meaning, between the individual and the people' (IC, p. 51).

Elsewhere in *The Inoperative Community* Nancy emphasizes the functional closure of this kind of self-representation/self-production: the community, in order to sustain its consciousness of itself *as* an organic community, needs to reflect back to itself images of its own completion (IC, p. 9). Seen from this point of view, the *closed* meaning system produced by the text also echoes and reinforces the closed nature of the community and its experiences. I have already indicated the extent to which the chronology of the narrative is a closed circle in which the past is reinstated as future:[9] the 'coumbite' taking place in the present time of the end of the narrative is as it were superimposed on the memory, at the beginning of the novel, of the lost 'coumbite' of the past, and this super-imposition is reiterated in the way in which Manuel's projects for the future are expressed in the form of repetition, as we have seen.

But the closure operates equally in the dimension of space. The narra-tive never moves outside the village; the town remains a hostile but shadowy presence which is never really confronted.[10] In contrast to the themes of migration and 'errance' that dominate more recent Caribbean fiction,[11] the characters in Roumain's novel are very attached to one, small, place – the village of Fonds-Rouge. The attachment is based on their intimate relationship with the land that provides them with a living; they are bound to the particular landscape of their home village, and the intensity of the bond is made very clear in Manuel's reaction to coming home: 'Si l'on est d'un pays, si l'on y est né, comme qui dirait: natif-natal, eh bien, on l'a dans les yeux, la peau, les mains […] c'est une présence, dans le cœur, ineffaçable, comme une fille qu'on aime' (p. 26). In its inti-macy, boundedness and stability, this is *per se* a nostalgic view of community, and the link between spatial immobility and the past is made entirely concrete in the villagers' additional reason for not leaving the village: namely, that their ancestors are buried there (p. 111). This fidelity to a place that preserves the community's past is thrown into stark relief by our gradual realization of how localized the drought is (Mahotière, where Annaïse goes to wash clothes in the river (p. 146), is not suffering from it, for instance), and yet how impossible it is for the main charac-ters to leave Fonds-Rouge. There are of course practical reasons which would make this difficult – they could not afford to buy land anywhere else, and there is little work available – but the reasons they themselves give for not leaving are not practical, but a question of loyalty to the ancestors and the land which has kept them alive for so many genera-tions. Those villagers who, forced by hunger, do reluctantly decide to leave are seen as traitors (pp. 100–102, 109–12); the others stay in the expectation that they will not survive. The closed space of the commu-nity, in other words, would have killed them had Manuel not found the spring – and conversely, were it not for this closure and the resulting immobility, the discovery of the spring would not have been necessary.

Spatial closure also results in a deep mistrust of anyone who comes from outside. Manuel himself is initially presented as a stranger. Although the first chapter establishes his identity as Bienaimé's and Délira's son, his first appearance in the novel, in the following chapter, is carefully anonymous: he is referred to as 'il', 'l'étranger' and 'l'homme' (p. 25) rather than by his name. The village children are fascinated by him because 'il était l'homme qui avait traversé la mer, qui avait vécu dans ce pays étrange de Cuba; il était auréolé de mystères et de légendes' (p. 76). Less positively, Gervilen uses his foreignness to denigrate him to Annaïse: he is 'un vaurien qui a vagabondé dans les pays étrangers comme un chien sans maître' (p. 92). Thus in order to persuade Larivoire and his men to listen to him, Manuel must first, before he even starts to make the logical case for the benefits of unity, prove that he is not a stranger, but one of them. He does this by reminding them that they all used to play together as children, and work together as young men:

> Pourtant, il les connaissait bien. N'étaient-ce pas là Pierrilis, Similien, Mauléon, Ismaël, Termonfis, Josaphat? Il avait grandi avec eux au milieu de ces bois, tendu dans la savane des pièges aux ortolans, chapardé ensemble des épis de maïs. Plus tard ils avaient mêlé dans les coumbites leurs voix et leurs forces de jeunes nègres fringants. (p. 74)

In other words, he only *seems* to be different, and hence untrustworthy; in reality, he belongs to the community just as much as they do.

The development of the narrative thus dispels the *illusion* of difference between Manuel and the other villagers, just as on a larger scale it demonstrates the illusory nature of the differences between the two opposing camps. André points out that the enemy, Larivoire, turns out to be exactly the same as Manuel: both have the same characteristics of wisdom, courage, and honour, both are described as 'rusé' (*Gouverneurs de la rosée*, p. 133, p. 151), and both recognize these qualities in the other (*Caraïbales*, p. 48). More generally, André argues, the novel as a whole is structured by the resolution of binary oppositions: 'le mouvement du récit s'ordonne autour de couples antithétiques: Manuel/Gervilen, les deux clans, arrosage/sécheresse, fécondité/stérilité, révolte/résignation – dont l'opposition contradictoire appelle la résolution dans une synthèse réconciliatrice' (p. 47). But what makes this reconciliation so easy to realize is that the key oppositions are not fundamentally real. We are reminded several times that the land has not really changed – the quality of the soil is still good, it just needs water[12] – and the feud has not altered the fact that the villagers are really all the same. They were united in the past, and they are reunited at the end of the novel; as André puts it, '[il n'y a] pas d'altérité irréductible mais seulement une aliénation du même dans l'autre, par définition provisoire' (p. 47).

Thus the achievement of unity is also made possible by the underlying homogeneity that is posited as the ideal of this conception of community, but is also revealed as something which has always existed: as Manuel says, 'Tous les habitants sont pareils [...] tous forment une seule famille' (p. 152). Unity, as we have seen in the description of the 'coumbite', goes beyond solidarity or common aims, fusing the men together into an illustration of Nancy's common being. Fusion of this kind implies a communal identity in which they are almost literally identical to each other. It is striking that when Manuel rehearses the conversation he plans to have with the enemy camp, he imagines each side repeating exactly the other's words – a ritualized speech that establishes the newly rediscovered absence not only of antagonism but of any difference at all between them:

> Et je vois arriver le jour quand les deux partis seront face à face...
> 'Alors, frères, diront les uns, est-ce que nous sommes frères?
> 'Oui, nous sommes frères, feront les autres.
> 'Sans rancune?'
> 'Sans rancune.'
> 'Tout de bon?'
> 'Tout de bon.'
> 'En avant pour le coumbite?'
> 'En avant pour le coumbite.' (p. 88)

* * *

A circular chronology in which the future is a repetition of the past, a closed space which confers a shared identity on all the people within it in opposition to those outside, a narrative dynamic which moves from discord to harmony and reconciliation, a repetitive system of imagery which encompasses every element of the text and makes it meaningful in terms of the overall system, and a community based on sameness and communion – in all these dimensions, *Gouverneurs de la rosée* seems to be characterized by closure, unity and consistency. It works, in other words, to eliminate difference and contradiction.

But one major contradiction appears to remain. Manuel's attitude to life is clearly, although never explicitly, Marxist, echoing Roumain's own commitment to Marxism and the Haitian Communist Party which he helped to found. The novel as a whole is overtly didactic, committed to convincing its readers that only a Marxist perspective can improve the lives of the Haitian peasantry. One prominent element of this is atheism; for Manuel (as for Roumain), the peasants' religious beliefs are largely to blame for their inability to assume responsibility for their actions.

Manuel, therefore, vigorously attacks their belief in the Christian God and in the *loas*, telling them that they must rely on their own strength and will-power:

> On prie pour la pluie, on prie pour la récolte, on dit les oraisons des saints et des loas. Mais la Providence, laisse-moi te dire, c'est le propre vouloir du nègre de ne pas accepter le malheur, de dompter chaque jour la mauvaise volonté de la terre […] et il n'y a d'autre Providence que son travail d'habitant sérieux, d'autre miracle que le fruit de ses mains. (p. 47)

On the level of the plot, the truth of this message is wholly borne out. But at the same time, Manuel's behaviour and the way in which he is described convey another message to the reader: that he is a Christ-like figure. He 'preaches' unity and reconciliation, in a series of pronouncements whose eloquence has a distinctly evangelical, parable-like quality; his words have an aura of obscurity and profundity – Annaïse tells him 'C'est comme pour l'eau, il faut fouiller profond dans tes paroles pour trouver leur sens' (p. 113) – but they are also clear (like the spring water) and illuminating (like the sunlight): Laurélien follows him with difficulty but finds that in his own mind 'un rideau de lumière commençait à se lever', and says: 'Ce que tu dis là est clair comme l'eau courante au soleil' (p. 70). Above all, the discovery of the spring is presented by Manuel in remarkably evangelistic terms: 'Et bientôt je t'apprendrai une grande nouvelle […] Il est trop bonne heure pour le dire. Mais ce sera une réjouissance, tu verras' (p. 97). His role as 'saviour' of the community is underlined in the family names, Sauveur and Délivrance, while his own first name recalls the Christian Emmanuel; and the details of his death – the stab wounds in his side, his crawling home in a kind of calvary, the way in which his 'gospel' is spread only after his death – insistently recall the death of Christ.[13]

Whereas some critics gloss over this co-existence of Christian imagery and atheist Marxist ideology,[14] others have seen it as deeply problematic. Having urged the villagers to relinquish their dependence on God, Manuel in effect adopts a God-like role himself and encourages them to follow him. The important article by Michel Serres, 'Le Christ noir', defines the contradiction in these terms: 'Le récit n'est pas libre, il n'est même pas isomorphe à la thèse [marxiste], il est un rêve religieux, celui-là même que l'auteur, le héros, tous ensemble, tenaient à congédier définitivement'.[15] His explanation of it takes as its starting point the difficulties inherent in transferring the Marxist model of proletarian struggle against capitalist employers, which Manuel has learnt in Cuba and which takes the concrete form of the successful strike of Cuban agricultural labourers in which he participated, to a very different society of peasant small-holders, whose main enemy, in Serres's analysis, is not capitalist exploitation but simply the weather. It is all very well, Serres argues, for Manuel to castigate the villagers for relying on prayer and sacrifices to persuade the gods to bring rain – but Marxism cannot make it rain either, and Manuel's luck in finding a spring that might well not have been there is a form of 'cheating' (p.14). The peasants' struggle to survive in the face of the elements is not susceptible of a political solution; and this in Serres's view induces a passivity and a fatalism that are objectively justified – and that can only produce a religious attitude towards life: 'Attendre. Quand la raison se fixe et que le corps s'arrête, le songe les prend. Toutes les religions, et quelques autres pans de la culture, sont nés de là' (p. 10). Therefore, the 'alien' Marxist project transplanted into an agrarian situation is inevitably assimilated to the mythical and religious world-view that more truly belongs to such a society; Manuel can only be represented as a messiah, not as a political leader.

It is certainly true that Roumain's attempt to adapt an orthodox Marxist perspective to rural Haitian society encounters various problems. While the novel does evoke the oppressive forces of the state (the policeman Hilarion, the market inspectors) and the villagers' class enemies (Florentine the money lender, and the townspeople in general) these are fairly peripheral to the central events of the narrative, and Serres's claim that the main enemies are simply the forces of nature is quite plausible. Moreover, although Manuel praises the solidarity of the Cuban cane-cutters, it soon becomes clear that he sees the real solution to their predicament not as higher wages and better working conditions, or indeed common ownership of the plantations, but as each individually owning their own piece of land; when asked whether in Cuba, 'il y en a des habitants comme nous?', he replies: 'Tu veux dire avec une portion de terre, la volaille, quelques bêtes à cornes? Non; seulement des travailleurs pour couper la canne à tant et tant. Ils n'ont rien que le courage de leurs bras, pas une poignée de terre, pas une goutte d'eau, sinon leur propre sueur' (p. 42). His ideal community, in other words, is not a socialist proletariat, but a society of small peasant proprietors, helping each other through collective practices such as the 'coumbite' but whose most basic attachment is to their own land; economically independent of each other, and in, fact, of everything except nature:

> – En vérité, il y a une consolation, je vais te dire: c'est la terre, ton morceau de terre fait pour le courage de tes bras, avec tes arbres fruitiers à l'entour, tes bêtes dans le pâturage, toutes tes nécessités à portée de main et ta liberté qui n'a pas une autre limite que la saison bonne ou mauvaise, la pluie ou la sécheresse. (pp. 29–30)

But it does not necessarily follow from this that the hybrid Marxist messiah defined by Serres is the inevitable result of the attempt to apply a Marxist world-view to a peasant society. Although the villagers of Fonds-Rouge are not primarily fighting a political battle against capitalist exploitation, some elements of the lessons Manuel learnt in Cuba are nevertheless wholly relevant to their situation; these elements are the importance of unity and collective action – which, as we have seen, is presented as a more important achievement than the actual irrigation project – and the importance of believing in one's own ability to change one's situation. And the second of these relies crucially on abandoning the religious attitude to reality: thus it is arguably the *atheist* dimension of Marxism that is most central to Roumain's use of it. While the refusal of religious fatalism is of course in no way specific to Marxism – it is in fact just as characteristic of a modernizing capitalist attitude to agriculture – it does mean that the confrontation between Manuel's Marxism and Christianity is entirely coherent in its own terms.

Serres does not explicitly address the question of community in his article. From his introductory comments on the fundamental dichotomy of agrarian and industrial societies, however, it is possible to deduce a vision of an 'organic' ideal agrarian community very similar to that presented in *Gouverneurs de la rosée*. On the one hand, the industrial urban society of the northern hemisphere has revealed itself to be a social failure and a historical dead-end: it is 'au bout de son histoire […] Elle constate dans l'inconscience l'échec de ses modèles d'évolution, d'économie, de culture, d'éthique et d'idéologie' ('Christ noir', p. 5). On the other hand, '[l'avenir] est au sud', as long as the 'agriculteurs de l'hémisphère Sud' (p. 5) do not try to imitate the norms of the industrial north but remain true to '[une] sagesse […] que donnent en entier les besoins de la terre' (p. 6). In the logic of this dichotomy, Marxism is very clearly seen as an 'industrial' product, atheist and rationalist: 'l'industrie est une pratique rationaliste athée, le rationalisme athée est la manière adéquate de parler les pratiques industrielles' (p. 4). Equally, Serres's view of Marxism excludes any consideration of its being also a philosophy of community, since for him the positive values of community are by implication associated with the traditional, essentially religious world-view of the 'Internationale non dite des cultivateurs, la classe humble, les hommes de l'humus' (p. 3).

It is however the literally *communist* dimension of Marxism that allows us to elaborate a more satisfactory explanation of the strange complicity of Marxism and Christianity in Roumain's novel. From this point of view, Nancy's formulation of community as work and communion offers a perspective from which Christianity and communism, while still significantly different, no longer form the two poles of a major opposition; it thus highlights what they have in common. For Nancy, that is, the relevant opposition is between a conception of community as essence, fusion, work and common being, and the sharing and 'spacing' of being-in-common. In this context, Christianity and communism both belong to the first type. In fact, they – together with fascism[16] – constitute its main historical exemplars. The communist ideal is based on 'human beings defined as producers [...] and fundamentally as the producers of their own essence in the form of their labor or their work' (IC, p. 2); the whole analysis of community in *The Inoperative Community* is in fact framed in its initial presentation of the *loss* of the communist conception of community, the disappearance of communism as what Sartre, quoted here by Nancy, called 'the unsurpassable horizon of our time' (IC, p. 1). Communism thus figures as one of the primary examples of the nostalgic illusion of lost community that Nancy goes on to develop in detail. The most exemplary illustration of community-as-communion, however, is Christianity: 'But the true consciousness of the loss of community is Christian: the community desired or pined for by Rousseau, Schlegel, Hegel, then Bakounine, Marx, Wagner or Mallarmé is understood as communion, and communion takes place, in its principle as in its ends, at the heart of the mystical body of Christ' (IC, p. 10).

Two aspects of this overlap between the two ideologies are particularly relevant to *Gouverneurs de la rosée*. Firstly, the death of the individual in both Christianity and communism is justified and redeemed as sacrifice for the sake of the community – religious or political martyrdom – and this theme is, as we have seen, prominent throughout the novel. Equally, Roumain's emphasis on what Nancy calls communion or fusion is apparent both in the context of quasi-Marxist collaborative labour in the 'coumbite' and in that of Manuel's Catholic funeral – although in this latter case the communality signally does not include the priest himself, who is satirically presented, in line with the Marxist critique of Catholicism as corrupt and oppressive. But the villagers' mourning is represented entirely sympathetically, as are Délira's anguished prayers to God and the *loas*. In both cases, moreover, the communion is expressed through the *singing* that accompanies both occasions, and the description of these two instances of singing makes of them a very striking example of the careful parallelism that is typical of the whole novel. In the 'coumbite', as I have already shown, the workers' singing fuses them into a single body: 'La ligne mouvante des habitants reprenait le nouveau refrain en une seule masse de voix' (p. 16), led by Antoine whose drumming inspires their 'élan unanime' (p. 15); in the funeral, the hymn-singing is kept going by a woman's voice which 'rassemble les autres voix et le cantique s'épanouit à nouveau dans un *élan unanime*' (p. 169, my italics).[17] In both 'coumbite' and funeral, too, the singing takes place in the early morning, and is heard from other parts of the community; it circulates around the landscape, drawing people together in their recognition of the communal reason for it. In the case of the 'coumbite', '[le] chant emplissait le matin inondé de soleil. Le vent l'emporterait au-delà des collines vers le plateau de Bellevue, et commère Francilla […] se tournerait vers la rumeur de la plaine: – oui, qu'elle ferait, c'est la bonne saison' (p. 17); while at the funeral, 'le cantique s'en va sur l'aile frissonnante de l'aube et les habitants qui se lèvent tôt à Fonds-Rouge l'entendent; "ah, oui, disent-ils, l'enterrement sera aujourd'hui"' (p. 175).

The differences of course remain, most generally perhaps in that Christianity is associated with passivity and despair, and communism with initiative and hope. But the rhetorical seamlessness of their juxtaposition in Roumain's text becomes far less difficult to explain if one focuses, as Nancy's insight enables us to do, on the essentialist nature of the community that both propose: a community in which dissension and difference are ultimately superficial, and in which an underlying homogeneity is the precondition for unity and collective consciousness.

However, if Nancy's theorization allows us to relativize the communism/Christianity polarity, it also focuses our attention on another aspect of the novel which, at least in Nancy's terms, could be said to constitute a different kind of contradiction. That is, there is one crucial exception to Roumain's otherwise extremely consistent representation of an organic community producing itself as essence. This type of community is necessarily self-sufficient; in Nancy's description no outside intervention contributes to the self-production of the community or to the reflexive process whereby 'it [plays] back to itself […] the representation, indeed the living offering, of its own immanent unity, intimacy, and autonomy' (IC, p. 9). The situation in *Gouverneurs de la rosée*, however, does not conform to this pattern. Fonds-Rouge does not simply save or heal *itself*; it needs the return of Manuel to initiate the process. And, although Manuel is not a stranger – and would not have been able to save them if he had been – the fact remains that it is only the knowledge and experience he has acquired abroad, in Cuba, that enables him to achieve his, and the community's, aims. Just as Laurélien becomes his 'disciple', so he too was earlier the disciple of a comrade in Cuba, who taught him the value of political analysis and struggle: 'Témoin ce compagnero à Cuba qui lui parlait politique, au temps de la grève. Il en savait des choses [...] et les situations les plus embrouillées, il te les démêlait que c'était une merveille' (p. 149). Although his experience in Cuba is not directly relevant to the very different situation at home, it is nevertheless his involvement in the cane-cutters' strike that teaches him what can be achieved if the workers overcome their differences and unite:

> dans les commencements, à Cuba, on était sans défense et sans résistance; celui-ci se croyait blanc, celui-là était nègre et il y avait pas mal de mésentente entre nous: on était éparpillé comme du sable et les patrons marchaient sur ce sable. Mais lorsque nous avons reconnu que nous étions pareils, lorsque nous nous sommes rassemblés pour la *huelga* [...] (p. 86)

– and he transfers what he has learnt to the predicament of the village.

In other words, the knowledge that saves the community comes from outside the community. In fact, it comes from a place that is represented throughout the novel as the exact opposite of the ideal community. The very lack of fit between a strike of Cuban agricultural wage labourers and the project of collectively digging canals to irrigate the privately owned plots of land of the Haitian peasantry merely throws into sharp relief the extent to which the community can realize its essence only through the external intervention of an *alien* experience – an experience which is not available to any of the community's members except Manuel. From Roumain's Marxist point of view, the necessary input of a politicized leader coming from outside is entirely congruent with the orthodox Marxist theory of the inability of the peasantry to lead its own revolution. But the weakness of this explanation is that Manuel, as we have seen, does not lead a revolution in Fonds-Rouge, but simply enables the villagers to return to a previous state of harmony and modest prosperity. This circularity, however, or this return of the same, can be accomplished only via the agency of an extraneous factor. Thus the necessity of outside intervention undercuts the closure and the completion that elsewhere dominate the representation of the ideal organic community. With this crucial inconsistency – which of course stands out more than it otherwise would given the uniform harmony of the rest of the representation – *Gouverneurs de la rosée* seems despite itself to designate the ultimate impossibility of common being. In so doing it points implicitly towards a more positive attitude to the *difference* which lies outside the bounds of the community. The novel, as I have argued, derives its exceptional power to move us from the concentrated unity of its characters' common being, and the streamlined narrative and metaphorical discourse that reflect this; its implicit but crucial recognition of the ultimate incompleteness of this view, however, provides an opening onto the outside world that is in a different way just as exhilarating.

CHAPTER 2

Past, Future and the Maroon Community in Edouard Glissant's *Le Quatrième Siècle*

Edouard Glissant differs from the other writers considered in this book in that he is known as a philosopher as well as for his novels and poetry. The concepts of 'Relation' and 'opacity' that he develops in the essays collected in *Poétique de la Relation* in 1990 resonate closely with Nancy's reworking, over approximately the same period of time, of the notion of community.[1] Nancy has written on mixed or creolized cultures in terms that are not unlike Glissant's treatment of this theme.[2] But his more general concept of 'being-singular-plural' also has striking similarities with Glissant's 'Relation'. In the first place, both insist on the primacy of the plural: the collective dimension of being is not something added on to an originary individual subject, but is itself originary. Like Nancy's singular beings, the component elements of Relation have no independent existence outside it: 'La Relation, nous l'avons souligné, ne joue pas sur des éléments premiers, séparables ou réductibles [...] Elle ne se précède pas dans son acte, ne se suppose aucun a priori' (*Poétique*, p. 186). But at the same time, both writers refuse to conceive of this 'primordial plurality' (BSP, p. 67) as a fusion based on closure and sameness. 'Relation' theorizes the *relation*, precisely, of *different* elements: 'non pas des indistinctions amalgamées, mais des écarts déterminants' (*Poétique*, p. 157); and Glissant projects a new literature 'par où le communautaire, sans s'effacer [...] initierait à la totalité sans abdiquer le particulier; et relativiserait de la sorte le spécifique sans avoir à confondre l'Autre [...] dans une transparence réductrice' (pp. 67–68).

The notion of opacity similarly defines a relation with the other that renders any kind of fusion or appropriation impossible: a relation that takes place, as Nancy would put it, on the limit between singular beings.[3] The prominence of opacity in Glissant's thinking needs to be understood in the context of the French colonial policy of *assimilation*, the inculcation of 'Frenchness' in France's colonial subjects, where resistance to fusion and appropriation becomes a particularly important issue. (Equally, Nancy's theorization of singularity thus has particularly valuable implications for a critique of assimilationism.) Therefore in 'Pour l'opacité' (*Poétique*, pp. 203–209) Glissant argues for the 'right to opacity', and he too defines it in terms of singularity:

> Non pas seulement consentir au droit à la différence mais, plus avant, au droit à l'opacité, qui n'est pas l'enfermement dans une autarcie impénétrable, mais la subsistence dans une singularité non réductible. Des opacités peuvent coexister, confluer, tramant des tissus dont la véritable compréhension porterait sur la texture de cette trame et non pas sur la nature des composantes. (p. 204)

Glissant here goes on to argue that opacity therefore embodies a notion of relations to others that – like Nancy's being-singular-plural[4] – is based neither on opposition nor on identification: 'Pensée de soi et pensée de l'Autre y deviennent caduques dans leur dualité [...] Ce qui est ici est ouvert, autant que ce là [...] L'ici-là est la trame, qui ne trame pas frontières' (p. 204). And he concludes that opacity – singularities in relation – is the only possible basis for community: 'C'est aussi que cette même opacité anime toute communauté: ce qui nous assemblerait à jamais, nous singularisant pour toujours. Le consentement général aux opacités particulières est le plus simple équivalent de la non-barbarie'(pp. 208–209).

Nancy's critique of the notions of origin and myth as a foundation for community also has an equivalent in Glissant's distinction between 'filiation' and 'étendue'. Glissant points out that Western myth and the epic literature of the West revolve around filiation, linking a community back to its original creation, as in the Old Testament; and argues that communities created through filiation are intolerant of outsiders: 'Il y a donc dans le Mythe une violence cachée, qui se prend aux mailles de la filiation et qui récuse en absolu l'existence de l'Autre comme élément de relation' (*Poétique*, p. 62).

For Glissant, the primacy of the collective comes into play with particular acuity in the situation of Antillean *writers*: in the earlier *Le Discours antillais* (1981), he promotes the project of the 'roman du Nous': the novel of the collective Antillean subject, rather than 'l'incarnation des devenirs particuliers' (p. 153). But here again, the 'nous' is *relational*, internally differentiated, and its novel is 'le roman de l'implication du Je au Nous, du Je à l'Autre, du Nous au Nous' (p. 153); 'Nous' and 'Je' form a structure of interdependent but discrete relations: 'Ce Nous qui est le sujet du dire, le parlant fondamental, oblige à faire le tableau de ses rapports au Je: Sur quel mode une communauté implique-t-elle les individus qui la composent? Ou inversement?' (p. 152). The terminology is different, but Glissant's double emphasis on the 'fundamental' status of the 'Nous' and the heterogeneity of the 'Je's' is strongly suggestive of Nancy's being-in-common.

Nancy's distinction between 'common being' and 'being-in-common' is a rejection of essentialist theories of community:

> Exposition and sharing do not make up an essence. [...] The thinking of community as essence [...] constitutes closure because it assigns to community a *common being*, whereas community is a matter of something quite different, namely, of existence inasmuch as it is *in* common, but without letting itself be absorbed into a common substance. (IC, p. xxxviii)

– and his replacement of the idealist immanent subject – the individual – with the 'singular plural being' is similarly anti-essentialist and relational. This emphasis is also echoed in Glissant's Relation. In *Le Discours antillais* Relation is contrasted with Being in the context of the transportation of slaves, to produce an anti-essentialist account of the formation of the Caribbean subject: the ontological violence of transportation *changes* its victims into *something else* (p. 28), and so forces them to abandon any idealist assumption of continuity of being – 'Nous renonçons à l'Etre' (p. 28) – and, *instead*, to 'entrer dans la variance toujours recommencée de la Relation (du relais, du relatif)' (p. 29). In *Poétique de la Relation*, this positing of Relation as the opposite of Being is further developed and generalized, becoming a major theme of the work: Relation 'ne vise pas l'être, l'entité suffisante qui trouverait en soi son commencement. La Relation est un produit, qui produit à son tour. Ce qu'elle produit n'est pas de l'être' (p. 174); '"L'Etre est relation": mais la Relation est sauve de l'idée de l'être' (p. 199), and so on.

There are however also important differences between Glissant's Relation and Nancy's being-singular-plural. Nancy's focus on 'beings', stripped down to the finitude of their bare existence, results in a rather abstract conception of collectivities, as existing in a social and cultural vacuum; and while this is in a sense the whole point of his representation, it means that he has nothing to say about culture. For Glissant, on the other hand, the elements which interact in Relation are preponderantly *cultures*, rather than human beings: Relation takes place in 'le champ inépuisable des variations nées du contact des cultures' (*Poétique*, p. 69). Glissant, in other words, is primarily interested in the multiple forms of relation between the cultures of the world:

> Comment ont cheminé jusqu'à nous les cultures chinoises ou basque, indiennes ou inuit, polynésiennes ou alpines, et nous jusqu'à elles? Que nous reste-t-il, et sous quelles formes, de toutes les cultures disparues, effondrées ou exterminées? Comment vivons-nous, aujourd'hui encore, la pression des cultures dominantes? Par quelles fantastiques accumulations de combien d'existences, de l'individuel at du collectif? (*Poétique*, p. 168)

The differences between the interacting elements are therefore not of the same order: we are dealing here with a different kind of difference. Specifically, there is nothing in Nancy's formulation that would necessarily presuppose *change* over time; whereas for Glissant, the contacts between cultures serve above all to generate, in a completely unpredictable fashion, new cultural combinations and new responses to situations:

> Est-il significatif, pathétique ou dérisoire, que les étudiants chinois se soient fait massacrer devant une reproduction en carton-pâte de la statue de la Liberté? Ou que, dans une maison roumaine, les portraits détestés de Ceausescu aient été remplacés par des photos, découpées dans des magazines, des personnages de la série télévisée *Dallas*? Poser seulement la question, c'est imaginer l'inimaginable turbulence de la Relation. (*Poétique*, pp. 152–53)

Thus, through being more closely involved with particular social and political situations, Relation is fundamentally dynamic, 'turbulent' in a way that being-in-common is not; reflecting Glissant's constant engagement with questions of social change, it works on 'ensembles, dont la nature est de varier prodigieusement dans la Relation' (*Poétique*, p. 156).

* * *

Thirty years earlier, however, in the 1960s, Glissant's position was significantly different. The concepts of Relation and opacity were already active in his thought, but they operated in a more narrowly Caribbean context and in conjunction with an active anti-colonial political stance. Glissant was influenced by the decolonization movements of the 1950s and 1960s; together with his friend Albert Béville, he founded the 'Front Antillo-Guyanais' in 1959 to campaign for the decolonization of Martinique and the other French Overseas Departments, and for the French Antilles to become part of a wider Caribbean federation of independent nation states. This led to his being banned from the Overseas Departments by De Gaulle until 1965; when he then returned to Martinique, it was to continue his political activity, working towards the political and also the *cultural* independence of Martinique – that is, working against the French policy of assimilation. To this end, he created the 'Institut Martiniquais d'Etudes' in an 'effort to break the cultural stranglehold of France on Martinique',[5] by teaching young Martinicans about Caribbean history and culture. The IME organized a number of research groups working on the social and cultural problems associated with Martinique's status as an Overseas Department, and their work was published in the journal *Acoma* which Glissant set up in 1971. In this period, in other words, Glissant was above all committed to the political task of building a national identity for Martinique; and this presupposed an entirely different conception of community from that of Nancy's being-in-common – and, indeed, from the 'Tout-monde' that he himself was to introduce in the 1990s. Peter Hallward formulates the difference in very absolute terms, arguing that 'Glissant's early work remains compatible with what might be called the *classically* post-colonial gesture, associated with Fanon and Césaire: the conversion of a "passively" colonized object into an actively post-colonial subject' – whereas '[in] the second moment, however (starting from the early 1980s), the specific, national moment is surpassed, and surpassed absolutely. In Glissant's later work, national mediation is a positive liability in the articulation of a deterritorialized, rhizomatic Reality'.[6] The transition is perhaps not quite such a clear-cut dichotomy as Hallward claims, but it is certainly the case that Glissant's intellectual and political work in the 1960s involved the asserting of an essentialist national community *against* the dominant colonial culture of France.[7] The community also had to be capable of political action, and this implied for Glissant that the individuals who belonged to it had to be autonomous subjects, able to overcome their alienation and instigate social change.[8] Hallward quotes Glissant's reservations concerning the European decon- struction of the humanist subject – 'We should develop a poetics of the "subject", for the very reason that we have been too long "objectified" (*Discours*, p. 257)' – and comments that '[the] preliminary task of the national subject is its own re-possession, the reversal of an inherited dispossession' (p. 443).

Le Quatrième Siècle, published in 1964, reflects the conceptions of community and individual that are required by this struggle for political independence, Caribbean solidarity, and cultural autonomy. It does not, therefore, conform to Nancy's articulation of 'being-in-common' and his concomitant rejection of the essentialist community founded on its oppo- sition to other communities. Indeed, the novel's representation of the maroon community – the ancestors of papa Longoué – initially seems to resemble more closely Nancy's mythical organic community. As the narrative proceeds, however, significant differences from this model become apparent. Like the 'coumbite' in *Gouverneurs de la rosée*, which, as I have argued in the previous chapter, does indeed replicate the features of the organic community, the maroon community is situated in the past; unlike the 'coumbite', however, it is a far more distant past, involving a gap of several generations rather than the fifteen years of Manuel's absence. More importantly, whereas the 'coumbite' is *reinstated* at the end of Roumain's novel, *Le Quatrième Siècle* recounts a non-circular historical process of irreversible change whereby the maroons cease to exist as a separate entity and a more open, mixed society emerges, with complex interrelations between maroons and slaves and their respective descendants.

Above all, however, whereas the golden age symbolized by Roumain's 'coumbite' is entirely positive, the portrayal of the maroons in *Le Quatrième Siècle* is a complicated mixture of good and bad qualities. I shall argue in the latter part of this chapter that the myth of the maroon community is 'interrupted': not, however, by the suspension of meaning that Nancy identifies with 'literature', but in so far as it is contradicted in various more substantive ways, by showing the maroons' own sense of their community and their superiority to the slaves to be an illusion.[9] Conversely, the heroic endurance of the slaves is also emphasized. This does not, however, mean that the novel operates according to a dialectical progression in which the contradiction between the cultural values of maroons and slaves leads to the maroons' becoming subsumed in a synthesis of the two. The mixed, creolized society that has come into existence by the end of the narrative does not provide a straightforward resolution of the ambiguities and antagonisms presented earlier in the text.[10] This is because the first interruption – of the maroon myth – is itself 'interrupted' by the novel's highly ambivalent attitude towards the new society that emerges in the twentieth century; this latter is criticized as being, in some ways, a regression to a condition of alienation, passivity and ignorance that was characteristic of slavery; as a result, the prestige of the maroons is ultimately, if ambiguously, reinstated.[11] (Thus rather than Nancy's view of a foundational mythical discourse that can only *be interrupted* and a qualitatively quite different 'unworking' literature that can only *interrupt*, we find in Glissant's novel a more complex and reversible relation in which each side interrupts the other.) This *second* 'interruption' arises from the novel's insistence throughout on the need to rediscover the past and 'root' oneself in it, in order to make political progress into the future. The prominence of this theme – Bernadette Cailler claims that it is 'la seule aventure' of the text[12] – means that on a subjective level, the past cannot simply be left behind. The historical movement forwards towards Relation and creolization that the novel narrates is accompanied by a simultaneous movement back in time: and this double movement, leading both away from and back to the maroons, is what gives the novel its peculiar complexity.[13]

* * *

At first sight, then, *Le Quatrième Siècle* represents the maroon community in a manner that has little to do with singularity, and is in fact much closer to Nancy's characterization of the mythical community. One of the latter's main features, for instance, is its self-definition in terms of its *origin*. The intimate connections that compose the community-origin-myth configuration have in fact also been criticized by Glissant in his more recent work; his essay 'Culture et identité', for instance, attacks 'atavistic' cultures for their dependence on the notion of a unique origin and the foundational myths which this generates:

> Le rôle principal des mythes fondateurs est de consacrer la présence d'une communauté sur un territoire, en rattachant par filiation légitime cette présence, ce présent à une Genèse, à une création du monde. Le mythe fondateur rassure obscurément sur la continuité sans faille de cette filiation et autorise dès lors la communauté dont il s'agit à considérer cette terre devenue territoire comme absolument sienne.[14]

And yet, *Le Quatrième Siècle* could be described as creating its own founding myth: telling the story of the origins of the maroon community founded and led by the ancestor Longoué ('l'initiateur, celui d'avant-garde, le découvreur du pays nouveau', p. 24), and tracing its connections through the subsequent generations to the present. Indeed, Jacques André describes it as 'une démarche fondatrice [...] La noble figure du "Marron primordial" [...] [assume] le rôle d'un véritable mythe d'origine' (*Caraïbales*, p. 117).[15] The title of the novel itself emphasizes this foundational rewriting of history: for papa Longoué at least, his ancestor the first Longoué is situated at the very beginning of history (i.e., of the 'four centuries'): 'il voulait commencer l'histoire qui est l'histoire pour moi [...] pour lui pour moi c'est le premier jour le premier cri le soleil et la première lune et le premier siècle du pays' (p. 74).

On the other hand, the 'lack of Being' resulting from transportation that Glissant analyses in *Le Discours antillais* is also clearly illustrated in the novel; the man who escapes from the plantation on his first night of captivity is presented to us in a kind of zero state of existence: 'Cet homme qui n'avait *plus* de souche [...] et qui n'était pas *encore* Longoué' (p. 83, my italics), and as filled with 'un vide infini [...] marque d'une déperdition d'existence, d'un flottement, d'un irréel vraiment futile et confortable' (p. 84). Here, however, lack of Being forms the starting point for a strenuous process of self-(re)construction, conveyed through the metaphor of 'enracinement' that is so prominent throughout the novel: thus 'l'homme qui n'avait plus de souche pourtant s'enracinait dans cette légèreté' (p. 104). It is, moreover, a continuing process that is more communitarian than individual: it is only with Melchior in the second generation that the 'enracinement' is finally accomplished: 'Ne peut-on pas dire qu'il s'était enraciné, lui le premier de sa lignée?' (p. 137).[16] Thus whereas in the model provided by *Le Discours antillais* lack of Being becomes a condition of possibility for an alternative non-essentialist conception of existence as Relation, in *Le Quatrième Siècle* it is merely the prelude to a *work* of self-production; here again we rejoin Nancy's characterization of the immanent community realizing itself through work. Thus although both slave and maroon communities are exceptional, involuntary and 'unnatural', since both came into existence out of the particular historical violence of transportation, the maroons, unlike the slaves, work to reconstruct themselves and found a community which in many respects is essentialist and homogeneous; it produces a sovereign subject – Melchior, 'le seul qui ait pu choisir sa destinée, la mener par la main sans dévier' (p. 149) – whose autonomy and rootedness is 'echoed' in the whole community: 'il était pour toute la famille (comme pour les marrons qui alentour étaient l'écho de la famille) la racine alourdie qui prend racine dans la terre' (p. 150).

The novel is not of course exclusively concerned with the Longoué family and the maroons; these are counterpointed throughout by the narration of the history of the Béluse family, starting off with their lives as slaves on Senglis's plantation. And this plantation community has none of the characteristics associated with the maroons. It is dominated by feelings of stagnation, passivity and indifference; the first thing Béluse notices on his arrival is 'ce silence [...] traversé d'indifférence et de résignation' (p. 60), and the fact that only one old man shows any interest in him. But later he too becomes equally indifferent to the sufferings of his fellow-slaves (p. 113). The plantation is also internally divided into a number of 'mondes différents qui se côtoyaient ou se superposaient dans l'espace de l'habitation' (p. 113), and which generate envy and mutual distrust.[17] The slave community, at least on this plantation, which is the only one in which daily life is described in any detail, thus has no consciousness of itself as a community. The only exception to this picture – but it is a significant one – occurs with the slave revolts; these are never successful, but the fact that they happen at all would seem to presuppose a degree of collective purpose.[18] Glissant in fact links them explicitly to the process of 'enracinement': 'La révolte d'un esclave n'est pas d'espoir, elle ne s'alimente d'aucun espoir [...] elle préfigure, elle inaugure l'action (l'opération) la plus sourde et la plus pénible: d'enracinement' (p. 101).

In other words, the revolts are not orientated towards a different, future state of being, but embody the only way in which the slaves can express their *refusal* of their condition, and it is only by doing this that they can achieve a degree of rootedness comparable to that of the maroons.

The maroons, however, define themselves in opposition to the slaves, as Self versus Other; the maroons are 'ceux qui refusèrent' and the slaves 'ceux qui acceptèrent' (p. 57), and this forms a major thematic binary opposition in the novel (more so, ultimately, than the opposition between master and slave or plantation owner and maroon).[19] It is imprinted onto a landscape structured through the contrast between 'le morne' (or 'le bois') and 'la plaine', in which the wild, mysterious interior of the island is consistently associated with natural beauty, freedom and daring as against the cultivated coastal plain on which the plantations are situated. The environment of the virgin forest contributes to the image of the maroon as a Rousseauesque noble savage, as André notes (*Caraïbales*, pp. 117–19), while also reinforcing the idea of the maroons' originary status by giving the impression that no previous human community has settled in this primordially natural landscape. The plain, conversely, is dominated by agriculture, commerce, and slavery.

The ever-present danger of recapture in which the maroons live creates a closed community which exists by virtue of its boundaries, that is, of what it excludes: 'la vocation du marron [...] est de se garder en permanence contre le bas, contre la plaine et ses sujets, de trouver ainsi la force de survivre' (p. 142). Confrontation with the Other provides the Self with a secure identity: it is only after Longoué's meeting with La Roche in the forest that he can feel that 'il était maître des hauteurs qu'à tout prendre l'homme blanc lui avait concédées. Non pas concédées mais reconnues, après un loyal combat' (p. 111). This defensive posture towards the outside world also ensures the maroon community's homogeneity – overcoming, for instance, the initial antagonism between Louise and Longoué: 'Ils vécurent ainsi en équilibre, chacun d'eux étouffant l'ancienne colère. La menace d'en bas les rapprocha encore' (p. 95) – and justifies the absolute authority of Longoué and later Melchior as the community's leader, whom the other maroons 'echo' as we have seen (p. 150).

The plantation community is of course equally closed to the outside world as far as the slaves are concerned, but this closure functions as an imposed imprisonment rather than a proudly assumed system of self-defence. Significantly, it is only through the periodic revolts of the slaves that their enclosure and separation from each other can be temporarily overcome: this rejection of their life as slaves remains largely symbolic, as the novel repeatedly makes clear, but it does have the real consequence that for the duration of the uprising they move between plantations and meet other slaves from elsewhere: 'Ils avaient brisé les barrières qui constituaient chaque plantation en une prison inéluctable' (pp. 101–102). Moreover, this aspect of the revolt – like the 'enracinement' mentioned earlier – survives its inevitable defeat: 'Car les barrières une fois brisées ne pouvaient plus être rebâties étanches; il y avait désormais un vent-courant dans les campagnes: c'était le résultat le plus précieux de l'affaire' (p. 102). The notion of closure, in other words, has opposite meanings for the maroon and the slave communities: the slaves' desire to break down the barriers between plantations contrasts with the maroons' dependence on the boundaries of their community – their inaccessibility in the forest – to ensure their survival.

The opposition between slaves and maroons in fact appears most dramatically at the very moment at which it is about to disappear. Following the proclamation of the abolition of slavery, two metropolitan French civil servants register the population and give them surnames. This applies not only to those who have hitherto been slaves, but also to the maroons, who, no longer outlaws, come down from the hills and wait to be processed along with everyone else. Visually distinguished by their dignity, their 'majestueux' and 'superbe' appearance (p. 176), they stand out in the crowd 'comme autant d'îles fermes dans la mer bouillonnante' (p. 176): that is, as possessing a solid, well-defined identity in contrast to the undifferentiated and chaotic mass of ex-slaves. Above all, they assert their distinctive superiority by choosing their own surnames; the theme of naming is prominent throughout the novel, and the capacity to name oneself or one's children, as opposed to being named by one's master, is used elsewhere as well as an index of self-determination of both individual and community.[20]

Abolition is at first greeted by the slaves in *Le Quatrième Siècle* with uncomplicated joy. Later they realize that their situation has not improved as much as they had hoped. But although the novel as a whole presents abolition as a hollow victory with extremely limited gains, in its immediate aftermath the ex-slaves do seem to acquire a sense of themselves as a united group: it is noticeable that the 'effervescence générale' (p. 179) which follows the declaration excludes those individuals who had already gained their freedom: 'Les affranchis […] n'étaient pas en mesure de goûter le plaisir collectif, eux qui n'avaient dû leur libération qu'à un mérite individuel […] à une cause particulière, étroite, distincte.

Ils étaient comme exclus du transport général' (pp. 179–80). Abolition, therefore, at least gives the slaves the sense of a distinct communal identity that they had previously lacked. The opposite, however, is true of the maroons, who greet abolition with deep ambivalence regarding the new status that it gives them; they are in effect exchanging the heroic superiority previously conferred on them by the dangers of their illegal existence for the security of a legal identity, and are therefore 'partagés entre la satisfaction de celui qui voit légitimer son existence ou ratifier son passé [...] et le vague regret des jours révolus, quand le danger de vivre les élisait au plus haut de l'ordre de vie' (pp. 176–77). The abolition of slavery signals the end of the maroon way of life too.

* * *

The maroon community thus appears to be a sovereign community of autonomous, rooted subjects; it is closed by definition, constructing and consolidating its communal identity through its opposition to the slaves and their masters; it is authoritarian, obeying and 'echoing' an unchallenged leader, and it draws its cohesion and strength from reference back to a unique origin and a foundational process of 'enracinement' in its territory. All of these features make of it a representation of the kind of common being and mythical community that Nancy not only castigates but describes as a pure phantasy.[21]

If, however, one does not consider this representation in isolation but replaces it within the structure of the novel as a whole, many of the above attributes are revealed to be either ambiguous or simply illusory. For instance, the process of 'enracinement' is eroded by a countervailing desire to leave the forest, or even the island.[22] On a more general level, the notion of the *sovereign subject*, whether individual or collective, is systematically undermined by the very complexity of the whole novel's construction: that is, the text gradually builds up an intricate web of causal connections, the effect of which is to radically limit the autonomy of individual characters. Stéfanise's decision to join the maroons in the woods, for instance, is not presented as a simple personal choice but as the result of an accumulation of other interconnected actions and events, of some of which she is not even aware:

> Ainsi, pour qu'un Longoué égaré parmi les Béluse montât, femme intrépide, de son plein gré sur les mornes [...] il avait fallu ce monotone entassement. Que Senglis entêté dans sa décrépitude s'obstine à garder sa plantation (que sa plantation ne soit pas ravagée par les marrons), que Béluse monte dans la case de Roche Carrée, qu'il se rapproche à mi-chemin des bois; que La Roche acharné à défricher laisse Longoué à ses hauteurs (que Longoué

protège l'*Acajou*, du moins qu'il se garde d'attaquer l'*Acajou*), et que 'la voisine sur le bateau' enfante la mère de Stéfanise. (p. 160)

There are also repeated instances of individuals *deluding themselves* as to the extent and efficacy of their agency, assuming that situations result from their own will and action when this is in fact untrue. The encounter in the woods between Longoué and La Roche provides two striking symmetrical examples of this. Their use of their own (mutually incomprehensible) languages is presented as a paradoxical sign of their respect for each other's opacity; but it also, far more ironically, allows the reader but not the two characters to realize that *each of them* is under the impression that he has protected the other. Thus Longoué has always believed that his survival as a maroon is due to his own actions, but La Roche says:

> Maintenant, pourquoi n'ai-je point continué de vous poursuivre? Mon caprice. J'escomptais armer une expédition contre vous, car enfin vous n'étiez pas inabordable. Mais je me suis entêté soudain de ces défrichements de terrain [...] Et puis, le temps aidant, vous m'êtes devenu précieux. (p. 110)

– while conversely, on the following page, Longoué 'cria, dans sa langue d'Africain: "J'ai eu ta vie entre mes mains. Je t'ai protégé tout le temps"' (p. 111).

The notion of subjectivity that underlies these incidents is one in which human beings are subject to complex determinations that seriously reduce the scope of their ability to impose their will on the situations in which they find themselves, despite any illusions they may have to the contrary – which is fundamentally incompatible with the myth of the primordial, self-determining maroon. And the text of *Le Quatrième Siècle* seems almost obsessive in its accumulation of such examples. Moreover, in the majority of them the countervailing causality is not another individual's action: rather, the illusion of the autonomous subject is repeatedly undermined by demonstrations of a *historical* and *economic* causality that bypasses human will. This is the case with all the various social groups that interact in the novel. The friendship between the slave Anne and the maroon Liberté, for instance, is the result of '[la] transformation du pays, la lutte et l'avancée de la forêt' (p. 118). Duchêne, captain of the slave ship, was 'jadis beaucoup plus tenu par ses employeurs qu'il ne l'avait avoué' (p. 183), and this is presented as the inevitable result of the economic exigencies of the slave trade: 'chaque capitaine se retrouvait, pensait Lapointe, comme un otage coincé entre les aléas de la course et les prévisions rigides de La Rochelle ou de

Bordeaux' (p. 183). The plantation managers allow Béluse to acquire the piece of land at Roche Carrée, because it saves them the expense of having to feed him and his family, but Béluse does not realize this: '*Il ne savait pas* que c'était là une situation rendue possible par l'évolution des choses. *Il croyait peut-être* qu'il avait arraché le droit de se retirer dans la case de terre rouge étayée de branches' (p. 117, my italics).[23]

This undermining of delusions of self-determination is however especially noticeable in the case of the maroons. Their collective identity is based on their courage in gaining their freedom and the constant struggle to keep it; and they despise the slaves for lacking that freedom and, by implication, that courage. But Longoué fails to realize that the maroons' freedom in fact *depends* on the slaves' lack of freedom, as the text very explicitly points out: '*Il ne savait pas* ce que leur lutte et leur souffrance avait d'utile. *Il ne comprenait pas* que toute la masse n'aurait pu monter. La forêt n'eût pas suffi à les abriter, encore moins à les nourrir. *Il ne savait pas* qu'ainsi leur tourment, et même leur acceptation, le protégeaient' (p. 94, my italics). But what is perhaps even more damaging to the maroons' illusion of autonomy is that they are shown to be equally dependent on the planters' lack of interest in them; and this itself is motivated by the economic and political constraints of the period. Thus we are told that, at the time when Liberté and Anne were still young boys (i.e., the early nineteenth century, well before abolition),

> [les] marrons étaient tranquilles dans leur retraite: la chasse qu'on en faisait n'était plus que par principe, pour ne pas perdre la main, pour maintenir un droit public dont à la vérité nul parmi les planteurs ne se souciait personnellement [...] Les marrons respiraient à cette époque, ils avaient presque cessé d'être une monstrueuse exception pour devenir une sorte de petite population tacitement agréée de tous [...] (p. 129)

– and this is because the planters are too preoccupied with more important problems: the economic situation, which is forcing plantations to amalgamate in order to remain profitable (p. 130); and the political and military situation, in which the English are trying to invade and take over the island (p. 131). Thus the maroons' freedom, their ability to survive as an *independent* community, is shown to be *dependent* on the existence of their 'opposites', the slaves, on the economic decline of the plantations, and on rivalry between two imperial powers: their community is demonstrated to be a mere by-product of large-scale historical processes rather than the result of their own prowess. In this way their belief in their own sovereign identity is quite ruthlessly dismantled by the text.

As for the notion of origin in the maroons' self-representation, its status is similarly undermined. The position of Longoué as the 'first' maroon and the original founder of the maroon community is revealed to be as objectively false as the belief in their autonomy:

> Le bateau de l'arrivage n'était pas le premier bateau. Parce que si Longoué a marronné dès la première heure, c'est on peut dire qu'il n'a pas pris la peine de connaître le bas, il est entré tout d'un coup dans le passé qui était debout à côté de lui; c'est pourquoi je l'appelle le premier. Il a rattrapé en une soirée les années amassées depuis le jour où on en débarqua devant la Pointe; et il est devenu le premier. C'est pourquoi le bateau est le bateau de l'arrivage. Mais les autres étaient là, qui avaient supporté avant lui. (p. 146)

Here the text makes it very clear that Longoué's originary status is symbolic rather than a matter of historical fact – he is 'le premier' only because, according to papa Longoué, he has 'entered into' the past and as it were absorbed it all into his individual self. The origin is thus revealed, almost exactly half-way through the narrative, to have been a purely discursive construct ('c'est pourquoi je l'*appelle* le premier'), a function of the narrator's desire to create, retrospectively, a 'primordial maroon'. The narrative here instantiates exactly Nancy's definition of myth as providing a phantasmatic origin of community which is inherently and avowedly fictional and, in the disjunction between these two propositions ('myth is a myth'), necessarily interrupts itself.[24]

Papa Longoué also attempts to consecrate the origin by re-establishing its continuity with the present – as he says, 'Qu'est-ce que j'ai fait, si ce n'était pas pour essayer de ne pas perdre la chaîne depuis le premier jour' (p. 236). But the novel as a whole undermines this project. It points out the difficulty of the task, even at times states its failure ('Et ainsi papa Longoué […] n'avait jamais pu rien raccrocher à rien, ni son père à son fils, ni par conséquent le passé à l'avenir', p. 19). At the same time, it comes to be increasingly dominated by a very different theme, namely, the unwilled historical process whereby over time the contrast between maroons and slaves, and hence the distinctive identity of the maroons, is gradually effaced through the interweaving of relations between them.[25] The binary opposition between the Longoués and the Béluses is disrupted by the emergence of two other families, the Targins and the Celats, who occupy an interstitial space in between maroons and slaves: the former as the descendants of a white foreman named Targin and a slave, living in freedom but destitution on the edge of the Senglis plantation, the latter as 'les Longoué d'en bas' (p. 267), descendants of the maroon woman Liberté Longoué but who have never lived in the maroon community. Similarly, the opposition between 'morne' and 'plaine' no longer accounts for the totality of the landscape: new indeterminate areas appear, making possible the relationship between Anne and Liberté, for instance ('Ils occupaient la zone neutre qui n'appartenait à personne', p. 118), or Béluse's settling at Roche Carrée, 'posée en équilibre sur la frontière indistincte de deux mondes' (p. 143). After abolition, life on the plantations becomes 'le cercle où il n'y aurait plus à distinguer entre des hauts et des fonds, entre celui qui refuse et celui qui accepte, entre un marron hagard et un esclave agonisant' (p. 224).

That *Le Quatrième Siècle* narrates the gradual hybridization of maroons and slaves is uncontentious and has been widely commented on.[26] What is much less clear, however, is the novel's attitude towards this process. It oscillates ambivalently between endorsing it as a positive movement towards Relation and creolization, and lamenting the loss of the maroons' special, distinctive status. Thus on the one hand the breaking down of barriers between slaves and maroons is celebrated, as in the comment that after abolition the continuing uprisings and revolts united all the different groups: 'Tous au même, levés avec ceux que les papiers appellent travailleurs des champs: anciens marrons, esclaves, affranchis' (p. 202). There is often a strong sense that the maroons ought to be more open to the world outside the forest; Melchior's curiosity regarding the townspeople is contrasted positively with his son's lack of interest in them which means that 'se recreusait le vide que Melchior avait franchi avec tant de patience' (p. 207). Mathieu himself argues vigorously that 'le monde est là et qu'il est ouvert et que nous devrons de toutes façons un jour dévaler nos mornes jusqu'à lui' (p. 58); and this stress on the openness of the world, and openness *to* the world – 'entrer en Relation' – is intensified with the lifting of the wartime blockade at the end of the novel: 'Et dans sa certitude, il y avait le monde enfin ouvert, et clair, et peut-être si proche' (p. 286).[27]

On the other hand, however, there is also a detectable counter-current of regret at the loss of the Longoués' original, distinct identity. Several critics have described the processes of historical change in *Le Quatrième Siècle* as an example of creolization;[28] and the central value of creolization, as Glissant theorizes it in his later work, is that it produces societies characterized by *diversity*.[29] But the way in which it is evoked in the novel more often presents it as the opposite of diversity: rather a *loss* of difference, a levelling down to an undifferentiated state that is entirely negative. The Longoués' 'descent' into the town, for instance, merges them with the slaves in a common lack of definition that is perceived as abject: 'Ainsi les anciens marrons n'étaient descendus de leurs mornes, les esclaves n'avaient tenus dans les fonds que pour finir par grouiller dans cette misère? Eux aussi, indéterminés; ni Longoué ni Béluse ni Targin? Et la longue histoire s'engluait dans la boue des taudis?' (pp. 220–21). The Béluse family is equally affected by this 'usure commune' (p. 231) and 'la destinée indivise' which reduces the whole landscape to a meaningless homogeneity, 'partout où la terre, unie, indifférenciée, ouvrait au poids du soleil des étendues désormais sans à-pics' (p. 231). But they, significantly, are later shown as reinvigorated by the changes – 'Les Béluse, multipliés, dispersés, nouveaux, commençaient une autre histoire' (p. 266) – while the Longoués are not. Overall, the novel gives the impression that it is the maroons who suffer most from the loss of their previous specificity. This negative view of hybridization, running alongside the novel's equally strong promotion of progress towards a more open and equal society, suggests that the existing contemporary society is not – at least not wholly – the desired result of the political struggle for progress to which the novel is dedicated.

This ambivalence is bound up with with the novel's attitude towards the significance of the past, which is not in fact restricted to the simple phantasmatic representation of the original maroon that I have already described. Rather, the novel gradually puts in place a crucial distinction between papa Longoué's impossible attempt to recapture the *origin*, discussed above, and a broader historical consciousness, associated with Mathieu, which places the emphasis on understanding the past as *process* and *change*. The value accorded to this latter conception (which I designated earlier as the novel's 'second interruption') is evident in the text right from the outset; the first exchanges between papa Longoué and Mathieu establish the problem of rediscovering the past as the principal project of the novel. What is important to Mathieu, however, is not *identification* with a mythical origin, but *knowledge* of the island's history, because only this knowledge, he believes, can provide a basis for *action* in the present.[30] This is made particularly clear in the last chapter thanks to the intervention of Mycéa (herself of maroon descent), who to some extent replaces papa Longoué as Mathieu's mentor and persuades him of the greater urgency of political action in the present. She knows '[pourquoi] un Béluse et une Celat, gardés secrètement au long de cette histoire, et appelés à la connaissance, dépasseraient ensemble la connaissance pour enfin entrer dans l'acte' (pp. 272–73) – and tells him 'le fait est qu'il faut apprendre ce que nous avons oublié, mais que, l'apprenant, il nous faut l'oublier encore' (p. 285).

Political agency is thus necessarily based on knowledge: in the first place knowledge of the past, but also, and indistinguishably, of oneself. Those who lack historical knowledge not only lack the ability to act, but also a self-knowledge whose absence is just as damaging: 'nous étions tellement ignorants, ignorants de nous-mêmes ce qui est le plus terrible' (p. 137). Mathieu as a boy cannot understand his own life because he lacks the necessary perspective that a knowledge of the past would give him (pp. 260–61). This lack produces an 'empty' self: 'nous essayons de tirer sur nous le jour du passé, nous sentons que nous sommes trop légers sous ce poids, et pour remplir notre présence nous sommes trop vides dans cette absence, cet oubli' (p. 58). Conversely, history gives individual and community a sense of their place in the world and the possibility of becoming a full, rooted, *knowing* subject that can move freely into the future: 'Le passé. Qu'est le passé sinon la connaissance qui te roidit dans la terre et te pousse en foule dans demain?' (p. 280).[31] In other words, knowledge of the past is important because it confers self-knowledge on the individual or the community, and both agency and identity are predicated on self-knowledge. In this way, the text proposes at least the *possibility* of a truly autonomous sovereign subject, to be distinguished from the illusory autonomy associated with the maroon community in so far as it is based on a real understanding of historical processes and a commitment to change and progress. The 'interruption' or contesting of the mythical community and its origin does not here produce as its alternative a community of singular beings-in-common, as in Nancy's theorization, but of full immanent subjects engaged in the political work of building a future.

The insistence on political and social change appears to marginalize the maroon community which obviously belongs to the past rather than the future: the new society, based in the towns, is more open and inclusive, and no longer willing to accord the maroons any special status. However, this society has come about through a haphazard and unwilled conjunction of historical circumstances; it is not the product of the political agency of self-aware subjects that *Le Quatrième Siècle* so insistently promotes. It is extremely imperfect; moreover its imperfections are seen in large part as stemming from its loss of any sense of its own history. Thus the text makes it clear that future progress depends on the political consciousness which itself depends on restoring and maintaining a connection with the past. It is at this point that the full irony of the status of the maroons becomes apparent: although the progressive political use which Mathieu wishes to make of the past is the opposite of their nostalgic relation to it, the basic sense of history which is necessary to his project is seen as the *unique prerogative* of the maroons – who at least have not simply forgotten the past. As papa Longoué tells Mathieu, 'Ils sont sots, par là-bas en bas. Ils disent "Ce qui est passé est bien passé." Mais tout ce qui passe dans les bois est gardé au fond du bois!' (pp. 15–16). Even as a young boy Mathieu is already aware of the dichotomy between papa Longoué's distinctive orientation to the past and the 'emptiness' of the town's existence in a meaningless present: 'Balancé entre le vertige de cette nuit où le passé réel (la lointaine filiation) s'était englouti et le clair lancinement du présent, ou plutôt de la vacance présente' (p. 261). Therefore, however inevitable and indeed beneficial the movement towards creolization, it inevitably conflicts with the desire to maintain a distinct maroon community as a basis for keeping alive the 'longue histoire' (p. 221) which alone can combat the stagnation from which contemporary Martinican society suffers.[32] This explains why the imminent end of the maroon way of life is at times described with such elegiac eloquence:

> Que la vie quitterait l'épais croisement et le tapis humide des bois pour s'ancrer autour de Roche Carrée, dans la région des tamis labourés, et partout où les hommes souffriraient et mourraient loin d'aucune sorte d'écho pour leurs cris. Et peut-être que Stéfanise comme Melchior prévoyait l'absence, le néant, l'oubli de mort qui en résulterait; – ce pour quoi elle monta dans les bois, afin qu'au moins il y en eut deux ou trois qui remuent, sur l'emplacement devant la case, les décombres et la cendre de l'incendie. (p. 173)

The last chapter attempts to overcome this contradiction by suggesting that the knowledge of the past ceases to be an exclusively maroon characteristic, to be shared by the whole society; it thus moves from the elegiac 'Les Longoué, seigneurs des hauts, étaient taris' (p. 286) to the optimistic claim that 'Taris, les Longoué reposaient en tous' (p. 287). The maroons' knowledge is not lost, but spreads down to the plain where, Mathieu hopes, it will become available to everyone: 'Et puisque s'ouvraient en effet d'autres chemins, puisque cette ombre de la case ne l'appelait plus là-haut mais au contraire allait peut-être (ramenant le passé dans le présent fébrile) désormais aider et conduire chacun sur les terrains alentour' (p. 278). Also, the novel definitely ends on a note of exhilaration, reaffirming Mathieu's confidence in life and the future. But at the same time, this final chapter also contains several indications that its overt message of a generalized, no longer purely maroon, consciousness of history remains extremely problematic. Whereas Mathieu himself 'voyait le Temps désormais noué à la terre' (p. 279), he doubts that many others do: 'Mais combien étaient-ils alentour à pressentir, à supputer, sous l'apparence, le sourd travail? Combien à connaître? (Une science pouvait-elle, ainsi non partagée, profiter? [...] le savoir n'est-il pas fécond, d'être avant tout commun?)' (p. 279). The majority of the people are not, or not yet, interested in the past; Mathieu realizes the scale of the task ahead: 'Et le temps, l'énorme, désespérant, désertique temps qu'il faudrait, simplement pour leur ouvrir la tête sur ce Temps passé noué à la terre, et pour les ramener vers le haut des mornes' (p. 280). The end of this sentence, moreover, in effect still equates historical consciousness with the inhabitants of 'le haut des mornes', in other words, the maroons; just as a later sentence, following 'Les Longoué étaient taris' implicitly identifies Africa (and hence the maroons) with a knowledge of the past that is in contradiction with, and repressed by, the rest of modern society: Africa is 'la source d'un passé suscité, la part qui, niée, à son tour niait la terre nouvelle, son peuplement et son travail' (p. 287).

In so far as the text thus finally identifies knowledge of the past exclusively with the maroons, it undercuts the distinction that it had earlier made between the attitudes of papa Longoué and Mathieu: between the past as origin and the past as process. Moroever, the *reason* for the maroons' commitment to keeping the past alive is that it provides the foundation for their distinct, originary identity. To appropriate this knowledge/identity configuration, as Mathieu tries to do, for the entirely different purpose of building the new society (by as it were injecting political agency into it) creates a perceptible strain within the novel, because of the conflicting pressures of the maroons' 'identité-racine' and the relational identity of creolization.[33] This is the reason for the ambivalent depiction of creolization; and also for the novel's inability, ultimately, to hold its forward and backward movements in a harmonious balance.

It would appear, therefore, that the creolization process is positive only on the condition that it retains intact, and generalizes, the value attached to historical knowledge that has actually been realized only in the maroon community. Not only is this presented as a difficult task, and a rather fragile hope; but it means that the maroon community itself survives as a privileged value within the larger society. The maroons themselves die out, and the novel accepts their passing as an inevitable and, to the extent that they are arrogant and unaware of their dependence on others, positive development. But it cannot relinquish its particular attachment to them in so far as they still represent a historical consciousness whose absence is seen as profoundly damaging in the rest of the population. Despite their limitations and blind spots, and the contradictions which their inclusion creates, the legacy of the maroons remains a necessary element in the political progress towards a better future.

CHAPTER 3

Living by Mistake: Individual and Community in Simone Schwarz-Bart's *Pluie et vent sur Télumée Miracle*

When *Pluie et vent sur Télumée Miracle* came out in 1972, its portrayal of rural Antillean society was attacked by Marxist critics for being depoliticized and defeatist, for ignoring the social and historical determinants of the reality which it depicted as timeless and irremediable, and for presenting a heroine who was relatively privileged and alienated from the community of cane-cutters.[1] Other critics later came to Schwarz-Bart's defence, notably Mireille Rosello, in an article first published in 1990, in which she argues that Télumée, far from being passive and resigned to her fate, embodies a specifically female type of resistance rejecting grandiose heroic gestures and martyrdom, and based instead on low-key tactics of day-to-day survival.[2] These two opposed views, however, have in common an emphasis on the heroine as an *individual*, suffering and surviving on her own. Télumée's independence is indeed prominent throughout her narration. There are other individuals whom she loves and cares for, but she does little to help the community as a whole; towards the end of the text she acts as a healer for a short period of time, but does not attach much importance to this.[3] Conversely, the community helps and supports her at times. But her dominant characteristic is her very strong sense of her *individual* identity – reinforced by her telling her story in the first person. The collective dimension, in other words, is not such an overtly important theme as it is in, for instance, *Gouverneurs de la rosée* or *Le Quatrième Siécle*. Nevertheless, *Pluie et vent sur Télumée Miracle* is a deceptively rich and complex text; its very unselfconsciousness allows it to accumulate clusters of meaning that are not made entirely explicit or organized into a coherent whole (unlike *Gouverneurs de la rosée*, again). Exploring these allows us to see that in fact Télumée's relation to the community is far more important than a superficial reading might suggest; but it is not at all straightforward.

When she is ten years old Télumée goes to live with her grandmother Toussine. Her reaction on entering the house for the first time is: 'je me sentis comme dans une forteresse, à l'abri de toutes choses connues et

inconnues, sous la protection de la grande jupe à fronces de grand-mère'
(p. 47). As this suggests, from this point onwards she is *protected* from
the outside world, and kept at a distance from the rest of the community. Toussine instils in her a sense of the superiority of her family – the
'lignée' of the Lougandor women – and tries to keep her away from the
bad influence of others in the village: she discourages her from playing
with other children (p. 68), later will not let her work in the canefields
(p. 86) but finds her a job as a domestic servant some way away from
the village, and so on. Télumée loves and admires her grandmother and
never questions any of her views; nevertheless, as she becomes an adult,
she does, as I will attempt to show, begin to acquire a rather different
attitude towards the community.

The novel's main theme is the battle between, on the one hand, happiness, emotional strength and the determination to control one's own
destiny and, on the other, suffering, despair and the 'folie antillaise' that
afflicts the whole community. The collective existence of the Antillais is
both cursed *and* saved by an ability to create happiness out of nothing.
Thus on the one hand the sense of malediction reflected in the place names
– 'L'Abandonnée', 'Fond-Zombi', 'Morne la Folie' – is reinforced by
frequent remarks such as 'le cœur du nègre est une terre aride que nulle
eau n'amendera, un cimetière jamais rassasié de cadavres' (p. 148). But
this is counterbalanced by Télumée's belief in people's ability to find
happiness despite everything: she reflects on 'tout ce lot de misère et la
malignité du nègre à forger du bonheur, malgré tout' (p. 112). Happiness
and suffering can, in the abstract, form a certain equilibrium – 'Chacun
semblait soupeser la vie, mettre en balance la misère du nègre, sa folie,
sa tristesse congénitales et puis le contentement mystérieux qui vous vient
quelquefois' (p. 129) – but their permanent, conflictual co-existence
produces a contradictory attitude to life, summed up in Maryse Condé's
definition, made in the course of her analysis of Schwarz-Bart's novel, of
Antillean oral culture as 'l'expression d'un profond fatalisme joint à un
indéracinable optimisme'.[4] Moments of happiness are thus rarely free of
anxiety; they are won against a constant background of fear and foreboding, and premonitions of disaster: 'Malheur à celui qui rit une fois et
s'y habitue, car la scélératesse de la vie est sans limites' (p. 23). (The most
prominent example of this is Télumée's and Elie's love for each other:
right from the start, their happiness is undermined by the fear that he
will end up destroying both of them (pp. 71–72) – an apparently quite
irrational fear that is nevertheless realized.)

This strange intimacy of happiness and misery is exacerbated by the fact that disaster is not primarily caused by external factors, but by the psychological fragility of the people themselves; as Amboise says, when Elie asks 'par quoi nous sommes poursuivis', 'Ami, rien ne poursuit le nègre que son propre cœur' (p. 147). The sense of doom is explained as a kind of collective madness: 'la folie antillaise' which, although imaged as an external force, tornado or bird of prey –

> Lorsque, durant les longs jours bleus et chauds, la folie antillaise se met à tournoyer dans l'air au-dessus des bourgs, des mornes et des plateaux, une angoisse s'empare des hommes à l'idée de la fatalité qui plane au-dessus d'eux, s'apprêtant à fondre sur l'un ou l'autre, à la manière d'un oiseau de proie, sans qu'il puisse offrir la moindre résistance. (p. 41)

– is in fact, precisely, a madness: the *psychological* legacy of slavery, the persisting, corrosive internalization of powerlessness and worthlessness. Conversely, therefore, as Toussine teaches Télumée, happiness derives from psychological strength: not the political strength to change and improve social existence, but the individual's ability to endure hardship and recover from despair and madness. In Toussine's view, 'Le principal était, après tous les avatars, les pièges et leurs surprises, oui, c'était seulement de reprendre souffle et de continuer son train, ce pour quoi le bon Dieu vous avait mis sur la terre' (p. 66). Happiness in other words is conditional on individual self-sufficiency – Nancy's 'immanent individual' – rather than on the relatedness of singular-plural beings. Toussine, again, exemplifies this in her 'plénitude' (p. 22) and her ability to 'se retirer à volonté dans les replis de son âme' (p. 22).

This strong, self-sufficient, *full* self is contrasted with images of the empty selves of those afflicted with 'la folie antillaise'. Thus Elie is tormented by 'ce gouffre dans sa poitrine où tout venait s'anéantir' (p. 149); Angebert, Télumée's father, also suffers from being 'la proie du vide' (p. 36), a disintegration in his case so profound that he doubts that he has any recognizable personality at all, anxiously stroking his little daughter's hair and asking her: 'c'est moi, c'est moi Angebert, est-ce que tu me reconnais?' (p. 36). Or else the self is described as *broken* – Man Cia, for instance, stresses the continuing after-effects of slavery by saying: 'sont-ils arrivés à nous casser, à nous broyer, à nous désarticuler à jamais? … Ah, nous avons été des marchandises à l'encan et aujourd'hui, nous nous retrouvons le cœur fêlé' (p. 190) – or torn apart like a piece of cloth: Germain exclaims: 'ah, la vie est déchirée, de partout déchirée, et le tissu ne se recoud pas' (p. 38), and the same image is taken up by Madame Brindosier: 'la vie est un vêtement déchiré, une loque impossible à recoudre' (p. 50).[5]

The legacy of slavery thus manifests itself in images of disintegration.

But on a deeper level it corresponds to a fundamental sense of *non-entitlement*, as though one had no right to exist.[6] The suicidal Ti-Paille, for instance, claims: 'je dis que le nègre mérite la mort pour vivre comme il vit' (p. 54). Télumée as a child, frightened by Mme Brindosier bitterly gloating over 'la dérision et la nullité de la vie du nègre' (p. 50), reacts with this same sense of illegitimacy: 'et soudain l'ombre descendait sur moi et je me demandais si je n'étais pas descendue sur la terre *par erreur*' (p. 50, my italics); two pages later, she even wonders whether her formidable grandmother does not also exist 'par erreur' (p. 52); and later still, as she tries to come to terms with the reality of slavery, it has extended to the whole of her universe: the stars 'semblaient posées là par erreur, comme tout le reste' (p. 63). Overcoming 'la folie antillaise' thus involves creating for oneself a sense of legitimacy; and this too would seem to imply the 'immanent totality' of Nancy's 'perfect individual' (BSP, p. 32).

As its name suggests, 'la folie antillaise' is a social rather than an individual pathology.[7] All the main characters, even the strongest and most lucid, succumb to it at one time or another; and some minor characters, such as Germain and Ti-Paille, serve solely to illustrate it. It deprives them of any ability to control their own actions, and Germain ends up murdering his friend Angebert – who forgives him because 'sa volonté ne lui appartenait plus' (p. 40). This powerlessness is expressed in repeated images of human lives as small boats tossed on a stormy sea, or as captive, mistreated animals. It is also reinforced by the overall narrative structure of the novel, which is dominated by an intricate structure of repetitions from one generation to another: the theme of kindness to a 'fou' being repaid with enmity is repeated from Angebert and Germain to Télumée and Médard; both Toussine and Victoire lose a child; both Minerve and Victoire have a child by a man who then abandons them; both Victoire's husband Angebert and Télumée's husband Amboise are murdered; both Amboise and Méranée burn to death, and so on.[8] It is as though, because people have no control over their future, they are doomed to an endless cycle of repeated misfortunes. This impossibility of any concerted collective action precludes any consciousness of community as 'work': it is significant that the only political project, the strike at the canefields, not only fails but is made to seem derisory, since the management eventually give the workers the pay rise anyway.

It is thus also impossible to imagine a future in any terms other than impending doom. In other words, 'la folie antillaise' is closely connected to the community's perception of *time*. The future impinges on the present only as a threat of imminent disaster; and so, as we have seen, even present moments of happiness are undermined by anxiety. The overall tone of the novel is strongly nostalgic; it ends with a clear rejection of the notion of progress, as the recent innovations of electricity, mains water and tarmacked roads are dismissed by Télumée as alien and meaningless (p. 248), and the final paragraph is a powerful statement of permanence – 'Comme je me suis débattue, d'autres se débattront, et, pour bien longtemps encore, les gens connaîtront même lune et même soleil' – but turned towards the past, in the form of the dead: 'et ils regarderont les mêmes étoiles, ils y verront comme nous les yeux des défunts' (p. 248).

This could be read as suggesting that one can take refuge in the past from the uncertainties of the future. But one could also argue that the repetitions of the plot engender another kind of fatalism and stagnation. It is not a dynamic history of lives changing over time; looking back to previous generations does not enable one to encounter difference, but only sameness; unable to move in either direction, time is frozen into stasis. In fact, the novel at one point seems to suggest that the community's past *of itself* makes the future impossible: 'Et dans ces instants-là, j'avais la ferme conviction que tout pouvait changer, que rien encore n'avait eu vraiment lieu depuis le commencement du monde' (p. 133). It is a sign of Télumée's being unusually carefree that she can momentarily imagine a future, but what is most significant here is the equivalence of the two final clauses: implying that for future change to be possible, the past would have had *not to exist*.

But there is a further reason for the community's inability to derive any emotional strength from the past, more closely linked to the notion of non-entitlement. In discussing *Le Quatrième Siècle*, I showed how the maroons legitimized themselves through reference to their origins; and this is precisely not available to the descendants of slaves in Schwarz-Bart's novel. Very few characters refer explicitly to slavery; as a child, Télumée learns to recognize a particular kind of bitter laugh as a veiled allusion to it (p. 50), and notices that her grandmother's voice changes when she sings 'les vieux chants d'esclaves' (p. 51). But there is an obscure sense of shame connected with being the descendants of slaves that inhibits open discussion of it; only Man Cia, the witch, articulates it clearly for Télumée: 'Si tu veux voir un esclave, dit-elle froidement, tu n'as qu'à descendre au marché de la Pointe et regarder les volailles ficelées dans les cages, avec leurs yeux d'épouvante' (p. 60). The slave, in other words, is non-human: an animal, and an object that is bought and sold.[9] Thus for a human community, slavery cannot function as an origin in the sense of a founding myth, but rather signifies, not even that lack of origin that features so prominently in many Caribbean novels, but a kind of actively corrosive *anti*-origin, generating only anxiety and confusion. As Ernest Pépin puts it, 'cette violence fondatrice [de l'esclavage] doit être conjurée, d'où l'obsession de Télumée sur le problème de l'origine du Mal, qui est aussi le problème de sa propre origine'.[10] Hence, for example, Abel's fear of being non-human: 'il se met à hurler dans son lit: est-ce que je sors du ventre d'une femme humaine?' (p. 72).

The 'folie antillaise' is destructive both of the self and of others, the source of violence and cruelty. It does not, however, *isolate* those affected by it, or completely negate their capacity to help each other. One of the most poignant aspects of the novel is the extent to which these damaged, apparently dysfunctional individuals do nevertheless form a community: they are not united in purposeful collective action, as in *Gouverneurs de la rosée* or (as we shall see) in *Texaco*, but they support each other in times of trouble. Angebert, as well as helping Germain, patiently cares for Victoire throughout her periods of drunken despair; and Adriana leads a group of women encouraging Télumée to emerge from her period of madness (pp. 162–63). Neither of these two characters has the stable, morally responsible, psychologically 'healthy' personality that might seem to be a prerequisite for this caring role: Angebert's extreme fragility and lack of identity ('il avait si bien effacé son visage qu'on ne sut jamais qui était mort ce jour-là', p. 41) are paralleled by Adriana's instability: 'Elle faisait partie de la cohorte d'épaves, d'errants, de perdus qui traî-naient de case en case, en quête d'un vertige' (p. 103). But both succeed in preventing the people they help from succumbing permanently to madness and despair, and in this they are typical of a community which lacks cohesion and collective identity, and most of whose members lack any stable selfhood, but who still manage to care for each other. In this sense it is close to Nancy's 'communauté désœuvrée' in which each being is '*inclined*, [...] outside itself, over that edge that opens up its being-in-common' (IC, p. 4), and in which '[the] relation (the community) is, if it *is*, nothing other than what undoes, in its very principle [...] the autarchy of absolute immanence' (IC, p. 4). And being-in-common, in so far as it is opposed to notions of entitlement and legitimacy, is perhaps also a matter of 'living by mistake'.

Fond-Zombi is not in fact the most extreme example in the novel of this kind of marginal, dispossessed and disintegrated community. There is also the 'confrérie des Déplacés', who live scattered over the hillside, and who are defined by their deviation from the norms of social existence: 'des nègres errants, disparates, rejetés des trente-deux communes de l'île et qui menaient là une existence exempte de toutes règles, sans souvenirs, étonnements, ni craintes' (p. 186). As the name they give themselves suggests, they have no legitimate 'place' in organized society – but they are a 'confrérie', a community. They look after Télumée, giving her food and helping her to get work in the canefield. Olympe keeps her fire going throughout the night so that each morning she can give all the others embers to start their own fires with; and every Sunday they go down into the town of La Ramée together to drink and enjoy themselves. Despite their lack of collective 'rules' (p. 186), in other words, they have a strong supportive collective existence. In fact, perhaps because of living 'sans souvenirs' (p. 186), they appear to be better able than the villagers to escape the psychological aftermath of slavery; whereas, as we have seen, most of the characters are fated to 'mourir silencieusement de l'esclavage après qu'il soit fini, oublié' (p. 244), the Déplacés' very marginality seems to liberate them from the weight of the past: Olympe is the only character in the whole novel to celebrate the *end* of slavery, drunkenly and scandalously shouting at the church-goers: 'l'esclavage est fini: aimez-moi, pourrez pas m'acheter… haïssez-moi pourrez pas me vendre!' (p. 201). But they, just like the more respectable villagers of Fond-Zombi, are a 'communauté désœuvrée' in the precise sense that they have not produced themselves as a self-conscious 'work' and are not 'working' on any other collective projects that would improve and define their lives. Their relationships with each other are limited to trying, in disorganized fashion, to ensure their day-to-day survival.

* * *

Toussine and Télumée themselves suffer periods of madness; for Toussine, it follows the death of her daughter in a fire which also destroys all their possessions, and in Télumée's case it is precipitated by the madness of her first husband, Elie, which makes him turn against her, beat and torture her. But unlike most of the other characters in the novel – most prominently Elie – both women find the strength to recover from these episodes. This, in fact, is the main moral lesson that the novel sets out to teach: like the reader, Télumée learns from her grandmother how to survive despair. But despite the parallels between the two women (Schwarz-Bart herself sees them as identical[11]) there are some significant differences in the ways in which they do this. In Toussine's case, following her daughter's death, she withdraws totally from the community members, who reciprocally make a point of not going near her house, and remains alone until she feels strong enough to go out in public once more (pp. 25–27); in other words, her return to normality is entirely due to her self-sufficiency as an individual. But Télumée's path towards recovery is somewhat different.

Up until this point she has defended herself against aggression by a tactic which is the exact opposite of the relatedness of the 'communauté désœuvrée': in a form of controlled hysteria, she mentally cuts herself off from her real situation , retreating into an imaginary world in which she can convince herself that she cannot be hurt by anyone. In her confrontations with the white family for whom she works for a time as a domestic servant, she preserves herself from being damaged by their contempt for her by deliberately imagining that she is *under water* (a pebble on the river bed, p. 92), thus removing herself from the situation, not reacting, but 'ne songeant qu'à me préserver, à demeurer intacte sous ces paroles de blancs' (p. 97). Her initial response to Elie's attacks on her, although far less controlled, is basically similar: not only does her madness take the familiar form of 'néant' (p. 150) and emptiness ('le vent qui passait sur moi rencontrait un autre vent', p. 150), but there is a further aspect to this 'nothingness': as she sits almost catatonically in her garden, 'inexistante et alanguie' (p. 151), her empty self becomes a 'bubble' which lifts her above the world: 'un rêve de bulle qui emplissait ma chair, m'élevant au ciel' (p. 151). Her tactic of survival, in this more extreme case, is the same hysterical detachment from an unbearable reality:

> Alors je m'allongeais à même le sol et m'efforçais de dissoudre ma chair, je m'emplissais de bulles et tout à coup je me sentais légère [...] ma tête et mon corps entier se dissipait dans l'air et je planais, je survolais Fond-Zombi de si haut qu'il ne m'apparaissait plus que comme un grain de pollen dans l'espace. (p. 153)[12]

Floating in the air and sinking under the water are equivalent ways of escaping life on earth.[13] But this is not the right way to respond to Elie, as she learns. Given his hallucinations, delusions and insane cruelty, there is something quite remarkable about the clarity with which he sees exactly what she is doing; he describes her as a 'négresse planante' (p. 159), 'un grand vent' (p. 154) and 'un nuage noir' (p. 150). There is also the suggestion that her inability to remain in touch with her immediate reality contributes to his own madness:

> Tu te crois toujours petite fille au Bassin bleu, mais si tu ne le sais pas, je t'apprends que tu es une grande femme aux seins lourds sous ta robe [...] Tu essayes de me fuir [...] tu grimpes dans les airs et tu planes, mais tu n'éviteras pas l'homme que je suis [...] tu crois que je te laisserai planer dans les airs, mais tu ne courtiseras pas les nuages car je suis là et bien là. (pp. 158–59)

The opposition between sky and earth is developed into one between evading and facing up to reality; and Télumée herself eventually accepts this. When Elie says to her, 'tes seins sont lourds et ton ventre est profond, mais tu ne sais pas encore ce que ça signifie d'être une femme *sur la terre*' (p. 155, my italics), she, despite dismissing these 'propos sibyllins' (p. 155), later seems to admit that he is right:

> Mais les voies du ciel m'étaient fermées, je ne pouvais plus prendre les airs pour refuge et [...] je demeurais en bas [...] avec le sentiment amer que j'étais loin du compte, la certitude qu'il me restait bien des découvertes à faire avant que je ne sache ce que signifie exactement cela: être une femme sur la terre. (p. 159)

Moreover, the reality of being 'une femme sur la terre' involves the recognition that one is part of a community. In fact, Télumée – unlike Toussine – begins to recover only when the other villagers start to help her. At first they do this simply by walking past her house while talking and singing cheerfully, just to remind her of their presence. Later, Adriana organizes a group of women to sit down outside her garden and talk about her, showing that they understand that she 'peut continuer longtemps à naviguer dans les airs' (p. 162) but reassuring her that she will eventually come back to earth: 'Quelque chose empêche cette petite négresse de toucher terre, et elle peut continuer longtemps à naviguer comme ça, longtemps... Et pourtant moi Adriana je frappe ma poitrine et je vous dis: cette femme abordera' (pp. 162–63). Thus the 'cure' consists in reminding Télumée that she is not isolated or exceptional, showing her 'qu'il ne pouvaient y avoir de coupure dans la trame, et que j'avais beau vouloir voler et devenir grand vent, j'étais pourvue de deux mains et deux pieds, tout comme eux' (p. 160). In other words, she is – at least temporarily – drawn back into the community.

A similar movement – that is, from a stance of detachment and apparent superiority towards a recognition that she does in fact share a common position with the rest of the community – occurs in the way in which Télumée's view of her ancestry changes in the course of the novel. Initially she follows Toussine's example and, in striking contrast to the other characters in the novel, turns to the past as a way of legitimizing her individual existence through filiation, by placing herself in the lineage of the Lougandor women, whom she repeatedly invokes in the course of the text as an example of wisdom and strength, and as the basis for her own sense of identity. The importance which Schwarz-Bart attaches to this is clear from a comment describing her battle with the editors who wanted her to cut out the first part of the novel, entitled 'Présentation des miens': 'Or, pour moi, il n'y a pas de roman sans cette première partie.

Car c'est notre mémoire. Il y a toujours une espèce de recherche, de filiation, toujours une recherche d'attache'.[14] This attempt to ground oneself
in the past, to counteract the sensation of existing 'par erreur' by claiming
a *right* to exist, a legitimacy deriving from one's position in a proud
history of strong women, has something in common with Nancy's definition of foundational myth. It is also, for Télumée, a way of dissociating
herself from the communal shame attached to the dehumanized anti-
origin of slavery. Her defiance represents a healthy refusal to internalize
such ideas, but in clinging to the counter-myth of the Lougandor filiation she also in a sense represses the historical truth of her descent from
slaves, and thus also what she shares with the rest of the community.

This however changes at the very end of the novel. In the final chapter
she looks back over her life, summarizes all the people and events that
have been important to her, and comes to the conclusion that it has all
been worthwhile; the tone is one of hard-won tranquillity and quiet
contentment at the achievement of her survival. In this context one might
have expected her to commemorate once again the female ancestors that
have inspired and supported her throughout her life. It is, therefore,
extremely significant that she does not do so. She does describe a dream
or vision of her ancestors – but, for the first time in the novel, these are
not the 'lignée de hautes négresses' (p. 203), but are identified as slaves
in the slave market. It is as though having almost reached the end of her
life she finally accepts, and gives the novel's fullest expression to, the terri-
fying enigma of what I have called the non-human anti-origin of slavery:

> J'essaye, j'essaye toutes les nuits, et je n'arrive pas à comprendre comment
> tout cela a pu commencer, comment cela a pu continuer, comment cela peut
> durer encore, dans notre âme tourmentée, indécise, en lambeaux et qui sera
> notre dernière prison. Parfois mon cœur se fêle et je me demande si nous
> sommes des hommes, parce que, si nous étions des hommes, on ne nous
> aurait pas traités ainsi, peut-être. (p. 244)

In reclaiming these ancestors – 'je soulève la lanterne pour chercher le
visage de mon ancêtre, et tous les visages sont les mêmes et ils sont tous
miens' (p. 244) – she as it were re-humanizes them, and this section ends
with a reaffirmation of their capacity for struggle and endurance,
although there is still no sense that their descendants will ever definitively
free themselves from the legacy of slavery.

* * *

Given her ambivalent, oscillating attitude towards collective social existence, what kind of role is Télumée able to play in the community? In the
first place, to what extent do the Lougandor women even feel that they

belong to it? Toussine and Victoire have a very definite sense of their separateness from the other villagers. Toussine is introduced as an exceptional person, un 'être mythique' (p. 11) and 'une femme qui vous aidait à ne pas baisser la tête devant la vie et rares sont les personnes à posséder ce don' (p. 11). Victoire refuses to let anyone see that she is suffering, repeating to herself 'les peines sont les mépris et mieux vaut faire envie que pitié' (p. 31). Télumée herself often expresses this same feeling of separateness, defining herself *against* the community, as an autonomous, self-sufficient subject. At the end of her life she has chosen to live alone, and relishes the peace of mind she feels 'debout au milieu de mon jardin, [...] jusqu'à ce que la mort me prenne dans mon rêve, avec toute ma joie' (p. 11). But at other times her happiness derives from feeling that she has a structured, legitimate position *in* the community, or, in a more extreme form, in moments of fusion *with* it. Thus setting up house with Elie counteracts, for a while, her sense of existing 'par erreur'; for the first time she feels 'in the right place': 'Le lendemain, je m'éveillai avec l'impression de [...] ne plus être étrangère sur la terre [...] Je regardai Fond-Zombi par rapport à ma case, ma case par rapport à Fond-Zombi et je me sentis à ma place exacte dans l'existence' (p. 125). The links between her and the other villagers appear as 'quelque chose de subtil [...] qui se tissait autour de moi, autour de la case' (p. 127) – which disappear when Elie abandons her (p. 153). Later, after her grandmother's death, working in the canefields produces in her an even more emphatic sensation of being 'in the right place': 'Et je me disais, c'est là, au milieu des piquants de la canne, c'est là qu'un nègre doit se trouver' (p. 200). To counteract her exhaustion she starts drinking and smoking, like the other workers; their collective endurance is conveyed in exuberantly rhythmic sentences expressing a new-found pride and solidarity with them:

> Et le jour se levait, et je reprenais ma route avec la sueur de la veille, les piquants de la veille, et j'arrivais sur la terre de l'usine et je brandissais mon coutelas, et je hachais ma peine comme tout le monde, et quelqu'un se mettait à chanter et notre peine à tous tombait dans la chanson, et c'était ça, la vie dans les cannes. (p. 201)

Occasional moments of an even more ecstatic loss of self and fusion occur when she is working in Abel's bar, for instance (p. 133), but most notably in the dancing that is part of the celebration accompanying her setting up house with Amboise (p. 209). The novel ends, nevertheless, with a reaffirmation of her self-sufficiency: living in contented isolation, feeling that she no longer belongs to modern society and looking forward to a peaceful death alone in her garden.

Télumée, then, alternates between detachment from and participation in the community. Correlatively, the community's relation to all the Lougandor women also oscillates: between envy at their good fortune (or gloating over their bad fortune) and being happy for them (or helping them recover). The ambivalence is never explicitly commented on, and it produces sudden, apparently fickle and unpredictable shifts of attitude from sympathy to envy. Toussine's and Jérémie's engagement, for instance, is celebrated by the fishermen giving away their catch in a feast of fish on the beach, in which the men 's'extasiaient... on pouvait le croire, mais en vérité, la race des hommes n'est pas morte' (p. 16), while the women are more sceptical. Later, however, the whole village becomes spiteful and jealous (p. 18). In particular, the unmarried women criticize Toussine 'avec une sorte de frénésie, d'emportement sauvage' (p. 19). But they all help to prepare the village for the wedding 'comme pour la fête communale', and all join in the celebration, the extravagance of which makes them realize that 'ils auraient une belle chose à raconter, au moins une fois dans leur vie. Ce fut cela qui soulagea les cœurs enflés de jalousie' (p. 20). In other words, the significance which is attached to the couple's good fortune fluctuates between the two poles of inclusion and exclusion: it is either an optimistic sign that such good fortune is possible for all of them, or a reinforcement, by contrast, of their own 'malédiction'. Conversely, the fire which kills Toussine's and Jérémie's daughter and destroys their house provokes an ambivalent response in the villagers: fascinated by the spectacle of the flames, they are 'entre deux âmes, voulant plaindre et trouvant dans cette fatalité comme un juste retour des choses' (p. 24).

The other Lougandor women elicit equally mixed feelings. Both Minerve (Toussine's mother) and Victoire are admired but also criticized for being snobbish (p. 12, p. 32). In the case of Télumée herself the balance is more clearly positive – the community helps and supports her – but she is still at times the victim of spiteful gossip. Such a mixture of sympathy and spite is in itself, of course, not unusual; indeed it is sometimes seen as typical of village communities.[15] But in this novel its very volatile dynamic is connected to the particular place that Toussine and Télumée occupy in the communities they live in. In other words, it is a situation in which the two individual women alternate beween detachment from and participation in the community, while the community's attitude to them fluctuates between admiration/sympathy and envy/spite. What makes sense of these two symmetrical oscillations is, I would argue, the ambivalent kind of leadership that is attributed to Télumée and Toussine.

The form taken by the community in itself precludes Télumée or anyone else acting as a leader comparable to Roumain's Manuel, or Marie-Sophie in Chamoiseau's *Texaco*. The assumption that human beings cannot exercise any control over what happens to them, that individual survival rather than collective change is all that can be aspired to, and the sense of static or cyclical time, mean that there is, simply, no collective project or 'work' for a leader to lead. Toussine and Télumée do not therefore organize the community or bring about large-scale material change. What they do, however, is to act as *role-models*. Each is an example of someone whose good fortune inspires hope, and whose strength in adversity counteracts the general assumption of 'malédiction'. It is their individual lives that have an impact on the community as models which others can attempt to emulate, and they have as a result to put themselves on display for the community's benefit. In order to do this they have to exhibit, even more markedly than would a more active leader, their exemplary status as full autonomous subjects whose psychological strength can act as an inspiration for others. In order to be a role-model the individual has to be, precisely, an 'individual' in Nancy's sense of 'the atom, the indivisible […] figure of immanence: the absolutely detached for-itself, taken as origin and as certainty' (IC, p. 3). Toussine's and Télumée's function is to provide an example of such an immanent subject: fully present to itself, autonomous, in control, and therefore admirable. Toussine passes the family role on to Télumée, instructing her in her duty to display her happiness publicly:

> Nous, les Lougandor, ne craignons pas davantage le bonheur que le malheur, ce qui signifie que tu as le devoir aujourd'hui de te réjouir sans appréhension ni retenue. Tout Fond-Zombi te regarde, et voit que tu es semblable à un jeune cocotier dans le ciel. Tout Fond-Zombi sait qu'il assiste à ta première floraison, alors fais ce que tu dois, c'est-à-dire: embaume-nous, ma fille… (p. 137)

– and, on her deathbed, making it even clearer how much the community *needs* a role-model: 'écoute, les gens t'épient, ils comptent toujours sur quelqu'un pour savoir comment vivre… si tu es heureuse, tout le monde peut être heureux et si tu sais souffrir, les autres sauront aussi' (p. 175).

It is their status as role-model that obliges the Lougandor women to be both part of and slightly apart from the others in the village, and generates a contradictory play between intimacy and distance, identification and separateness. But the same relationship produces a similar ambiguity in the community's attitude to the role-model; and here one can perhaps develop the implications of common being in a direction that Nancy himself does not consider. The notion of role-model posits *per se* an ideal of common being in the sense of homogeneity; it is leadership based on imitation. But it also presupposes that the ideal is not already achieved, in other words, it assumes a gap between the role-model herself and the rest of the community. She has to be both different from them, offering something they can aspire to, and sufficiently similar to them for them to be able to emulate her; this explains the oscillation in her attitude to them. But, equally, the role-model can only function if the other members of the community do indeed identify with her, and they can only do this if they see her experience as something that they too could potentially achieve. And, as we have seen, they do not consistently do this; the alternative reaction of jealousy and *Schadenfreude* is always open to them as well, and comes into play when she appears to be too distant and snobbish. Hence the unpredictability of their reactions; *their* oscillation between admiration and spite is an inevitable result of the inherent instability of the relationship to the role-model. Thus identical situations can produce opposite reactions: while Jérémie and Toussine's engagement is met with envy, that of Télumée and Elie gives his friends hope that such good fortune is possible for them too, and a collective satisfaction that 'un nègre est quand même quelque chose, sur la terre' (p. 129).

The role-model is thus completely incompatible with the 'communauté désœuvrée' that in other ways is strikingly exemplified in the novel. In the first place, the individual who acts as role-model has to be a full self-sufficient subject. Secondly, it defines the community in terms of an aspiration towards homogeneity, achievable through a *specular* relationship with the role-model – as in the mirroring effect in which Télumée sees herself reflected in the faces of the villagers listening to her: 'Et mon âme se relevait et flottait sur tous les visages' (p. 192). In relation to Nancy's conception, then, the novel presents the contradictory co-existence of a 'communauté désœuvrée' and an immanent individual subject. The ambiguity of the role-model, in other words, introduces a kind of split or fault-line within the common being that it both endorses and problematizes, and therefore also the possibility of a community that combines – paradoxically, in relation to Nancy's oppositional formulation of the two – features of both common being and being-in-common, coded respectively as success and failure.

However, despite the early indications that Télumée will play the same role as her grandmother, she does not in fact do so consistently. Within the dominant perspective of the novel this has to be seen as a failure; but it also opens up the possibility of a different model of community, one that accords a more positive and straightforward place to being-in-common. Télumée adopts her position as role-model very consciously and proudly, describing herself in almost religious terms as a beacon of hope: the procession of women who come to visit her after she has moved in with Elie sit in reverent silence:

> elles touchaient ma robe avec un léger soupir d'aise, et puis me regardaient en souriant, avec une confiance absolue, tout comme si elles se trouvaient dans l'allée latérale de notre église, sous la compréhension de leur saint préféré, celui qui éclairait les ténèbres de leur âme, les renvoyait vivre dans l'espérance. (p. 131)

But Toussine has already hinted that, despite her pride in Télumée, she is also aware of her vulnerability. Immediately after reassuring Elie that the Lougandor women are a race of 'coqs de combat' who are never destroyed by defeat, she – rather contradictorily – whispers in his ear 'Si tu fais naufrage, mon nègre, elle sombrera avec toi' (p. 121). This, of course, is what happens; and although Télumée's crisis is presented as a necessary initiation into suffering from which she emerges with renewed strength, she in fact continues to experience moments of psychological disintegration. The most striking of these occurs when she is happily in love with Amboise but nevertheless feels herself *torn apart*; and, significantly, she expresses this in an image of the same fighting cocks that for Toussine were the emblem of the Lougandors' strength, but which are now made to signify compulsive violent internal conflict and self-destruction:

> Parfois je me voyais au centre de l'arène d'un pitt, en plein milieu du combat, sanglante, tantôt un coq et tantôt l'autre, les éperons, les coups de bec, tantôt l'un, tantôt l'autre, et ces impressions me venaient toujours à l'improviste, dans les moments les plus inattendus, lorsque je me mettais à rire soudain. (p. 207)

Even in the final chapter, her tranquil dignity is disrupted by a return of the old feeling of non-entitlement: 'et je me sens impuissante, déplacée, sans aucune raison d'exister' (p. 244). The immanent selfhood required by the role-model, in other words, is never definitively achieved. This may explain Télumée's withdrawal from any kind of collective social existence at the end of the novel. Her friends from Morne La Folie plead with her to come back to them (p. 243) – but she refuses. Soon afterwards, she rejects Elie's final pitiful attempt to make contact with her; and we leave her preparing herself for a solitary and peaceful death. One could perhaps see this as evidence that the contradictory tensions involved in being a role-model have proved impossible to sustain.

The preceding chapter, however, is devoted to the very significant encounter between Télumée and Médard. At first this appears to be just another demonstration of her habitual strength in overcoming adversity; in other words another example of her acting as a role-model, consecrated by her being given the name 'Miracle' (p. 239). But I want to argue that it actually enacts a very different relationship from that of the role-model, which in turn implies a very different conception of community: not the role-model's ideal of self-sufficiency and homogeneity, but something closer to Nancy's concept of the 'partage' – both *sharing* and *division* – that is constitutive of singular beings.

In fact we have already seen, much earlier in the novel, a brief evocation of such a relationship. The 'confrérie des Déplacés', marginal as they are, are contrasted with an even more marginal group existing on the very limits of human sociality: further up the mountain, in the depths of the forest, 'vivaient quelques âmes franchement perdues auxquelles on avait donné ce nom: Egarés' (p. 187). The 'Egarés' do not (unlike the 'Déplacés') work, use money, or grow their own food, and Télumée's reaction to them stresses how alien and almost sinister she finds them: 'Ils avaient des visages impassibles, des yeux imprenables, puissants, immortels' (p. 187). But the very next sentence expresses her feeling that she is *like them*: 'Et une force étrange déferlait en moi à les voir, une douceur alanguissait mes os et sans savoir pourquoi, je me sentais pareille à eux, rejetée, irréductible'. For Télumée they are thus both same and other – but *simultaneously*, as distinct from the oscillation between identification and distance that characterizes the role-model: and this is exactly the relation of 'sharing', in which the opposition between same and other ceases to operate:

> We are alike because each one of us is exposed to the outside that *we* are *for ourselves*. The like is not the same (*le semblable n'est pas le pareil*). I do not rediscover *myself*, nor do I recognize *myself* in the other: I experience the other's alterity, or I experience alterity in the other together with the alteration that 'in me' sets my singularity outside me and infinitely delimits it. Community is that singular ontological order in which the other and the same are alike (*sont le semblable*): that is to say, in the sharing of identity. (IC, pp. 33–34)

The later encounter – less than twenty pages from the end of the novel – between Télumée and Médard is a far more extended example of this 'spaced out' relationship which does not involve similarity or affinity, and has a transformative effect on the singular beings that it places in relation to each other. Médard is an outcast; sarcastically baptized 'l'ange Médard' by the villagers, he is 'evil' – 'un être créé pour le mal' (p. 230) – and the metaphors of cracks and brokenness that have throughout the novel been associated with madness are made entirely literal in his case, since his skull has been split open by a machete.[16] As a result, his other nickname is 'l'homme à la cervelle qui danse' (p. 230). Persuaded by her adopted daughter Sonore to be kind to him, Télumée accepts him into her house, but distrusts him from the start. They first meet in the village shop, where the proprietor mocks and humiliates Médard, giving him a bottle of petrol when he tries to buy rum. Télumée gives him the rum she has bought for herself: 'je le poussai sur la planche du comptoir, près de l'ange Médard, cependant qu'un filet de voix grêle et désagréable sortait de ma bouche… vous m'avez bien mal regardée, savez-vous?… et avez-vous jamais remarqué que moi aussi, j'ai la cervelle qui danse?' (pp. 231–32). This ambiguous mixture of dislike and not only kindness but a strange solidarity – sharing his madness – intensifies as the chapter progresses. When he turns Sonore against her, persuading the girl to return to her own village, Télumée starts to hate him; guessing that he will return to torment her further, she buys a large pair of scissors. It is unclear whether this is purely for self-defence, or whether she intends to murder him; but when he does indeed return he accidentally kills himself, in a slow and particularly horrible fashion, by falling and impaling his wounded skull on the corner of her table. Unable to move, he takes several hours to die; Télumée sits with him, holding his hand and talking to him, and in a mysterious way this releases him from his life-long anger and hatred of the world: 'Je savais maintenant ce qu'il voulait, ce qu'il avait toujours voulu au fond de lui-même, par-dessous la poche de fiel posée sur son cœur' (p. 237).

Various aspects of the episode differentiate it from the operation of the role-model. Médard has in fact previously undermined Télumée's status as role-model by invoking it in an openly cynical way, to ingratiate himself with her: 'J'étais une personne à chance, disait-il, et toute sa joie était de me contempler, lui, le mort sans bonheur' (p. 233). More generally, his effect on her prevents her from being wholly sane and in control of herself: he makes her brain 'crumble away' ('les jours allant, mon cerveau s'émiettait peu à peu', p. 234). Yet she cannot dissociate herself from him; ostensibly this is because of Sonore's affection for him, but it is noticeable how Télumée follows a very hostile remark about him with an expression of their *shared* experience: after his death she describes him as poisonous, but then as someone who had found that life suffocated him, squeezing the breath out of his lungs – and concludes: 'Voilà ce qui en avait été de nous deux, l'ange Médard et moi' (p. 238). In other words, the interaction between her and Médard is based on an unindividualized common experience which unlike the role-model relation has no specular dimension, which brings them into relation with each other without transcending difference and without eliminating or compensating for personal hatred, but in a way which nevertheless redefines their 'singularity'.

It is highly significant that Télumée's relationship with Médard culminates in his death. For Nancy, death as 'the unmasterable excess of finitude' (IC, p.13) undermines the concept of the immanent subject: my own death escapes me, but in the deaths of others my own mortal finitude is exposed to me, and for this to happen I must be part of a community defined as singularity and being-in-common as opposed to the substantive essence of common being. The other's death exposes my finitude to me: crucially, it is not a *specular* relation:

> it is in the death of the other, as I have said, that community enjoins me to its ownmost register, but this does not occur through the mediation of specular recognition. For *I* do not recognize *myself* in the death of the other – whose limit nonetheless exposes me irreversibly [...] I recognize that in the death of the other there is nothing recognizable. And this is how sharing – and finitude – can be inscribed. (IC, p. 33)

This is made particularly clear in the sole, cryptic, fragment of direct speech that occurs in this scene; Télumée's response to having intuitively realized what Médard wants from her is to say: 'nous voyons les corbeaux et nous disons: ils parlent une langue étrangère... mais non, les corbeaux ne parlent pas une langue étrangère, les corbeaux parlent leur propre langue et nous ne la comprenons pas' (pp. 237–38). It is this ability not to see others in comparison to oneself, this acceptance of alterity and singularity as opposed to the fusion of communion, that marks the difference between Télumée's relation to Médard and her previous 'role-model' relationships with the community, and makes of the former an example of Nancy's 'sharing'. (It is also relevant, given Nancy's insistence that the 'senseless meaning' of death must not be sublated or reabsorbed into any kind of 'immortal communion' (IC, pp. 13–14), that Médard's death is described without any reference to the supernatural – unlike the deaths of Toussine and Amboise, which conform to the fairly dominant presence of the supernatural throughout the novel.)

Another aspect of the episode is its impact on the villagers. They have watched Médard's long-drawn-out death, giving it a dimension of *spectacle* that could be wholly congruent with the performance of the role-model. But in their collective presence they could equally be seen as enacting the reciprocal 'revelation' of death and community. And, although they admire Télumée's behaviour, their response is less a desire to imitate it than to try to *understand* what is going on: specifically, to turn the event into a meaningful narrative: 'Les gens s'amassaient en silence, devant ma case, contemplant la scène qui se déroulaient sous leurs yeux et s'efforçant d'en tirer une histoire, déjà, une histoire qui ait un sens' (p. 238). They are, in other words, learning something new; and this suggests a possibility of collective change which is quite distinct from the identification and repetition inherent in the role-model.

This possibility is not pursued in the next and final chapter, which reverts to the perspective of the survival of the individual self and emphasizes the value of reconciliation with existing realities rather than any hope of change. Notably, Télumée cannot do for Elie, who dies in the last chapter, what she has done here for Médard. However, the shift that I have outlined in relation to Médard, from role-model to 'sharing', does in itself point to the potential for a different kind of change, and a different conception of community.

CHAPTER 4

Singular Beings and Political Disorganization in Vincent Placoly's *L'Eau-de-mort guildive*

Unlike Roumain, Glissant and Schwarz-Bart, who all appear regularly on francophone literature courses in Europe and North America, Vincent Placoly is almost unknown outside the French Caribbean. He died while still in his forties, in 1992, having written three novels, a number of shorter literary pieces, and a large amount of political journalism.[1] *L'Eau-de-mort guildive*, his second novel, came out in 1973 when he was twenty-seven. Placoly was a student in Paris between 1963 and 1969; he was introduced to Maurice Nadeau, who encouraged him in his writing and published his first two novels in the 'Lettres nouvelles' series at Denoël. They have affinities with some of the other, much better-known, writers whom Nadeau published and/or wrote on: Malcolm Lowry, Blanchot, Raymond Queneau and the Nouveau Roman in particular. But *L'Eau-de-mort guildive* is also an extremely original work, characterized by a surreal atmosphere and a chaotic structure. There is no continous narrative:[2] the novel's sixteen short chapters relate a number of unconnected or very loosely connected events involving an open-ended group of characters who appear and disappear more or less at random, and whose conversations make up the greater part of the text.

The novel's cryptic title is an indication of the kind of language that characterizes the novel. 'Guildive', unknown in standard French, is the local name for a cheap rum that was originally produced for the slaves: an 'eau-de-vie' that here is rather associated with death. The title thus both exemplifies Placoly's inventive use of language, delighting in obscurity, and alerts the reader to expect the atmosphere of drunken delirium, underscored by consciousness of death, that prevails in the novel. This is perhaps the single most striking feature of Placoly's text: its refusal to conform to the norms of intelligibility of realist fictional discourse. The narrative, although it follows a roughly chronological progression, is broken up into short sections which are difficult to place in relation to each other, in terms of either their locations or the people who appear in them; there are many gaps and inconsistencies, and the novel is spectacularly open-ended, ending on a note of suspense rather than resolution. Similarly, the characters and their surroundings, rather than being described in realist terms, are presented in fleeting images that seem to belong to poetic rather than fictional discourse. Nor is the dialogue that makes up such a large part of the text realistic, either in the sense of trying to reproduce the typical speech of the Martinican poor, or in the sense of providing functional information that would help the reader to follow what is happening. In fact, its main effect is to disorientate; it is a free-wheeling, delirious, 'wasteful' proliferation of language – as the novel itself remarks, 'Ce sont les gens qui conversent, librement, comme si la parole leur avait été donnée pour rien, sans dommages ni pour eux-mêmes, ni pour les autres' (p. 55). These are not rational subjects in control of their discourse; their language is always so to speak running away from them, escaping the constraints that would enable it to 'make sense' in a conventional fashion. The overall impression one gets from reading *L'Eau-de-mort guildive* is thus one of *unworking*: rather than constructing a coherent representation of a fictional world and suggesting conclusions that can be drawn from it, the text illustrates Nancy's conception of literature as 'désœuvrée', based on the suspension, inter-ruption and deferral of singular meanings.

Placoly's elusive, fragmentary representation of a chaotic reality is particularly surprising in that its author was throughout his life a very active and committed Marxist.[3] *L'Eau-de-mort guildive* is quite different from the orthodox novels of political commitment that both French and Caribbean readers had come to expect: there is no structured represen-tation of organized political struggle, no clear 'message', no concern to be intelligible to a wide readership, nor even any individual characters that are sufficiently developed for the reader to identify with them. The contrast with the didactic clarity and streamlined narrative of Roumain's *Gouverneurs de la rosée*, for instance, is striking. Placoly's Marxist colleagues, in a slightly uneasy attempt to explain this apparent aberra-tion, can only fall back on the traditional aesthetic defence of art as distinct from propaganda; René Ménil, for instance, who had been his teacher, describes Placoly's writing as inspired by 'une esthétique qui sait dire non à la banalité du sentiment et du langage pour bien asseoir la liberté et l'indépendance de la création littéraire', and concludes: 'Heureusement, ici, la littérature garde son autonomie pour dire ce qu'elle seule peut dire et qu'elle apporte à l'action politique'.[4]

But one could also argue that Placoly's transgressive attitude towards the conventions of the politically committed novel translates into a discourse which is *political* in Nancy's sense of 'the in-finite resistance of sense in the configuration of the "together"' (SW, p. 119). Writing confronts established political power 'through the resistance of significance to being captured or subsumed by signification. Which is nothing other than the resistance of the "community" to to its hypostasis' (SW, p. 119). In other words, the refusal to conform to a discourse of established political meanings is itself political in so far as it refuses to obscure or cover up the being-in-common that for Nancy is the only reality both of the political and of meaning, and also the justification for writing:

> 'Political' would mean a community ordering itself to the unworking of its communication [...] a community consciously undergoing the experience of its sharing. To attain such a significance of the 'political' does not depend, or in any case not simply, on what is called a 'political will'. It implies being already engaged in the community, that is to say, undergoing, in whatever manner, the experience of community as communication: it implies writing. We must not stop writing, or letting the singular outline of our being-in-common expose itself. (IC, pp. 40–41)

The 'question of thinking sense in the absencing of sense' is, he claims, not only political, 'it is revolution itself: the destitution of the authority of sense or of sense as authority, and the entry into the unheard-of. For the unheard-of, one has to get one's ears ready'.[5]

One can argue that Nancy's equation of literature-as-unworking *per se* and being-in-common means that *all* literature (as he defines it) is inevitably political (as he defines it), and that the equivalence between them is therefore too generalized to be illuminating, or indeed convincing.[6] But, while it is certainly true that 'one has to get one's ears ready' to read *L'Eau-de-mort guildive*, the events narrated in this particular novel are also political in an entirely conventional sense. The fraudulent criminal charges brought against the building workers by their employer Hamelin, the arrests of Clothaire and Ignigni, and the violent clashes between the police and the rioters all illustrate the unending struggle between the poorest inhabitants of Fort-de-France and the forces of law and order, and of capitalism. But this conflict does not result in any concerted effort of opposition. In other words, this community does not conceive of itself as a 'work' – its disorganized and habitually inebriated members are incapable of 'producing' themselves in or as a communal work, and even the politically conscious Mettiviers, who proclaims 'qu'il ne peut pas vivre en homme libre dans un pays où on enferme l'innocent malheureux pour préserver l'intérêt des puissants' (p. 42), does not organize his fellow workers to unite in struggle against Hamelin.

Equally, the community does not attempt to root itself in the past or project itself forwards into a better future. The setting is urban and contemporary: the poor quarters of Fort-de-France in the 1960s. In comparison to the three novels I have discussed so far, there is very little reference to the past, and the traditional rural life of Martinique is evoked, occasionally, only to stress its absence – as when Mettiviers, now working for Hamelin, looks back with mixed feelings on his earlier life in the canefields:

> – la poudre de ciment mangeait mes yeux de telle façon que continuellement, c'était déjà la nuit. J'en venais à regretter l'esclavage de la canne, ses heures perdues. Mais je n'aurais pas quitté pour un empire le volant de la Ford et sa ferraille, puissante comme une usine. C'est la jeunesse. Pendant que les champs de canne, vieillis, raidissent sous la poussière des siècles […] (p. 52)

Martinique is rapidly industrializing – 'L'industrie, beuglante sur des milliers d'hectares de terre grise, de fumée et de cendres, de cendres et de fumée' (p. 54) – and Roumain's idealized 'coumbite' is now just an irrelevant memory: 'Parce que monsieur Hamelin nous avait dit que l'exploitation des terres se restreint, adieu le cumbite [sic] et la cagnote des soucis, des peines, des espérances et des devoirs' (p. 54). But the novel does not represent this move away from the plantations as progress. The traditional exploitation of agricultural workers is being replaced by an equally exploitative industrial sector, and while the present is to some extent celebrated – for all their hardships, the lives of the urban poor have a mobility and exuberance that is absent from the lives of Roumain's villagers, for instance[7] – the future is not viewed with any confidence. Indeed, the sense of foreboding expressed in the numerous allusions to the future echoes that of Schwarz-Bart's (very different) characters. A description of Rachel laughing, for instance, is interrupted by an evocation of vague but imminent disaster:

> Dans la salle à manger, […] Rachel riait. Fenêtres ouvertes sur aucune chose que sur l'indécision des jours. Le futur encore et encore , frappant d'un doigt sec sur le linteau des portes, jusqu'à les faire béer de crainte et appeler à la rescousse bourrasques de vents, typhons, chutes de pluie: invitation sourde au désastre. […] Rachel riait. Et elle riait si fort qu'elle en risquait de tomber. (p. 155)

Thus the people in Placoly's novel neither look back nostalgically to a communal past, nor do they plan and work for a better future; they exist purely in a chaotic present.

The treatment of death in the novel also echoes the role of death in the 'désœuvrée' community as revealing the finitude of existence. The text conveys throughout the general awareness of the omnipresence of death that is foreshadowed in the 'eau-de-mort' of its title; life in the present is experienced as constantly vulnerable to it, as though death is the under-lying truth of life: 'Un sursaut d'énergie quand rien n'est possible que la mort' (p. 141); 'ainsi qu'obscurément en l'agonie la mort patauge dans la vie' (p. 142); 'Il faut la mort, car c'est à son pas que la vie marche' (p. 166). This impression is made more acute by the way in which the narra-tion of very ordinary incidents is frequently interrupted by unexpected allusions to death. For instance, the police are rounding up drunks in the market-place: 'On les y entendait disputer aussi de qui est-ce qui gagn-erait la sortie en premier. La vie n'ouvre sur rien. La mort ouvre-t-elle... sur quoi?' (p. 129). And a few pages later, the police lieutenant says: 'furieuse mort aux dents de congre! Ah cesse donc de mordre et de tourner, ennassée que tu es dans les joncs de la vie...' (p. 132).

At the same time, the novel 'unworks' the treatment of death as heroic self-sacrifice, its recuperation into immanence, that is characteristic of the Marxist novel. Five characters die in the course of the narrative: Loïs, La Tortue, Synge, Giap and Hand-Ball. The last three of these deaths are sudden and violent: Synge is shot by the police as he runs away from a shop that he is accused of robbing; Giap is murdered, presumably on the orders of his employer Hamelin; and Hand-Ball is shot dead by the police in the early stages of the riot that the two other deaths have provoked. We are told that '[la] découverte du cadavre de Giap fit fumer le feu des manifestations de rue [...] La mort d'Hand-Ball fit mèche: artificière et guerrière, elle déploya son van de feux' (pp. 219–20). In other words, all three deaths act as triggers for spontaneous collective action. But the characters are nevertheless not treated as *martyrs*. Synge's death is reported almost flippantly: 'Au même moment, une balle, partie d'un de ces bons-dieux de pistolets, sillonna l'air, rasa les têtes et troua l'œil étonné de SYNGE. Adieu, SYNGE!' (p. 110); and that of Hand-Ball in a brief fragment of dialogue as his comrades flee from the police:

    – Hand-Ball! Hand-Ball!
    – Trop tard! Trop tard! Déjà, sous le vent de son âme, il a passé
    le cap de notre humanité. Sauvons-nous!
    – O mort! (p. 219)

The murder of Giap is given more serious attention, and its effect on the rioters is made quite explicit – Ignigni says 'Dis-lui [à Hamelin] que nous danserons dans la gaieté des balles tant que Giap saignera en notre mémoire encore' (p. 216). But the riots last only a few days, and none of the three deaths results in anything other than immediate violent action; they are not *interpreted* by the community, no particular meaning is elab-orated around them – and, of course, they occur in the context of numerous other violent deaths at the hands of the police and army, as well as the more peaceful deaths of Loïs and La Tortue. Synge, Giap and Hand-Ball are not regarded as martyrs in the way that Manuel in *Gouverneurs de la rosée* is; his death, as I have argued in Chapter 1, is built up into a central component of the community's representation of itself: he strengthens the community's organic unity by dying for it. There is no sense in Placoly's novel of that process of 'reabsorption', in Nancy's formulation, of death into the community. Here there is a different relationship, between the pervasive evocation of death in the abstract as a permanent threat underlying life, and the fairly matter-of-fact way in which the actual deaths of individual characters are treated. On one level both of these aspects are explicable simply by the fact that even untimely death is sufficiently common as to be almost unremarkable. But perhaps there is more involved here than just an attitude of taking death for granted. The brevity with which the deaths are recounted could be linked to the fact that the novel ends just as the police are beginning to move in on the area they have surrounded, which includes the bar in which most of the characters are gathered; in other words, it stops short of describing their deaths, which we are nevertheless led to believe are about to happen. If death is, in Nancy's terms, the 'unmasterable excess of finitude', then it is also barely representable:[8] and it is this conception of death that ultimately determines the text's treatment of it.

* * *

In Placoly's novel, then, we find a close correlation between the 'unworking' characteristics of *literature* and the type of *community* that is evoked. This is above all evident in the novel's representation of people as neither immanent individuals nor a collective common being, but the 'singular plural' of being-in-common. One of the most immediately obvious ways in which the text distances itself from conventional realism is simply in the frequency of *plural* nouns, which often dominate whole pages of text, creating the impression of a vague, unspecific and uncircumscribed scene. Among many examples, this is typical:

> Le ciel tremblait; du moins, ce passage de lueurs poursuivies par des ombres, où l'on entrevoyait, au hasard d'une clairière, des tuiles dans des arbres et des arbres dans des oiseaux, rondes d'épées plantées comme en des bivouacs de chevalerie, tables rondes de l'écho, brillantes comme des cuivres, ruminations de la terre... Les quartiers se renfermaient, chacun dans sa solitude, laissant libres de larges espaces de rues où la police furetait, sentinelles hantées par la peur de la mort. Ponceaux de lune. Rivières dormantes. Sauts de carpe de la nuit humant l'épaisseur des gaz. (pp. 211–12)

Thus the whole text bathes in an atmosphere of plurality; and this is especially significant when it applies to human beings. There are, of course, many individual characters, but their very numbers, together with the fact that they are not organized into any hierarchy of importance but all exist in the text on the same level, serve to create a similar impression of plurality. Moreover, the reader's attention is often focused on groups of people rather than isolated individuals: building workers, prisoners, prisoners' wives, lawyers, police, gamblers, street entertainers – but also less easily recognizable groups such as 'les porteuses de seau qui ne parlent d'amour que la nuit, et ceux qui flânent les mains serrées dans leurs poches, parce que quand on a les mains dans les poches on a l'air plus encore de flâner' (p. 28); or 'un peuple aux dents de loups, portant à bout de bras des nuages d'incendie et des bombes meurtrières' (p. 213). Here, plurality goes together with anonymity. Either we do not know the names of any members of a particular group – the lawyers in Chapter 4, for instance, whose dialogue spans the whole chapter, are all anonymous – or, alternatively, named characters are presented as part of a group whose other members remain nameless: Valdes and Papayito are two of the troop of street entertainers, but the others are anonymous; Rachel and Mettiviers' wife are waiting among a larger group of other prisoners' wives who are not identified; Seguy Montanaes is the only one of the policemen to be named, and so on. No single character exists in isolation, but only in relation to other characters in a group whose membership is usually only very vaguely delineated.

In this sense, *L'Eau-de-mort guildive* offers a striking literary representation of Nancy's core concept of being-in-common as 'a dimension of "in-common" that is in no way "added onto" the dimension of "being-self", but that is rather co-originary and coextensive with it' (IC, p. xxxvii). It is exactly this originary being-in-common that is enacted by the dynamic of Placoly's text, first of all in the way in which single characters typically emerge against the background of an unspecified plurality of other characters.[9] For instance, Chapter 3 opens with dawn breaking over the prison; the first signs of human presence are simply the sounds of keys being turned in locks, footsteps, water running from taps and buckets clattering on the floors of the latrines. This is followed by a reference to '[têtes] grisonnantes de la captivité' (p. 33). Then the prisoners are again evoked collectively, but this time in a rather oddly constructed sentence in which the use of 'chacun' serves also to present them as 'singular beings' rather than an indistinct mass: 'chacun ne s'était pas encore désempêtré du rêve rouge sang de l'injustice et de la captivité' (p.

34). But then one of them starts crowing like a cock; another voice complains about him to the sergeant, and is only then, after he has spoken at some length, identified: 'C'est l'Indien [i.e., Ignigni] qui hurlait, les dents collés aux barreaux de sa cellule' (p. 34). And two paragraphs later, we learn the name of the prisoner who has been imitating the cock crowing: 'Mais Siméon Baptiste n'arrêtait son manège que vers les sept heures du matin' (p. 34).

Or, as the last night of the 'fête aux Années Lumière' draws to an end, the text first stages the gamblers collectively by using the inclusive pronoun 'on' alternating with subjectless infinitives: 'Aux tables de jeu, l'argent avait fondu. On ne pensait plus. Ne plus penser à ce qu'on avait perdu. On oubliait. Oublier ce qu'on avait gagné, pour un temps, le temps de se fourrer les mains dans les poches, cracher, hennir, suer, souffler comme un cheval parce que l'aube se lève' (p. 138). Only then do we learn that Dolminche is one of them: 'Mais Dolminche que la terre surprend vieilli, buté, sale [...]' (p. 138). Or, to give just one more example, the police are wondering how to deal with all the 'petit peuple de la nuit' (p. 176) that they have arrested for being drunk and disorderly. The reader does not know for certain who these are, although we assume they include some of the people we have already met. They are referred to first simply as 'ceux-là', and described in a way that does not help us to identify them: 'Ceux-là, sur qui planait l'ombre de sa majesté la lune [...] attendaient, qui pionçant à demi, bougonnant à demi rêvant, qui ressassant l'heure et son silence, qui parlant pour soi tout seul' (p. 176). Then, however, two of them are named, and their individual attitudes are distinguished: 'Seul, Le Lermot Clément semblait vivre sa vie à terre, attendant, dignité, qu'on veuille l'interroger, reconnaître qui il est, et le relâcher avec excuses pour son dommage. Emehu, lui vivait mal; assis droit, crépu de visage, il ne voyait rien n'entendait rien, semblait-il' (p. 176).

The fusion of common being is completely absent from these people, whose groups are always very loosely defined and their 'members' only temporarily interconnected. As in the sharing of being-in-common, they remain separate without being individualized (or, sometimes, even identified); this is often achieved through syntactic means, either by the 'qui' construction which develops out of 'ceux-là', as quoted above: '*qui* pionçant à demi, bougonnant à demi rêvant, *qui* ressassant l'heure et son silence, *qui* parlant pour soi tout seul' (p. 176, my italics), or by the use of 'chacun', as discussed earlier in the case of the prisoners in Chapter 3, and frequently throughout the text (as in this movement from 'on' to 'chacun', for instance: 'On est là, on s'agite comme si l'on dansait sous les lampions. Chacun quitte son échoppe, poussiéreuse tel l'oubli. Chacun tourne autour de sa musardise', p. 107; or the prisoners again: 'A leur entrée, chacun s'était tu. Ils ne parlaient pas, depuis bien un moment, mais chacun grommelait dans son coin', p. 172). On a more general level, also, it is important that the groups of characters are never stable; with the exception of the family relations centred on Ignigni (his wife, children, brother and sister-in-law) and possibly Bougie's gang (Chapter 15), they are temporary, more or less accidental groupings of people who happen to be working together or simply meet up in bars or in the street.

Thus while the description I have given above of single characters emerging, textually, out of plural groups may appear to suggest a figure/ground relation in which the single figure has a more privileged status than those who remain in the background, the hierarchy which that implies does not really exist. On the one hand this is because the 'background' is extremely fissile and unstable: a 'groundless ground', in the sense which Nancy elaborates.[10] On the other hand, also, the single figure who is momentarily picked out never remains in the foreground for long, and is not individualized to any significant extent. Sometimes s/he is not even named; the confused night-time scene in which Clothaire and Ignigni quarrel over the exchange of their respective animals takes place in front of a crowd of onlookers, out of which a third character suddenly emerges:

> Panique et mangement de paroles [...] La nuit tourbillonnait, en jouant de l'éclat de la lune comme du jour. *Celui qui* vient de déboucher sur la place, furieux, excité plus qu'un artilleur, et brandissant en même temps que son fusil sa cartouchière, menaçait de tuer raide tous ceux qu'il soupçonnait d'avoir participé au vol de son bétail. (p. 29, my italics)

This man, who turns out to be the legal owner of Ignigni's cow, starts a fight which ends in the arrival of the police and the arrests of all three men, but is never named and never appears in the narrative again

These fleeting appearances and rapid disappearances are one aspect of a lack of realist substance, and hence of *identity*, which also takes various other forms in the text.[11] Placoly's characters are both extremely vivid and extremely elusive. They are given no psychological or circumstantial description: there is no 'characterization' in the normal sense of the word. Sometimes, indeed, they have a ghostly, inhuman quality: 'Les rares gens qui venaient à passer n'avaient ni yeux ni bouche, ni visage, ni mains. Ils passaient [...] grattant la nuit comme d'un mur son écaille' (p. 127). They exist above all through their speech – and yet it is often difficult for the reader to identify who is speaking at any particular point. The text does not attach them unambiguously to their own words, but enacts the kind of '*fading* des voix' that Barthes describes in *S/Z*.[12] Occasionally the text actually comments on this; in the courtroom scene, for instance: 'Qui parlait? Mettiviers? Giap? Condre? Ou Clouette? […] Qui essaie de se désempêtrer de la tourbe des culpabilités grossissant à chaque mot qu'il dit, sans savoir, pauvre, que toute parole est coupable. Giap? Condre? Mettiviers? Ou Clouette' (p. 49). More often, though, the reader is left on her own to deal with the ambiguities and indeterminacies of the dialogue – in the crowd protesting at Bougie's arrest (pp. 108–109) for instance, or the conversation between Valdes's troop and the other people in Antinéa's bar (pp. 90–96).

Another sign of the characters' lack of identity is the strange fluidity of names. Some characters, as we have seen, are simply not named. But what is even more baffling is that others have *more than one* name. The man who gets out of his car to help Clothaire pull his cart out of a pot-hole in the road eventually gives Clothaire (and hence the reader) his name: 'demande monsieur Broquoteur' (p. 17). But later, to the prison guard, he is 'Monsieur Brockhearst! En personne!' (p. 45) – and although he corrects this by replying 'Broquoteur, mon ami, Broquoteur… C'est ainsi qu'on m'appelle le plus souvent' (p. 46) it is only to add immediately 'Mais les noms, c'est si peu de chose'; and in fact in his subsequent appearances he is usually referred to as Brockhearst (or 'Brock-a-hearst', p. 102, p. 132). Similarly, Ignigni's brother is called Dolminche, but also Bélisaire and Vildefonce, the text switching for no apparent reason between the three names; Valdes is also Sante (p. 89, p. 91), and Victor-Patte is also Gratien-les-quinze-pieds (p. 87). Thus Placoly exploits the Antillean fondness for nicknames to add to the referential confusion of his text; the owner of the bar is 'Antinéa Museau, surnommée Les-Mille-Dents tellement son sourire était doux, lumineux, et brillant comme un ciel' (p. 88); but in the last chapter, set in the same bar, she is not mentioned, but there is a reference to someone of a very similar name and, separated only by a comma, someone *else* called Mille-Dents: 'Autour d'elle [Rachel], Antenaïs, Mille Dents… cousaient leur crainte' (p. 221). The old woman who sells ice cream from her bicycle at night goes through the most elaborate sequence of changing designations; at first, she is 'la marchande de sorbets' (p. 28), and 'la sorbetière' on the next page. Nearly fifty pages later, she reappears as '[la] femme qui ne vit que la nuit, sans homme et sans progéniture, à vendre ses friandises de lait de coco et de glaces' (p. 74); from then on this is abbreviated to 'la femme qui ne vit que la nuit', which is repeated several times in the text before metamorphosing once more into 'la marchande de bonbons [...] Qui ne connaît la Tortue Ventrue et sa dent torte!' (p. 78). She remains 'La Tortue' – with slight variations such as 'Ventre-de-Tortue' (p. 101) – until the moment of her funeral, at which we seem finally to learn her real name: 'madame Flore Mackennah, surnommée La Tortue' (p. 165) – only to find that on the next page she has become 'Alma Mackennah' (p. 166).

This 'désœuvré' style of the novel, its suspension and deferral of meaning, contributes to the lack of solidity of the characters and minimizes reference to a consistent diegetic world. Sometimes it creates an effect of suspense that is fairly classical: the gradual identification of the corpse found in the rubbish dump with Giap, for instance (Chapters 14, 15 and 16). But more often the ambiguities are not resolved. For instance, Brockhearst's entry into the novel, in Chapter 1, is conveyed as follows:

> Fatalité troublée par l'aile d'une automobile, arrondie comme une bourrade. Descendre de voiture, l'aborder franchement des deux mains, envahir et charrette et mulet d'un univers de sueur, d'alcool et de tabac, tout cela ne prit pas une seconde à celui qui condescendait à aider le misérable dans sa peine. Il lui manquait toute une rangée de dents de devant, ce qui rendait sa bouche semblable à un clapoir. (p. 9)

The series of infinitives ('Descendre... aborder... envahir') describe his actions without any overt reference to their grammatical subject, at this point hardly distinguishable from his car; then his presence becomes perceptible by virtue of what he smells of ('sueur', 'alcool', 'tabac'); then he is designated as 'celui qui [...]'. But even this minimal characterization is blurred by the following sentence, whose subject ('Il') could refer either to 'celui qui' or to 'le misérable' (i.e., Clothaire, although we do not yet know his name either).

The suspension of fictional reference points is to some extent palliated by a very different technique, more usual in poetry than fiction, of *repetition*. That is, certain characters are habitually accompanied by certain phrases or indeed complete sentences or paragraphs, which, once the reader has realized this, help to identify them. In the first chapter, Brockhearst's remark 'mes yeux dansaient une danse d'ombre et de buée' (p. 10) is echoed in the middle of an anonymous fragment of speech later in the chapter (p. 17), allowing us to guess that the speaker is in fact Brockhearst. An image of the sky as being obstructed with ruts and potholes, just like the road, is twice associated with Clothaire (p. 9, p. 11). In the case of the ice-cream seller, the mention of her name on page 78 generates a whole paragraph of imagery which could be read as a metaphorical evocation of her state of mind – 'Etrange lutte de la mer boueuse et du chemin des rivières [...]' – but is not in any conventional sense a description of her; nevertheless it is repeated, with slight variations towards the end, the next time she appears in the text on page 101. In other words, the characters are 'placed' in the text by means of, and *as*, fragments of discourse rather than by consistent references to them or solid descriptions of them. Lacking any realist guidelines, the reader is set afloat in a sea of chaotic language.

But the relation between elusiveness of characters and obscurity of meanings is not simply a way of disorientating the reader; it also has implications for the deconstruction of the 'individual'. For a subject to be in control of signification, eliminating ambiguity, organizing language to convey an intended message, that subject has to be a sovereign, immanent individual.[13] This implies a self-consciousness – 'a subject in the sense of the relation of a self to itself' (BSP, p. 32) – that is crucially absent from the 'singular beings' that we find in Placoly's novel, 'où la parole est dispute, confusion des sens, marché du rien et commerce du non plus' (p. 79). From Clothaire 'qui ne sait pas très bien où il en est de la vie' (p. 7) to Ignigni who is unable to tell the police even who he is and what he has been doing (p. 179), the people who appear in *L'Eau-de-mort guildive* almost without exception lack the autonomy and control that is implied by the classic conception of the individual subject in its 'relation to itself'.

Another way to express this is to say that they have no *interiority*. They are often evoked in terms of absence: 'songes plafonnant sous l'absence' (p. 127), 'Quand on s'est absenté de la vie [...]' (p. 167), 'ils magnifiaient leur absence au monde' (p. 142). Perhaps the strongest image of this is the description of La Tortue when the police find her and at first think she is dead: 'Ainsi qu'une maison vide, aux volets épars, engloutis sous la poussière, son être vivait son sommeil, hanté de souvenirs fuyants, obsessifs et futiles. Fuites' (p. 131). Empty, dispersed, 'leaking' or 'fleeing' out of herself, the old woman is an extreme example of the lack of inner substance that is shared by almost all the characters and underlies our impression of their strange fluidity. While there are passages of interior monologue in the text, these are never introspective; they record impressions or memories of the outside world, but the characters never reflect on themselves.

For Nancy, this lack of immanence is a necessary condition for being-in-common to be realizable. Singular beings exist only in their exposition, 'the exposed face of what subsists, existing only in so far as it is exposed,

forever unavailable and beyond appropriation for the interior of subsistence and [...] for its inexistent center' ('Of Being-in-Common', p. 4).
There is a strong affinity between Nancy's theoretical formulation of the
correlation between lack of immanent selfhood and being-in-common,
and Placoly's literary representation of characters lacking any psychological content and existing solely in their relations to each other. The
question Nancy poses in the preface to *The Inoperative Community*, is, I
suggest, the same question that Placoly is implicitly asking throughout his
novel: 'How can we be receptive to the *meaning* of our multiple, dispersed,
mortally fragmented existences, which nonetheless only make sense by
existing in common?' (IC, p. xl). It is in this sense that *L'Eau-de-mort guildive* is profoundly concerned with the question of community.

On the simplest level, the characters are never alone.[14] The text stages
a series of encounters, often between people who have not met before,
and which usually, given the lack of any structured plot in the novel,
happen by chance; and it is through these encounters that the characters
are brought into existence, as in Nancy's 'compearance' (in which
singular beings 'appear only to the extent that they compear (*compara-
issent*), to the extent that they are exposed, presented, or offered to one
another', IC, p. 58). Thus in the first chapter, Clothaire and Brockhearst's
interaction reciprocally constructs their 'characters'; a similar process
occurs with Clothaire and Ignigni in the second chapter, with the respective wives of Ignigni and Mettiviers in the third, and so on: it is only the
initially anonymous dialogue between them that gradually and tenta-
tively reveals who they are. The main point of Chapter 14 is the
witnessing of Giap's murder by Hamelin's hired gangsters, but even there
the witness – a new character, Man Ciment – is introduced together with
a blind man whom she has found trying to cross the road, and who has
no further role in the book. It is as though Man Ciment cannot appear
in the text without 'compearing' together with someone else, and the
dialogue between them (pp. 182–83, 185–86) is a necessary condition
for her to exist.

By the same token, these meetings also serve to undermine any notion
of consistent identity in the characters. A person can be one thing with
one other person, and something different with somebody else. Or,
conversely, two people can turn out to be the same one: the 'voyante'
visited by Dolminche in the fairground in Chapter 9 is in fact his sister-
in-law Rachel in disguise, for instance. But a more striking example of
this kaleidoscoping of identities involves Mettiviers' wife, whom we first
meet in Chapter 3, in the yard outside the prison, giving Rachel the food

she had brought for her husband. Then, Chapter 7 introduces a new character: 'l'amie Délice', who is shown trying to cure the sick Loïs with magic spells. Délice then reappears much later, in Chapter 12, together with Rachel and her children – and starts to talk about her husband, Darius Mettiviers (p. 160). Thus two figures – Mettiviers' wife and 'l'amie Délice' – who previously have been not only distinct but totally unconnected with each other are suddenly revealed as being the same person.

The novel also allows us to see that there is a close connection between Nancy's concepts of exposition and compearance, on the one hand, and the apparently unrelated *narratological* concept of point of view. In realist fiction, the existence of a clear narrative point of view (even if it changes in the course of the novel) is the basis for the text's organization of the self–others relation: the narratological concept of focalization is entirely based on this relation. But in Nancy's philosophical vision, instead of the overarching perspective of a subject which places all others in relation to itself as *other*, precisely, there is only the 'sharing' of singular beings, who are 'distributed and placed, or rather *spaced*, by the sharing that makes them *others*: other for one another' (IC, p. 25). In literary terms, this would mean that the text has no overview of the relations between its characters; there is no one single point of view from which, as subject of representation, it surveys the landscape of its other characters; and this is indeed what we find in *L'Eau-de-mort guildive*.

In Placoly's novel, in other words, the textual evidence which might allow the reader to identify a clearly defined narrative point of view is minimal and indeterminate. In the first place, this is due to the preponderance of direct speech throughout the text, long stretches of which read more like the script of a play than a novel. Chapter 7, for instance, opens with a dialogue between Loïs and Délice which continues for five pages (pp. 83–87), uninterrupted except for one paragraph describing the 'cour de la maison' where they are talking. This includes the sentence 'Du lit de paille […] elle apercevait ça […]' (p. 83): as we gradually realize that Loïs is dying (and therefore in bed), it is possible to assign the narrative point of view of this paragraph to her. But then a comment she makes, about death, is followed by a fragment of speech – 'Des deux chemins, celui de la vie n'est pas le moins tortueux' (p. 87) which we at first attribute to Délice, only to be told that 'C'était l'avis de Victor-Patte' (p. 87) – and we suddenly find ourselves in a different dialogue, involving Victor-Patte, Clément le Lermot and, given the reference to 'l'hilarité générale', an unknown number of other people. On the following page, we realize that the scene has shifted to Antinéa Museau's bar, where the conversation continues until, in the final paragraph of the chapter, Délice rushes in with the news that Loïs has died (p. 97). But the change of location is not signalled explicitly, and this fluidity of place – typical of the novel as a whole – underlines the marginalization of a controlling narrative point of view that would as one of its basic functions indicate where the events were taking place. The second part of the chapter, in the bar, lasts for ten pages and is again dominated by uncontextualized direct speech, unbroken except for four paragraphs (pp. 88–89, 89–90, 94, 96–97). The first two of these appear to be from the point of view of someone in the bar, describing some of the people present and a donkey grazing outside. But the third reverts to the earlier scene of what Loïs can see from her bed, although without mentioning her. One sentence clearly positions this point of view as outside, and distant from, the bar – only the donkey outside it can be seen: 'Du bar d'Antinéa Museau, rien ne passait de la beuverie. Dehors, l'ânon, seul, broutait sa longe' (p. 94). But then, as though the donkey acts as a point of transition between the two locations, the point of view migrates to one in which it is Loïs's house which is seen from a distance, i.e., presumably, from *inside* the bar again: 'Dans l'horizon gris, la maison d'Eloïse élevait sa forme mortuaire. Du tapage de la morte et de sa surveillante, rien ne trespassait non plus' (p. 94). In other words, the separation of the two places is emphasized – nothing from one can be heard in the other – but at the same time the narrative point of view of the paragraph is neither 'inside' nor 'outside' either of them.[15] It echoes 'the singular logic of an inside-outside' ('Of Being-in-Common', p. 6) that constitutes the exposition of singular beings. In other words the narrative situates itself, here and elsewhere, *as* this spacing, 'in the paradox of that proximity where distancing and strangeness are revealed' (BSP, p. 35).

* * *

The lack of self-consciousness already discussed in relation to single characters has an equivalent on the level of the community, which also lacks any awareness of itself as a community (even on the level of family: Clothaire's numerous relations do not know that they are related, p. 17). It has no clear boundaries: not even, in fact, between human and non-human. On the one hand 'humanity' in the abstract is treated with derision – 'Mais qu'est-ce qu'une humanité? S'asseoir à la table d'un débit, saisir à plein poing la délicatesse du cristal d'un verre de rhum, et plonger ses yeux dans le visage de l'autre, le terreau de la fraternité? [...] Serait-ce cela l'humanité?' (pp. 193–94) – and on the other hand, the text frequently blurs the boundaries between the human, the animal and the inanimate, attributing thoughts and speech to animals, machines, buildings, etc. The first piece of 'speech' in the novel is that of Clothaire's mule (p. 7); planes get tired and fall asleep like animals ('Un avion pique du nez sur sa piste et va droit s'endormir dans sa grange, comme un cheval fourbu', pp. 23–24); houses 'laissent voir leurs pensées d'intérieur' (p. 24), lorries 'crachotent indistinctement de lourdes pensées d'huile et de cambouis' (p. 16), and so on. Conversely, people make noises like animals – Bélisaire 'bêtifiait comme un âne tttbrr tttbrr tttbrr' (p. 106), the 'enfant de la nature' speaks a magic language made up of bird calls (p. 60), Papayito's act consists of imitating bird calls as well – or like inanimate objects: the troop as a whole engage in 'un fracas de clochettes et de cris onomatopéiques, imitant la chanson de la pluie et jusqu'au roulement du train de canne sur ses jantes' (p. 89); this latter is in fact a kind of *mise-en-abyme* of the novel, whose human dialogues are constantly interrupted by onomatopoeic representations of the noises of the city: 'gdhe ghe gdhe ghe faisait la ville, ses immeubles, usines, trafic, commerces et chasses, comme un maître tambour' (p. 20). As well as contributing disconcertingly to the novel's general disruption of sense, this reluctance to attribute special status to the human as distinct from the animal or inanimate components of the city also works against any conception of a self-conscious closed community.

This, then, is a community which has no awareness of its boundaries. (The textual presentation of groups in which, as I have shown, the reader does not know how many people are involved in a particular scene, replicates and reinforces this idea.) No one is excluded, and strangers are welcome: the crowd watching the quarrel in Chapter 2 are on Clothaire's side 'parce qu'il était nouveau' (p. 24). This inclusiveness and openness to others means that acts of kindness take place not only in the context of established friendships (Délice trying to cure Loïs, Victor-Patte wanting to pay for her treatment, p. 92) but also between strangers. It is on the face of it unlikely that a powerful rich man such as Brockhearst would stop and get out of his car to help the shabby and rather pathetic figure of Clothaire pull his cart out of a pot-hole, but he does, and this incident is prominently placed at the beginning of the novel. Man Ciment stops to help the blind man across the road (p. 181); Délice, learning that she will not be able to give Mettiviers the food she has brought for him in prison, gives it to Rachel, who has no food to give Ignigni – Délice does not know who Rachel is, but decides that 'si je lui donnais ma gamelle, mes fruits et mon linge, ce serait une manière de partager mon inquiétude' (p. 42). In this fashion the community of *L'Eau-de-mort guil-dive* realizes its open-ended being-in-common.

The community is not so inclusive that it has no enemies. Most of the characters whom we meet in the course of the novel (Dolminche and Clément are the only exceptions) see the police, the legal system, and employers such as Hamelin as their enemies. This opposition comes across clearly in the courtroom scene in Chapter 4, where the four workers whom Hamelin has had arrested on a false charge of stealing building materials are on trial, and where Mettiviers attempts, in a long speech (pp. 51–56) that is interrupted by the conversations of the lawyers who are clearly not listening to him, to prove the innocence of himself and his three fellow workers. Their wives sit in the courtroom anxiously following the proceedings, and the text, in the characteristic way I have described, presents them as surrounded by an indistinct group of other people. In this case, however, the 'background' group is shown as silently supporting them, linked to them by solidarity in the face of the superior forces of law and order:

> dans la salle où quatre femmes, au milieu d'un maigre public composé de *parentés vagues mais sûres* et de curieux, *d'amitiés lugubres mais incondi-tionnelles*, où quatre femmes essayent, sourcils froncés sur des yeux d'inquiétude, de suivre les tours et détours d'une justice qui les dépasse. (p. 50, my italics)

But the community's resistance to its enemies is never *organized* in a manner that would also organize the community itself into a unified, disciplined entity. One might of course argue that this is why Placoly's characters do not succeed in overcoming the forces ranged against them. But the novel's representation of the balance of power suggests, rather, that on the one hand definitive victory is in any case out of the question: the people are not in a position to overthrow the state. On the other hand, however, the forces of law and order – the police, the courts, and ulti-mately the army – are *also* shown as incapable of preventing spontaneous outbreaks of rebellion; while they always defeat these in the end, they remain unable to stop them happening – in other words, to establish a permanently peaceful and law-abiding society. The people, therefore, can gain a certain kind of freedom through their very *dis*organization: it is this that most effectively challenges the authorities' attempts to contain or impose order on the community.

The prison acts as an important metaphor for the concept of social control by *containment* – and as such it is shown to be strangely inef-fective. Clothaire, Ignigni, the owner of the cow that Ignigni stole, the four building workers, Bougie, Dolminche, Clément and Emehu Loisir are all arrested and put in prison at various points in the narrative, but none of them stays there for long.[16] Whatever the particular reasons for these releases (or escapes?), the idea that prison cannot contain them is also linked to the fluid, fissile quality of these singular beings. The prison guard tells the men who have been arrested after the game of dice that they are so insubstantial that they cannot be contained in prison: 'Où vous garder? Et à attendre quoi? J'ai l'idée que les prisons riraient de vous contraindre. Vous êtes vapeur et pluie' (p. 170).

The same quality of protean elusiveness and evanescence characterizes the community as a whole: a few pages later, one of the civil servants visiting the prison complains that '[cette] société fuit sous nos mains' (p. 174). Thus it is strongly implied that the community's capacity for resistance lies primarily in its *disorganization*: it is because it has no collective consciousness of itself and its boundaries – because it is constantly unravelling and escaping itself – that the community can also escape the authorities' attempts to control it. In other words, it escapes and resists because it is not a *subject* and so does not participate in the 'politics of self-sufficiency' that Nancy critiques in *The Sense of the World*.

The riots that dominate the second half of the novel provide the main example of this subjectless political resistance, which offers an alternative to Mettiviers' attempts to fight for justice through legal, constitutional channels. The rioters are 'uncontainable', anonymous and elusive: 'l'écho fuyant, invisible, armée de tout ce qui peut donner la mort dans l'ombre' (p. 212); not an identifiable faction but 'un peuple' who 'se faisait pour se défaire' (p. 213), who start fires in the town at night, so that in the darkness no one can see who they are (p. 213). Their actions are a political protest and rebellion, but in no sense a consciously organized struggle. It is as though the only form of political action that is possible in this situation is a spontaneous revolt which has no precise aims but spreads rapidly by word of mouth ('le vent télégraphie l'insoumission', p. 217) and sows *disorder* throughout the city: 'DESORDRE faisait tanguer la nuit […] DESORDRE tortueux soufflait dans la corne de l'ombre' (p. 135).

The riots do not achieve any concrete gains, and are eventually put down by the police and army, with considerable loss of life. In this sense the rioters are no more successful than Mettiviers in his attempt to take on the justice system. But they do at least succeed in shifting the battle onto their own ground and putting the police on the defensive. Right from the start, in the initial incident of Bougie's arrest for theft from Dolminche's shop, which attracts a crowd that becomes violent, the police are struggling to keep things under control: 'Le flic perdait tous ses esprits. L'inculpé se fout de lui, certainement' (p. 99). From then on, with the death of Synge from a police bullet, the situation escalates until the police patrolling the streets are 'sentinelles hantées par la peur de la mort' (p. 212). Not only the police, but the army too are frightened: Bougie's gang is protected by 'la peur de la mort silencieuse, celle qui fige et décatit les troupes régulières' (p. 218).

Also, for the people involved in the rioting it is a meaningful form of revolt against oppression, in which they experience a sense of liberation and exhilaration in risking their lives: they 'prétend s'égaler aux dieux de la guerre, boute-feu, maîtres en ruses, et marchant cavalièrement côte à côte avec la mort' (p. 213). The crowd gives in to its 'ardeur au combat où la nuit les appelle' (p. 214); Ignigni exultantly proclaims that now '[la] ville nous appartient' (p. 216) and brushes aside Rachel's tearful plea to him to calm down: 'Apaiser? Quand, au plus fort de sa vie, un homme peut arrêter le cours d'une ville?' (p. 221). In fact the mood in the last chapter comes close to a Fanonian view of self-affirmation through violent struggle.[17] According to someone who may be Ignigni (it is not entirely clear), the rebels' ability to *invent*, to find new ways of acting and resisting, combined with their fearlessness in the face of death, renders the police powerless against them: 'S'il ne nous reste pas d'autre pouvoir que celui d'inventer... Regarde la ronde des autos de police circulant... Quelle belle mort! Aurais-tu peur?... Mais ils ne parlent pas; figés dans leur silence, ils ne peuvent rien contre nous' (p. 221).

It does not last, of course, and in the closing scene of the novel the group is, precisely, *contained*: trapped in the bar surrounded by police. But the narrative comes to an abrupt end at this point; it stops short of recounting the final stage of the rioters' defeat, and, although we may assume that many of the remaining characters will be killed by the police, we are left with this *suspension* that is not only the central characteristic of literature as unworking, but also prevents the characters' deaths being made available for the process of reintegration into common being that for Nancy is incompatible with being-in-common. The awareness of death as revealing the finitude of life – 'Il faut la mort, car c'est à son pas que la vie marche' (p. 166) – remains as pervasive as it has been throughout the text, because it is not allowed to crystallize into a tragic climax. At the same time, the novel has shown how the sharing of being-in-common generates an explosive freedom that is possible when nothing else is; in so doing it embodies, in Placoly's phrase, '[un] sursaut d'énergie quand rien n'est possible que la mort' (p. 141).

CHAPTER 5

Conquering the Town: Stories and Myth in Patrick Chamoiseau's *Texaco*

Texaco is set against the background of the steady influx of Martinique's population from the countryside into the towns, a process which started in the mid-nineteenth century with the abolition of slavery and continued in successive waves up until late in the twentieth century. The building of new communities and the polarity between town and country are thus important themes. The first words of the text, introducing a chronology of the historical and fictional events covered by the novel, are:

> Afin d'échapper à la nuit esclavagiste et coloniale, les nègres esclaves et les mûlatres de la Martinique vont, de génération en génération, abandonner les habitations, les champs et les mornes, pour s'élancer à la conquête des villes (qu'ils appellent en créole: 'l'En-ville'). Ces multiples élans se concluront par la création guerrière du quartier Texaco et le règne menaçant d'une ville démesurée. (p. 13)

For the workers on the plantations, in other words, the towns appear as beacons of freedom – Saint-Pierre and Fort-de-France '[tenaient] lieu de flambeau dans la nuit close des chaînes' (p. 223) – but also as formidable enemies whom they have to fight in order to gain a foothold in them: Marie-Sophie says of Fort-de-France 'Nous étions venus pour ses promesses, son destin, nous étions exclus de ses promesses, de son destin. Rien n'était donné, il fallait tout essoucher' (pp. 404–405).

With the new arrivals from the countryside a circle of slums known as 'les Quartiers' grow up around Fort-de-France. Texaco is the most recent of these, but 'le Quartier des Misérables' and Morne Abélard also figure in the narrative, and Texaco is always seen in the context of the other Quartiers, thus acquiring a kind of exemplary status. Its starting point is Marie-Sophie Laborieux's decision to build her shack on the outskirts of Fort-de-France, on land belonging to the Texaco oil company; she is gradually joined by other people, and the new community takes shape. It is, of course, illegal (and also dangerous, because of the petrol stored on the site), and is the object of constant police raids which destroy the residents' shacks and attempt to drive them out. But they always refuse to leave, rebuilding their homes and gradually improving their defence systems. Their life there is thus one of a constant battle with the CRS (i.e., the police), the site owner, and the town council; Marie-Sophie always describes it as a 'war' and complains that 'il y avait mille guerres à mener pour seulement exister' (p. 410).

The community does not, in other words, have a 'natural' existence that can be taken for granted; rather, it is the result of a sustained effort of will, a collective determination to continue to live there in the face of the hostile forces surrounding it and attempting to get rid of it. In this it exemplifies Nancy's notion of the community that produces itself as a 'work' – a *creation* ('la création guerrière du quartier Texaco', p. 13) that wills itself into existence, and whose members are united in the struggle: Marie-Sophie refers to them as 'mes compagnons de lutte' (p. 387). There is great emphasis on a fusional unity: the women are 'soudées par le malheur. Nos cases furent détruites bien souvent ensemble. Ensemble bien souvent, nous nous retrouvâmes sous la bourrade des céhêresses' (p. 429).

Texaco is a new community not only because it has only recently come into existence, but also because its inhabitants have left behind the traditional life of the countryside and are learning to survive in a very different situation on the margins and in the interstices of the town. They have to create new forms of social organization: 'Nous réinventâmes tout: les lois, les codes de l'urbain, les rapports de voisinage, les règles d'implantation et de construction' (p. 406). But this newness, the 'espace créole de solidarités neuves' (p. 410), is balanced by the equally important theme of survival through the adaptation of their inherited rural expertise to the new situation; they still possess the traditional skills of building, growing food, etc., and the culture of resourcefulness, ruse and cooperation that, Chamoiseau implies, has been lost by the inhabitants of the city. In this sense, the old rural society helps them to adapt to the new urban one, and the emphasis on innovation goes hand in hand with a celebration of the past. There are distinct echoes here of Glissant's concern in *Le Quatrième Siècle* to recover and preserve the lost knowledge of the past. But whereas for Glissant the major spatial opposition was between the hills and the plain, in Texaco it is between the hills and the town – and it is not a simple opposition.

The relationship is given its most developed expression in the counterpointing of the creation of Texaco with the earlier episode of the 'Noutéka des mornes'. After the abolition of slavery and the subsequent realization that the ex-slaves are not going to receive any land, Esternome (Marie-Sophie's father) and Ninon make their way up into the hills to find land that is not owned by anyone. They are joined by others in the same situation, and Esternome becomes the founder and leader of this new community just as his daughter will do later in relation to Texaco. This is thus the first experiment in creating a free community; they learn how to survive and become self-sufficient. They also acquire, for the first time, a strong self-conscious collective identity; Esternome's account (relayed by Marie-Sophie) of their experiences is so dominated by the pronoun 'nous' that Marie-Sophie's name for the community is the 'Noutéka ['we used to' in creole] des mornes', and she comments: 'C'était une sorte de *nous* magique. A son sens, il chargeait un destin d'à-plusieurs dessinant ce nous-mêmes qui le bourrelait sur ses années dernières' (pp. 160–61). Unlike Texaco, this community in the hills has no obvious enemies. But it is nevertheless eventually defeated by the town, because its inhabitants are gradually drawn down from the hills by the prospect of working in the new factories. Thus the town's destructive force proves more insidiously effective when it is exercised at a distance than when the community is immediately confronted by it, as in the case of Texaco and the other 'Quartiers'. The 'Noutéka' community, in other words, failed because it suffered from the 'illusion' (p. 217) that it could exist independently of Saint-Pierre; the towns, even in the nineteenth century, had become such a powerful centre of attraction as sources of employment that not even those living in the remote hills could afford to ignore them.

The Quartiers, on the other hand, attempt to preserve their independence while being closely imbricated in Fort-de-France. When Esternome later comes to live in the Quartier des Misérables, he sees the multiple, complex, conflictual but also beneficial links between it and the town itself (pp. 220–21), and reflects bitterly on his previous attempt to found the community in the hills, 'sa montée glorieuse dégonflée par l'Usine. Leur échec collectif se traduisait alors en vagues sur cet En-ville qui n'était pas l'En-ville' (pp. 221–22). But the relation between the two communities is not merely one of contrast; the experience gained from living in the hills is brought to bear on life in the Quartiers, so that he exclaims: 'Les mornes sont descendus En-ville, seigneur' (p. 221). The original rural community of Noutéka provides both an inspiration and a fund of practical knowledge for the later urban ones. Marie-Sophie says of Texaco:

> Quand nous vînmes, nous amenâmes la campagne [...] Nous nous comportions comme dans cette vie du Noutéka des mornes que mon Esternome m'avait longuement décrite, avec un entretien sans faiblesse des espaces libres à l'abord de la case, un rythme soumis aux saisons de la lune, de la pluie et des vents. Et nous voulûmes, face à l'En-ville, vivre dans l'esprit des

> Mornes, c'est dire: avec notre seule ressource, et mieux: notre seul savoir.
> (pp. 406–407)

Texaco thus represents a new *synthesis* of rural and urban, and this is its value. By the 1980s, the town is characterized by its soulless, inflexible, geometrical order and its dedication to a process of modernization, inspired by Europe and North America, that threatens to destroy the countryside around it. The country, in contrast, is organic, living and 'poetic'. The country – in the guise of the Quartiers – is therefore needed by the town, to irrigate the latter's aridity with its life-giving qualities. The town planner whom Marie-Sophie converts to the cause of saving Texaco, and whose 'Notes' addressed to the 'marqueur de paroles'[1] interrupt the main text at frequent and apparently arbitrary intervals, comments repeatedly on the importance of its implantation of rural life within Fort-de-France; it restores its humanity: 'Texaco était ce que la ville conservait de l'humanité de la campagne. Et l'humanité est ce qu'il y a de plus précieux pour une ville. Et de plus fragile' (p. 360). Texaco, as he also says, has the capacity to 'reinvent' both the town itself and its relation to the countryside:

> Mais la ville est une menace. [...] sa logique est inhumaine. Le désert y naît sous la joie mécanique des néons et les dictatures automobiles. [...] Il faut désormais, à l'urbaniste créole, réamorcer d'autres tracées, en sorte de susciter en ville *une contre-ville*. Et autour de la ville, *réinventer la campagne*.
> (p. 462)

While the town is dominated by modernity, the countryside is not only, as we have seen, the source of the practical knowledge and traditional values of an archaic way of life, but also the guardian of the island's collective *memory*. Bringing the country into the town, as Texaco does, is thus a way of restoring collective memory to it: paradoxically, the new Quartiers embody a sense of history that the old town centre has lost – the town planner distinguishes between 'le centre historique vivant des exigences neuves de la consommation' and 'les couronnes d'occupation populaires, riches du fond de nos histoires [...] Au centre, on détruit le souvenir pour s'inspirer des villes occidentales et rénover. Ici, dans la couronne, on survit de mémoire' (p. 218). In his view, clearly shared by Chamoiseau, the future of urban life depends, paradoxically again, on rejecting modernization and incorporating the memory of the past preserved in the country. In this non-linear conception of time, the future lies with memory – as the town planner puts it: 'Rayer Texaco comme on me le demandait, reviendrait à amputer la ville d'une part de son *futur* et, surtout, de cette richesse irremplaçable que demeure la *mémoire*' (p. 430, my italics).[2]

However, these precious attributes of the Quartiers are not immediately apparent to the observer. Viewed from the outside, Texaco looks like a chaotic, unhygienic, unaesthetic conglomeration of rubbish: hence the authorities' determination to get rid of it. As the town planner once again comments, 'L'urbaniste occidental voit dans Texaco une tumeur à l'ordre urbain. Incohérente. Insalubre. Une contestation active. Une menace. On lui dénie toute valeur architecturale ou sociale' (p. 345). But it is in fact constructed in an entirely rational and purposeful manner, making the best possible use of every inch of space and of the inclines of the land, the direction of the sun and the wind, and so on. Marie-Sophie describes in detail the ingenious planning that has gone into its construction (pp. 407–409), before concluding: 'Mais qui aurait pu comprendre cela à part mon Esternome ou bien Papa Totone? Ces équilibres demeurent indéchiffrables pour les gens de l'En-ville et même de Texaco. Qui nous voyait, ne voyait que misères enchevêtrées' (p. 409). Unlike the overt geometrical order of the town, Texaco's order is not obvious. Rather, one has to 'decipher' its subtle balances and interdependences – like the 'subtile touffaille d'équilibres' (p. 340) of Morne Abélard.[3] It is organic rather than mechanical; the town planner describes it as an 'ecosystem'. But it had remained invisible to him until Marie-Sophie explained it to him: 'La Dame m'a enseigné à percevoir la ville comme un écosystème, tout en équilibres et en interactions' (p. 328). Through listening to her, he learns to see beyond the apparent chaotic destitution of Texaco and grasp its underlying order:

> Au-delà des bouleversements insolites des cloisons, du béton, du fibrociment et des tôles, au-delà des coulées d'eaux qui dévalaient des pentes, des flaques stagnantes, des écarts aux règles de salubrité urbaine, il existait une cohérence à décoder, qui permettait à ces gens-là de vivre aussi parfaitement, et aussi harmonieusement qu'il était possible d'y vivre, à ce niveau de conditions. (p. 313)

Only those who live in Texaco, or who are initiated into its secrets, are aware of its 'coherence'.

Moreover, this relation between superficial disorder (incoherence, multiplicity, chaos) and an underlying secret order (coherence, unity, organization) is in fact a major structure which works on several levels in the novel. Notably, it defines the structure of the *narrative*, which the parallel with the (dis)order of Texaco allows us to see as also concealing a unified coherence beneath the appearances of disorganization and digression. Faced with this 500-page novel covering two centuries, involving an enormous number of characters, incidents and settings, in which the main narrative recounted by Marie-Sophie to the 'marqueur de paroles' is frequently interrupted by quotations from her 'Cahiers', by notes from the town planner, from the 'marqueur de paroles', and various other textual fragments, the reader's first impression is of a deliberately chaotic and heterogeneous multiplicity.[4] For instance, the information conveyed by the narrative is not always reliable: Marie-Sophie forgets things, gives alternative versions, and so on.

The novel also appears to proceed by an accumulation of detail: even its minor characters are the subject of digressive anecdotes, and one of its main stylistic techniques is the relentless listing of numerous diverse items: to take just one example, Marie-Sophie's description of the alley-ways of Morne Abelard (pp. 357–58) is a list of 26 different 'passes', each with its own picturesque characterization ('La passe de la soupe de pieds-bœuf sur des cendres cuisantes [...] La passe où il est plus facile de voir une bourrique travaillant à onze heures qu'un nègre sans verre à midi', etc.).

These characteristics have led to the novel's being described as post-modern; Maeve McCusker, for instance, writes that it 'can be considered to exemplify many of the principles of postmodernism in, for example, its questioning of any monolithic "truth" or stable narrative perspective, its ludic disregard for narrative linearity and in its self-referential under-mining of canonical History'. She concludes that '*Texaco* preserves its protean fluidity, working to multiply and disperse meanings rather than to fix or delimit them'.[5] I want to argue, however, that although these postmodern aspects of the narrative certainly exist, they merely serve to camouflage its underlying unity of purpose: that like Texaco itself, the novel dedicated to it has a 'secret order' that organizes its apparently disparate textual surface and limits its overt commitment to multiplicity and diversity.[6] It is significant that Marie-Sophie, in her distrust of the 'deathliness' of writing as opposed to speech, envisages an ideal form of writing that would convey all the 'living' mobility and capaciousness of speech, *but* without sacrificing an elusive underlying unity:

> Oiseau Cham, existe-t-il une écriture informée de la parole, et des silences, et qui reste vivante, qui bouge en cercle et circule tout le temps, irriguant sans cesse de vie ce qui a été écrit avant, et qui réinvente le cercle à chaque fois comme le font les spirales qui sont à tout moment dans le futur et dans l'avant, l'une modifiant l'autre, sans cesse, *sans perdre une unité difficile à nommer*? (p. 413, my italics)

Texaco itself seems to be attempting to achieve a similar balance; but there is in fact a certain tension between the chaotic diversity I have already described and a more fundamental drive towards unity. Not only does the novel have one strong central theme, but this theme in itself embodies a thrusting momentum that carries the narrative forward: it is the 'conquête des villes' which repeatedly signposts and orientates the narrative, and is usually expressed as a series of 'élans' or forward movements; the initial chronological summary of the novel is titled 'Repères chronologiques de nos élans pour conquérir la ville', and the phrase 'pour s'élancer à la conquête des villes' recurs in the paragraph immediately below (p. 13). It is the basis for Marie-Sophie's relationship with Esternome: 'il n'avait à m'offrir que l'ultime gambade de sa mémoire autour d'une volonté de conquérir l'En-ville' (p. 249). It explicitly justifies the long rambling narrative of the first half of the novel, as Marie-Sophie explains: 'Pour comprendre Texaco et l'élan de nos pères vers la ville, il nous faudra remonter loin dans la lignée de ma propre famille' (p. 48).

The situational context of the narrative contributes to this singleness of purpose. The story Marie-Sophie tells to the 'marqueur de paroles' is a second version of the story she has already told to the town planner, and this first act of story-telling has a single, clear and very powerful aim: to save Texaco. The town planner has come with the intention of destroying the community; only Marie-Sophie can save it, and she can only do so by telling him about its history and what it means to its inhabitants. She tells the 'marqueur de paroles' that on meeting the town planner, 'j'avais soudain compris que c'était moi, [...] avec pour seule arme la persuasion de mon parole, qui devrais mener seule – à mon âge – la décisive bataille pour la survie de Texaco [...] je commençai à lui raconter l'histoire de notre Quartier et de notre conquête de l'En-ville' (p. 41). The story becomes a 'weapon' in the final battle, and the coherence and rationale of the whole narrative are thus assured from the start: its purpose is to save Texaco and everything in it – however apparently irrelevant – will be designed to achieve that goal.

In fact the narrative is also overwhelmingly linear. Given its overall length, the amount of jumping back and forth in time is relatively minor; it proceeds for the most part in a straightforwardly chronological manner, narrating the life of Esternome and then that of Marie-Sophie; and this progression is underlined by the titles of the subsections which refer to the historical succession of building materials, moving from 'Temps de paille' through to 'Temps de béton'. The text flirts self-consciously with the idea of non-linearity, telling us that it will try not to digress, as though it finds this a difficult and unnatural constraint: 'Mais ne perdons pas le fil, et reprenons l'affaire maille par maille, avec si possible une maille avant l'autre' (p. 21); 'J'aurais pu raconter en ciné-

mascope cette histoire d'amour [...] mais le détour serait risqué'(p. 25);
'Là encore, le détour eût été édifiant [...] mais je n'ai pas cela à dire' (p.
26). It thus creates the impression that it is more digressive than it really
is. Another way in which it evokes an atmosphere of disorder without
actually becoming disordered is by exploiting the slippage in between
what Marie-Sophie tells the 'marqueur de paroles', and the text that he
writes and that we are reading. In his postscript he stresses how disorganized her oral narrative is: 'Elle me raconta ses histoires de manière
assez difficultueuse. Il lui arrivait, bien qu'elle me le cachât, d'avoir des
trous de mémoire, et de se répéter, ou de se contredire' (p. 493). But he
edits her words, and uses her 'Cahiers' to fill in gaps and correct distor-
tions (p. 494); moreover, he 'organizes' her story around the central
figure of the town planner, in accordance with his own idea of appro-
priateness: 'Je réorganisai la foisonnante parole de l'Informatrice, autour
de l'idée messianique d'un Christ; cette idée respectait bien la déréliction
de cette communauté face à cet urbaniste qui sut la décoder' (p. 497).
Thus evocations of the oral narrative of Marie-Sophie serve to endow the
written narrative of the novel with an atmosphere of greater uncertainty
and shapeless proliferation than the latter actually exhibits.

Finally, there is the question of narrative point of view – one of the
major criteria of the unicity or plurality of a literary text. Despite the
various relays of the narrative – from Esternome to Marie-Sophie and
then from her to the town planner and the 'marqueur de paroles' – the
point of view throughout belongs to Marie-Sophie. We only hear what
she remembers of her father's words; the main interpolations in the text
are from her own 'Cahiers', and even those of the town planner are based
on what he has learnt from listening to her.[7] The 'marqueur de paroles'
is dedicated to reproducing her words as faithfully as possible, merely
editing out the inconsistencies, and considers himself subordinate to her
authority. Above all, there is no conflict or disagreement between these
four figures: they are all united in their desire to realize the project of
Texaco's 'conquête de la ville' – the project on which the whole narrative is centred. Beneath the superficial multiplicity and heterogeneity of
the text, there is a 'secret order' of unity and coherence.[8]

Thus while *Texaco*'s ludic, postmodern aspects could be seen as constituting the 'share of literature' in the work, its underlying unity and
concentration on telling the story of the long struggle to found the
community of Texaco allow us to see in the novel the main characteristics of Nancy's conception of myth, as always narrativizing and glorifying
the foundation of a community (IC, p. 45). Moreover, mythical *language*

has a special status and power – Nancy describes it as 'a primordial language: the element of an inaugural communication' (IC, p. 48) – and this is also prominent in *Texaco* through the interventions of the Mentô figures, who represent the power of African magic: it is a Mentô who first tells Esternome that he must leave the countryside and start the process of conquering the towns (pp. 73–74). Christine Chivallon argues that this confers on the quest a sacred origin which defines the narrative as 'le mythe fondateur de "Texaco"' (p. 26), sacralizes the role of memory and unifies the text.[9] But the language of myth is more explicitly associated with Papa Totone – 'le dernier Mentô' – who communicates to Marie-Sophie the force of '*La Parole*', telling her that '[une] parole est tombée dans l'oreille de ton Esternome. Une parole l'a porté. C'est venu *La Parole*' (p. 373), and that she must learn to acquire this power: 'C'est quoi *La Parole*? Si elle te porte, c'est *La Parole*. Si elle te porte seulement et sans une illusion. Qui tient parole-qui-porte tient *La Parole*. Il peut tout faire. C'est plus que Force' (p. 374). The mythical force of Marie-Sophie's 'parole' is demonstrated by her ability to convince the town planner to save Texaco – by, precisely, recounting its *origins*. The time she spends living with Papa Totone is presented as a period of initiation, and serves to link her closely to his magic power. He tells her to choose a secret name for herself, and this magically endows her with a new war-like identity, capable of fighting for Texaco: 'Je me levai – […] je dis "je", mais en fait la personne qui se leva n'était plus moi, non. C'était une autre personne forte de son nom secret, qui pouvait esquinter Castrador [the oil company's guard on the site] à coups de paroles mais à coups de roches aussi' (p. 382).

Marie-Sophie also possesses many of the other attributes of the mythical heroine. She comes from a heroic lineage: her grandfather rebelled against slavery by poisoning the animals on his plantation, and died imprisoned in an underground dungeon (pp. 50–51); her father Esternome founded and led the 'Noutéka des mornes' and his telling her the story of his life enables her to 'produire pour moi-même l'énergie d'une légende' (p. 256). Throughout her life she is enveloped in this 'legendary' aura which is enhanced by her subsequent heroic deeds: when she stands up to Julot-la-Gale, she comments: 'Branche neuve à ma légende: j'avais stoppé un Major au combat'; and her relationship with Irené the shark fisherman means that '[ma] légende s'augmenta: plus que jamais matador-Texaco, j'avais domestiqué le destructeur de monstres' (p. 483). There is of course a slightly humorous tone to these pronouncements, but the fact that she is describing herself renders the humour anodyne, so that her heroic status is not undermined. And it is greatly reinforced by the description of her by the marqueur de paroles in the final section: 'Je n'avais jamais perçu autant d'autorité profonde irradier de quelqu'un' (p. 493); 'Une câpresse de haute lutte, impériale, dont les rides rayonnaient de puissance' (p. 495).[10]

Above all, she is the founder of Texaco ('moi, Marie-Sophie Laborieux, ancêtre fondatrice de ce Quartier', p. 38). Texaco exists only because she willed it into existence.[11] She is also responsible for its continuing survival: while she cannot succeed without the help of others – including the local communist politicans and, of course, the town planner – it is clear that had the community succumbed to the police raids nothing would have saved it. She is its undisputed leader, organizing the resistance and leading her troops into battle.[12] She is repeatedly described as the 'centre' of the community, with the others grouped around her: 'De toute évidence, l'on s'était installé *autour de moi*: un espace vital plus large qu'ailleurs instituait mon foyer en centre rayonnant de Texaco-du-haut' (p. 463).

Another very striking feature of her representation in the text is her total *identification* with Texaco. The fact that her secret name is 'Texaco', as she reveals at the very end of the narrative, sums up a number of passages in which she asserts the complete fusion between her individual self and the community of Texaco. As she talks to the town planner, she is speaking 'en notre nom à tous, plaidant notre cause, contant ma vie' (p. 41); that is, not only is she the spokeswoman for the community, but there is an implied equivalence between 'notre cause' and 'ma vie'. Indeed, 'moi' and 'nous' frequently overlap: 'ce fut bon pour moi – et "moi" c'est comme dire "nous"' (p. 402). Where there is a slight disjunction between them, it only serves to affirm her special status as founder, as when she says: '*Mon* intérêt pour le monde se résumait à Texaco, *mon* œuvre, *notre* quartier, *notre* champ de bataille et de résistance' (p. 39, my italics).

To describe Texaco as 'mon œuvre' succinctly brings together the foundational dimension of her discourse with the idea of community as a 'work' in which the individual members – as we have seen with Marie-Sophie herself – are fused together in a common identity.[13] It is this closed community of common being that in Nancy's theorization produces and is produced by myth. It is, however, a significantly different conception of community from that normally associated with 'créolité'. The 'créolité' movement, led by Chamoiseau, Raphaël Confiant and Jean Bernabé, insists upon the diverse, mixed, and hence *open* nature of creole society.

In their *Eloge de la créolité*[14] they write:

> Du fait de sa mosaïque constitutive, la Créolité est une spécificité ouverte. Elle échappe ainsi aux perceptions qui ne seraient pas elle-mêmes ouvertes. L'exprimer c'est exprimer non une synthèse, pas simplement un métissage, ou n'importe quelle autre unicité. C'est exprimer une totalité kaléido-scopique, c'est à dire *la conscience non totalitaire d'une diversité préservée.* (pp. 27–28)

To argue, as I have been doing, that Chamoiseau's novel recounts the founding myth of Texaco therefore goes against both the general emphasis in the 'créolité' movement on the diversity, openness and fluidity of creole communities, and the impression that *Texaco* itself gives of diversity, which has dominated most critical accounts of the novel. David Dabydeen, for instance, reviewing the English translation of it in *The Times*, writes:

> We are given a collage of characters inhabiting masks of sorcery, rebellion and revelry. Each is individuated but each belongs to interlocking commu-nities: there are maroons, field-negroes, house-negroes and *chabins* […] whose various presences testify to the chaotic social and sexual history of the island. Stories and characters gyrate and jostle for space.[15]

The large number of stories about different individuals, the long time-scale of the narrative, and the sheer length of the novel, might indeed seem to suggest that this is a community which cannot be *defined* by any generalizing formula, but can only be *evoked* by an accumulation of stories about individuals. Diversity, in other words, would seem to be the justification for the overwhelming prominence of detail and the prolif-erating quality of Marie-Sophie's 'foisonnante parole' (p. 497). It is also true that ethnic diversity features quite strongly in Texaco.[16]

On the other hand, one cannot help noticing the extent to which all the inhabitants of Texaco conform to the dominance of certain types of character in the literature of 'créolité': they are very similar to characters found in Chamoiseau's other novels and those of Raphaël Confiant. There is the sinister, violent 'Major' Julot-la-Gale, the exiled Haitian intellectual Ti-Cirique, the gossip Marie-Clémence, and a large group of women who all have the same characteristics: they are physically and mentally strong and resourceful, they dominate the men in the commu-nity, they have all been badly treated by men in the past, and they are prepared to fight physically as well as verbally (Marie-Sophie, confronted by Mano Castrador assumes 'la pure pose de guerre des femmes créoles', p. 383). The diversity of the characters is thus limited to instantiating a fixed set of stereotypes.[17]

Texaco, in Richard Burton's words, 'incarne le génie créole de la débrouillardise' (*Le Roman marron*, p. 182): that is, its inhabitants also all have the same moral values and the same attitude to life. These values are stamina and endurance, traditional practical knowledge, the use of ruse and trickery to compensate for their lack of power (e.g., exploiting the police's reluctance to destroy homes where there are children by sharing the children out between as many shacks as possible), and the supreme importance of helping and supporting each other. It is this last quality that more than anything else defines the community of the Quartiers where, unlike the atomized existences of people living in the town centre, extreme interdependence is the necessary basis for their collective survival. It is shown to be a feature of all the Quartiers; in the Quartier des Misérables, Marie-Sophie is 'environnée de la sollicitude que les Quartiers développent' (p. 337); in Morne Abélard, even the shacks form a 'communauté', 'portées l'une par l'autre, nouées l'une par l'autre à la terre descendante, chacune tirant son équilibre de l'autre selon des lois montées du Noutéka de mon pauvre Esternome' (p. 355). In Texaco itself, both buildings and people are similarly intertwined: 'Chaque case, au fil des jours, servait d'appui à l'autre et ainsi de suite. Pareil pour les existences qui se nouaient par-dessus les fantômes de clôtures ondulant sur le sol' (p. 408). But it is in the 'Noutéka des mornes' that this principle of mutual support is first formulated, and claimed as an explicitly creole characteristic: 'Quartier créole c'est des gens qui s'entendent [...] C'est *l'entraide* qui mène. Un Quartier même s'écrie comme ça' (p. 172). Texaco's 'ecosystem' thus incorporates social behaviour as well as the physical environment: people who are united in their battle against the authorities and whose survival requires a tightly knit and consciously 'creole' system of interdependence, so that the 'quartier', as Milne comments, becomes a perfect reflection of the culture as a whole.[18] As a system, i.e., made up of interlocking elements, it is by definition closed; as a living ecosystem, it is an exemplarily *organic* community. The ideals of diversity and openness promoted by the 'créolité' movement are not very evident in Chamoiseau's representation of the community of Texaco.

However, the text of *Eloge de la créolité* is in fact itself ambiguously poised between the kind of affirmation of diversity cited above, and a countervailing determination to define and celebrate the unique attributes of 'créolité' that results in a far more essentialist conception of creole culture and society. While on the one hand it affirms the inclusive, mixed nature of this culture – 'La Créolité est *l'agrégat interactionnel ou transactionnel*, des éléments culturels caraïbes, européens, africains,

asiatiques, et levantins, que le joug de l'Histoire a réunis sur le même sol'
(p. 26) – its opening words present exactly the same situation in a manner
which on the contrary stresses exclusion and distinctiveness: 'Ni
Européens, ni Africains, ni Asiatiques, nous nous proclamons Créoles'
(13). The mixed nature of the society has thus become essentialized into
a unitary category – creole – which is, moreover, claimed to be the ontological *foundation* of all Caribbean existence, the 'fondement même de
notre être, fondement qu'aujourd'hui, avec toute la solennité possible,
nous déclarons être le vecteur esthétique majeur de la connaissance de
nous-mêmes et du monde: *la Créolité*' (p. 25). Creole society may be made
up, historically, of a mixture of races – but that is precisely what gives it
a unique, essentialist identity, different from any other society.[19]

In Nancy's discussion of myth, the past is a fundamental reference
point. In looking back through time to the origin of the community,
myths reinforce the nostalgia that according to Nancy always surrounds
the ideal of organic community. The myths that he has in mind situate
the moment of foundation in the distant past, rather than the twentieth
century as is the case with Texaco. But Chamoiseau is nevertheless very
attached to Martinique's past; as we have seen, his project for its future
is to counteract the modernization of the towns by implanting in them
the traditional culture of the countryside. He has been criticized for his
nostalgic view of creole society, and for peopling his novels, set in the
1980s, with characters whose real-life equivalents have not existed in
Martinique for generations. Maryse Condé, for instance, protests: 'et puis
finalement ces Antillais dont il parle, où existent-t-ils? Où sont-ils? Où
les voit-il? Peut-être qu'ils étaient comme ça il y a cent cinquante ans,
peut-être, mais bien avant que Chamoiseau ne soit né, bien avant que je
ne sois née, donc maintenant on parle de mythes'.[20] In this sense too,
then, his representation of Texaco can be seen as mythical. The novel
itself contains one indication of the author's awareness of the disappearance of a distinctive creole culture: the 'marqueur de paroles' notes
in his concluding section that while Martinicans were able to withstand
the French colonial attacks on them, they are now threatened by a more
insidious loss of identity – ' l'érosion des différences de leur génie, de leurs
goûts, de leurs émois [...] – de leur imaginaire' (p. 493) – against which
their traditional means of resistance are powerless. In this context
Texaco's insistence on the values of the countryside and the importance
of living close to nature – as in Marie-Sophie's idyllic period staying with
Papa Totone, in which 'nous avions pris le rythme de l'eau, la texture des
écorces, le mouvement des oiseaux qui se posaient par terre' (p. 370) –

emerges all the more clearly as a conservative attempt to fight against the disappearance of the authentic traditional culture of the island.

Equally prominent is Chamoiseau's investment in folklore and the supernatural. This runs through all his novels, and also features strongly in those of Confiant and in the programme of the 'créolité' movement in general. It has attracted particular condemnation from the movement's critics, who see it as a simple evasion of the difficulties facing contemporary Martinican society; Michel Giraud, for instance, writes that the literature of Chamoiseau and Confiant 's'attache plus à la célébration nostalgique de la particularité d'un passé déjà révolu et à l'évocation conservatrice d'un folklore dans une large mesure en déshérence qu'à la prospection d'un avenir commun particulièrement incertaine' ('La créolité', p. 801). In the same vein, Richard and Sally Price argue that the rapid modernization of Martinique has created a nostalgic need for folklore that the 'créolité' movement both endorses and exploits, presenting its readers with 'a picturesque and "pastified" Martinique that promotes a "feel-good" nostalgia for people who are otherwise busy adjusting to the complexities of a rapidly modernizing life-style' ('Shadow-Boxing', p. 15).

The principal manifestation of the supernatural in *Texaco* is the figure of the Mentô. Since a Mentô is the source of Esternome's original inspiration to go and 'conquer the towns', and another Mentô, Papa Totone, gives Marie-Sophie the magic strength necessary to found and lead Texaco, the ideal of community is throughout associated with supernatural wisdom and powers. More generally, the Mentô constitute another instance of the 'secret order' that structures both Texaco and the narrative. The 'marqueur de paroles' describes them as providing both a thread of continuity through time and also, significantly, as *unifying* the scattered diversity of cultural beliefs: 'Les Mentô avaient de tous temps mobilisé notre imaginaire *mosaïque*. Ils lui avaient imprimé une *convergence* – une *cohérence*. Dans l'*éparpillée* des croyances caraïbes, africaines, européennes, chinoises, indiennes, levantines […], ils avaient noué des fibres restituées en bonne corde' (p. 492, my italics).[21] But there is also a more diffuse presence of the supernatural that goes beyond the Mentô. It often has to do with the past, or more precisely the spectral traces of the past in the present; Idoménée, for instance, tells Esternome of the stories about the ghosts of the Caribs which continue to haunt Fort-de-France (pp. 223–24), and he replies, 'C'est légende […] L'En-ville c'est ça aussi. Mais légende c'est mémoire plus grande que mémoire' (p. 226). In this way the distinction between historical memory and legend or myth is blurred, and the boundary between real and supernatural becomes very fragile.

This is in fact true, it is suggested, of Marie-Sophie's narrative as a whole. In the novel's final paragraph, the 'marqueur de paroles' laments his inadequacy in transcribing and transmitting her story in these terms:

> Puis, j'écrivis de mon mieux ce Texaco *mythologique*, m'apercevant à quel point mon écriture trahissait le *réel*. Elle ne transmettait rien du souffle de l'Informatrice, ni même évoquait sa densité de *légende*. Et j'abondais dans le jugement de Ti-Cirique, ce cher Maître, sur mon incapacité générale qu'il soulignait dans de longues épîtres. Pourtant, ses sentences m'encourageaient à poursuivre le marquage de cette chronique *magicienne*. (p. 497, my italics)

The juxtaposition of 'mythologique' and 'réel' in the first sentence would normally be read as an opposition; for the 'marqueur de paroles', however, they are synonymous: that is, his writing betrays the real *because* it fails to capture fully the 'mythological' quality of Texaco, and Marie-Sophie's 'densité de légende'. And if the whole of her narrative is finally described as 'cette chronique magicienne', then the implication is that the story of Texaco is 'real' *in so far as* it is supernatural. Folklore and magic, in other words, play a role similar to that which Nancy attributes to myth, of being simultaneously foundational and fictional: 'Mythic thought [...] is in effect nothing other than *the thought of a founding fiction, or a foundation by fiction*. Far from being in opposition to one another, the two concepts are conjoined in the mythic thought of myth' (IC, p. 53). Thus whereas on some levels the novel is commited to an almost documentary realism – implicitly endorsed by André Lucrèce,[22] and in the citation at the end of the text of the real figure of Serge Letchimy as the inspiration for the character of the town planner, and of various other real inhabitants of Texaco[23] – its concluding passage in effect retrospectively situates the whole novel in a very different world of myth and legend. The logical conclusion is that Texaco itself is indeed a mythical community.

The passage quoted above has, however, a further implication. If the version of Marie-Sophie's story relayed by the 'marqueur de paroles' is inadequate in the way he outlines, then her original oral narrative is actually *more* supernatural – as well as more chaotic – than the text we have been reading. The figure of the traditional story-teller on the plantations is accorded great importance and great value in the 'créolité' movement; indeed, the central character of Chamoiseau's previous novel, *Solibo magnifique*, was such a *conteur*. *Texaco*, in contrast, contains no major characters who are *conteurs*; but Marie-Sophie's long oral narrative, in its 'magical' quality, its digressions and so on, is clearly analogous to a *conte*. The novel thus brings into play the familiar opposition between oral, rural, traditional, creole, 'living' stories and written, urban, modern, French, 'dead' novels. Dominique Chancé in *L'Auteur en souffrance* interprets the figure of the 'marqueur de paroles' as a compromise between *conteur* and author, arguing that writers such as Chamoiseau are reluctant to assume the status of author because of its European and colonial connotations.[24] Like the Quartiers themselves, the 'marqueur de paroles' can also be seen as a compromise between rural-traditional and urban-modernizing. In Chancé's rather acerbic analysis, he attempts to recreate a community which includes him as an important and respected figure equivalent to the *conteur*; in his narratives, therefore, 'la quête des histoires à recueillir et celle d'une communauté à fonder ne sont pas dissociables' (*L'Auteur en souffrance*, p. 20). This is a double nostalgia, therefore: for the united community of the plantations, and for the value accorded to the story-teller in them: 'Ce sont les romans d'une créolité mythique où la collectivité est réunie, formant le destinataire immédiate, du moins imaginairement, du narrateur-conteur qui s'adresse à elle et la suscite' (p. 23). Chancé interprets the balance between diversity and unity in *Texaco* as a way of coming to terms with the disappearance of the united community by evoking a far more disparate one which is nevertheless pulled together by the work of the 'marqueur de paroles' (p. 36).

Whether or not Chamoiseau's use of the 'marqueur de paroles' is motivated by a phantasy of identification with the *conteur*, as Chancé suggests, the positioning of the 'marqueur de paroles' in relation to Marie-Sophie and her narrative is certainly an important factor in the novel's representation of community. In the first place, it is a rather old-fashioned technique of the realist novel: the narrator does not tell his own story, but receives and transmits a story from someone else and guarantees its 'reality' by explaining the circumstances in which the narrative came into his possession: finding a manuscript, for instance, or listening to the hero recount his story, as in many eighteenth- and nineteenth-century novels. The novel is presented to the reader not as a straightforward fiction but as a real-life testimony. In the case of the 'marqueur de paroles', however, this supposed reality is also approached from a quasi-ethnographic point of view: he describes Marie-Sophie as 'l'Informatrice' (p. 493, p. 494, p. 497).[25] His role in *Texaco* is therefore parallel to that of the town planner: neither of them belongs to the community, but both are initiated into its way of life by Marie-Sophie and so come to understand its 'ecosystem'. Defining her as a native informant has two implications: what she tells him is, precisely, *infor-*

mation, i.e., factual rather than fictional; and she belongs to a 'native' *community* which is the object of the ethnographer's research and therefore valuable and distinct: Marie-Sophie is of interest not for her individual life, but as a representative of and spokesperson for her community.

From this point of view, the confessed inability of the 'marqueur de paroles' to convey the full richness and magical quality of Marie-Sophie's narrative merely serves to reinforce the reality effect already introduced by the reference to its existence: if he is failing to conform to an original model, that model must by definition exist, even if the reader has no access to it. Equally, although the 'marqueur de paroles' is unable to reproduce the full living quality of Marie-Sophie's speech, and although he edits her narrative and incorporates into it excerpts from her written texts and the notes of the town planner, it remains the case that he does not add anything of his own to it.[26] He is, he claims, as faithful to it as he can be. In other words, nothing in the text that we are reading is fictional; it is all taken from the supposedly true account of 'l'Informatrice', which has all the force associated with an authentic member of an oppressed community telling her own story in her own words.

In this respect, Marie-Sophie's narrative could be considered similar to that of Télumée in *Pluie et vent sur Télumée Miracle*. But the difference is that the latter is simply presented directly to the reader: it is not surrounded by the extensive comment and explicit legitimation that we find in *Texaco*. Here, the reader cannot help but be aware of the fact that the original oral narrative attributed to Marie-Sophie, in its proclaimed superiority to the text that we are actually reading, in fact has no real existence; *Texaco* is a novel, written by Chamoiseau.[27] The assumed humility of the 'marqueur de paroles' – a mere transcriber of the words of others rather than an original creative author – is therefore ultimately self-defeating; the reality effect backfires. Had Marie-Sophie's own narrative been presented to us without any external comment – specifically, without all the explicit guarantees of its authenticity which the text constantly impresses on us – then we would have accepted it at face value, as we do in the case of Télumée. But, ironically, the more emphasis is placed on the authenticity of a supposedly 'real' original of which we are reading the copy, the more our attention is drawn to the fact that Chamoiseau is, to put it simply, making it up.

This tightly paradoxical situation – the more it claims to be real, the more we see it as fictional – can be seen as a rather unexpected variation on Nancy's theme of myth as inseparably foundation and fiction: the claims to documentary realism give Marie-Sophie's story the status of a foundational discourse, but simultaneously, by as it were forcing us to decide whether we 'believe' in it or not, betray its real status as fiction.[28] There is therefore, finally, a further sense in which the representation of community in *Texaco* can be seen as mythical. Chancé concentrates her attention on the 'créolité' writers' phantasy of integration within the creole community that their status as middle-class intellectuals in fact makes impossible. But one can also argue that, just as Chamoiseau is actually inventing the oral narrative of the informant that he claims to be transcribing, so he is in reality *creating* the community of Texaco that he claims to be recording via the 'authentic' testimony of Marie-Sophie. The phantasy is perhaps not so much one of his inclusion in this community, but of the existence of the community *per se*. Rather than the nostalgic phantasy which Nancy describes for an authentic community that is imagined to have existed in the past, Chamoiseau presents us with a similar phantasy set in the present. Texaco is not, ultimately, the physically real 'œuvre' of Marie-Sophie: it is the mythical creation of Patrick Chamoiseau.

CHAPTER 6

Community, Nature and Solitude in Daniel Maximin's *L'Ile et une nuit*

Daniel Maximin has written three novels, the so-called 'Caribbean trilogy' consisting of *L'Isolé soleil*, *Soufrières*, and *L'Ile et une nuit*; they are all set in Guadeloupe, and many of the same characters appear in all three.[1] The main focus of this chapter will be on *L'Ile et une nuit*, but I shall also refer quite extensively to *Soufrières*, because these two novels also have in common the central theme of natural disaster. *Soufrières* is the name of the volcano that was thought to be about to erupt in 1976, while *L'Ile et une nuit* recounts the 'one night' in which Hurricane Hugo hit the island in 1989. In both texts, therefore, the community of Guadeloupe is defined in relation to the forces of nature, and by its capacity to resist them. As the blurb introducing *Soufrières* puts it, 'Tout un peuple habitué des apocalypses de l'histoire et de la géographie se prépare la résistance'; and on the last page of *L'Ile et une nuit* Marie-Gabriel 'entendait déjà sourdre la résistance de l'île au travail sous le masque du désastre en cours' (p. 172).

These kinds of extreme natural phenomena lend themselves readily to allegorical use; in particular, the volcano has a long history in Caribbean literature as a metaphor for social unrest and revolution.[2] Most critical work on Maximin's writing has followed this trend: thus, for instance, Chris Bongie equates the volcano of *Soufrières* with the modernist anti-colonial revolution that never happens, and Nick Nesbitt interprets the hurricane in *L'Ile et une nuit* as a depoliticizing metaphor for the colonization process.[3] The hurricane does indeed acquire metaphorical resonances in the course of *L'Ile et une nuit*, although these are in fact more politically liberating than Nesbitt suggests. The word 'hurricane' derives from the Carib deity U Ra Kan, 'diable du ciel' (p. 26), and as such it is seen as avenging the deportation of the Carib Indians from Guadeloupe and Martinique to Dominica and St Vincent (p. 27); later, because it travels across the Atlantic from the West African coast, it is 'la force du cœur d'Afrique venue par le fleuve et l'Harmattan, pour enfanter l'eau de foudre, fils d'Oya, et transporter un pêle-mêle d'ancêtres et de divinités marchant sur l'océan pour apporter la mort et la survie' (pp. 73–74).

But to see its significance as solely allegorical is an unnecessarily restrictive and perhaps even rather Eurocentric reading: the societies of the Caribbean are fundamentally affected by the forces of nature, and it is important to start, at least, by taking these literally. In the opening pages of *L'Ile et une nuit*, Maximin sets out a typology of natural disasters and their differing effects on the population:

> Car pour nous qui l'avons vécu, nous savons que le tremblement de terre catastrophie nos pieds, embarquant le sol en lames de fond sans eau [...] Et pour nous qui l'avons déjà vécu, nous savons que l'éruption catastrophie nos têtes. Courbé sous le feu des cendres, le ciel s'abaisse sur nous sans étoiles ni soleil [...] Mais le cyclone, lui, sans pied ni tête, voleur d'eau de mer sans feu ni lieu, faufilé entre cimes et racines, dédaigneux des continents, c'est en plein cœur des îles qu'il vient de très loin nous frapper. (pp. 14–15)

The text makes it clear that the ever-present possibility of a hurricane, a volcanic eruption or an earthquake represents a constant risk of death, often on a large scale – 'Milliers de morts. Et par familles entières. Blotties ensemble dans leurs refuges massacrés' (p. 26) – and that this creates a particularly acute awareness of the uncertainty of life, which in turn affects relations with other people. Indeed, if we take seriously Nancy's view that '[death] is indissociable from community, for it is through death that the community reveals itself – and reciprocally' (IC, p. 14), then the placing of the people of Guadeloupe in relation to the hurricane is bound to have profound consequences for the conception of community. The fact that their resistance is directed against a *natural* rather than a social or political antagonist shapes both a particular kind of community and a particular kind of resistance.[4] For instance, the community extends beyond human beings to include animals – the birds and cows, more sensitive than humans to changes in air pressure, give the first warnings of the approach of the hurricane and the direction it will come from (p. 23) – and also trees and houses: 'Tous solidaires, les humains, les cases et les arbres, mais chacun si possible chez soi, les familles enfermées, les maisons barricadées et les arbres en sentinelles' (pp. 13–14).[5] Marie-Gabriel is as emotionally attached to her house and her mango tree as she is to her human friends; and as the eye of the storm passes over her house she becomes aware of the 'dialogue rompu des amis inconnus autour de la maison' – that is, the mountain, the trees, the river and the stars (pp. 76–77). Human beings, in other words, have no absolutely privileged status in comparison with the rest of the natural world.

One of the most important differences between natural and social phenomena is temporal: nature operates, for the most part, according to a cyclical time-scale which excludes radical, irreversible change; and this will determine the form that resistance to the hurricane takes. Here, however, we are confronted with an apparent contradiction between the literal meaning of the hurricane and the cultural, metaphorical connotations that it is given by the text – because one of the most dominant of these is the *apocalypse*. The hurricane in *L'Ile et une nuit* and the volcano in *Soufrières* are both regularly and matter-of-factly referred to as an 'apocalypse'. But at the same time, both novels also insistently undermine the notion of apocalypse – that is, of a cataclysmic, irreversible end of the world. In the case of *Soufrières*, this is simply because the major eruption that has been predicted never happens. As his chapter title – 'The (Un)exploded Volcano: Daniel Maximin's *Soufrières* and the Apocalypse of Narrative' – suggests, this significant absence forms the framework for Bongie's analysis of the novel. His starting point is the contrast between the modernist 'apocalyptic' sensibility of Césaire's writing, with its privileging of the image of the erupting volcano ('the explosive promises of this apocalyptic voice with which the literature of decolonization begins', p. 350), and Maximin's 'purposefully anticlimactic story' (p. 368) and postmodernist decentring of the teleological apocalyptic narrative from which it nevertheless cannot entirely break free.[6] One of *Soufrières'* chapter titles is 'Apostroph' Apocalypse',[7] which Bongie analyses in some detail (pp. 364–65). The word 'apostrophe' is itself interrupted by an apostrophe, an omission mark which Bongie, in a rather convoluted argument, sees as indicating the relationship between Maximin's first two novels.[8] But there is a far simpler interpretation: that it signals the 'omission', the non-event, of the apocalypse itself (especially if we bear in mind the etymology of the Greek word: 'apostrophe' means 'turning away' or deflecting).

In *L'Ile et une nuit*, the hurricane does of course happen; but here too, its apocalyptic significance is contested throughout the text.[9] Marie-Gabriel sees the fascination with apocalypse as a dangerous form of desperation: 'Laissons à d'autres le désespoir si commun parmi nous des rêves de ruine et d'apocalypse bien totale pour asseoir les projets de renouveau' (p. 22) – which is characteristic, according to her, of the Antilleans: 'Ou alors, allons-nous tous ensemble succomber à cette soif antillaise de tout détruire pour mieux tout commencer?' (p. 59). The text makes it clear, in contrast, that resistance is not a matter of this kind of grand space-clearing gesture; resistance is the *opposite* of apocalypse: 'Ce n'est pas seulement une nuit d'apocalypse. C'est aussi le grincement des résistances, le crissement des clous qui arc-boutent les tôles aux madriers' (p. 53).

Marie-Gabriel's assertion that dreaming of apocalypse is a typically

Caribbean temptation conflicts strikingly with Antonio Benítes-Rojo's well-known opposition between apocalypse and chaos, according to which the Caribbean is temperamentally incapable of an apocalyptic sensibility.[10] He claims that 'the Caribbean is not an apocalyptic world [...] The notion of the apocalypse is not important within the culture of the Caribbean. The choices of all or nothing, for or against, honor or blood, have little to do with the culture of the Caribbean' (p. 10). But for that very reason his position accords with Maximin's own perspective, and Benítes-Rojo's promotion of an alternative 'chaotic' world-view, although rather vaguely formulated, is illuminating with regard to the text of *L'Ile et une nuit*. Chaos dissolves the confrontations and binary oppositions of Western thought into a fluid, all-inclusive, endless process based on rhythmic plurality and varying repetition, which 'carries the desire to sublimate apocalypse and violence' (p. 16) and creates 'a realm where the tensions that lead to confrontation are inoperative' (p. 20); 'in this paradoxical space, [...] there appear to be no repressions or contradictions; there is no desire other than that of maintaining oneself within the limits of this zone for the longest possible time, in free orbit, beyond imprisonment or liberty' (p. 17). In the same way, in its depiction of the effects of the hurricane the text of *L'Ile et une nuit* continually recasts oppositions as paradoxical co-existences: as it states on the first page, 'Nous allons chercher ensemble les mots qui disent à la fois la tragédie de la lumière coupée et la résistance de la dernière bougie' (p. 11). This results in a particular style of writing in which antinomic phrases such as '[à] travers espoir et désespoir maillés' (p. 38), 'les mêmes eaux donnant mort ou renaissance' (p. 39), '[cyclone] fertile' (p. 79), '[les] Flamboyants, tombeau des renaissances' (p. 82), 'un riche fourbis de petites résistances et de fragiles agonies' (p. 90), and so on, are prominent throughout the text, creating and reinforcing the idea that the hurricane is not *simply* a disaster. For instance, it also has the positive effect of levelling out the island's inequalities: '[le vent] disperse les cartes comme ce soir pour une donne nouvelle et plus égale: qui a le moins perdra le moins, qui a plus aura plus perdu' (p. 98).[11] In this way Benítes-Rojo's view of the Caribbean's ability to defuse potentially apocalyptic situations is borne out; this is true not only of *L'Ile et une nuit*, but also of *Soufrières*, which repeatedly emphasizes the people's relaxed good humour as they await the eruption, and their lack of any morbid or melodramatic fascination with the prospect of imminent death: the volcano comments: 'Décidément, la mort ne passionne pas ce peuple qui cherche toujours la survie à toutes les perditions sans remords ni expiation' (p. 146).[12]

It is however the text's questioning of the notion of *finality* that has the most far-reaching implications for its representation of the community's resistance to the hurricane. The idea that it could be a real apocalypse is undermined by Marie-Gabriel's ironic reference to it as 'une petite fin du monde à endurer sans forcément mourir' (p. 25); a 'little' ending which is not really the end. Indeed, the apocalypse – supposedly the end of everything – is *itself* seen as coming to an end: 'Après la fin de l'apocalypse des autres îles dévastées [...]' (p. 55). A survivable apocalypse is a contradiction in terms; and the emphasis thoughout *L'Ile et une nuit* is on the work of rebuilding and reparation that will start as soon as the hurricane is over. No ending, the text tells us, is definitive: 'Toute fin est celle du paon: abattu par la tête, mais qui déjà commence, par la queue, sa renaissance' (p. 156); and one of the many intertextual links between the two novels is the song 'La Vida Continua', to which the characters dance in *Soufrières* (p. 226), and which is mentioned again in *L'Ile et une nuit* (p. 113, p. 119) as a source of reassurance and encouragement that life will, indeed, go on.

In this context, Benítez-Rojo's emphasis on process rather than completion, and the 'endlessness' of the Caribbean vision of reality – 'a continual flow of paradoxes' (p. 11) – is obviously relevant. He also links it to the ideas of plurality and repetition (primarily, in his case, the 'repeating island' of his title), and one can see a further connection here with Maximin's novels. Bongie's argument against apocalypse rests on the claim that the volcano, in the course of the narrative, never actually erupts. But this claim relies on a distinction between 'magmatic' and 'phreatic' eruptions; while there is no major magmatic explosion, there is a series of smaller phreatic ones which, while less dangerous, nevertheless cause a considerable amount of damage and injury, and lead to the evacuation of the population from their homes. One could therefore equally well argue that the single, devastating, once-and-for-all magmatic explosion is replaced by a plurality of smaller, less climactic, events which repeat each other and so are never final. In the case of the hurricane, the recurrent nature of the phenomenon is even clearer: the hurricane is not the end of the world because it is a natural phenomenon which follows a cyclical time-scale, and the novel brings this to our attention by its many references to previous hurricanes – for instance by the personified 'eye' recalling its previous visits to the island:

> Il profita de cet éclairage pour faire le tour de l'île, qu'il n'avait pas revue depuis dix ans [...] *chaque fois* que le cyclone arrivait, l'île se masquait en un désert de chlorophylle et de béton aux yeux du vent, lui cachant la population *chaque fois renouvelée* des humains calfeutrés. (pp. 72–73, my italics)

In fact the hurricane perfectly illustrates the 'chaotic' rhythm of Benítes-Rojo's Caribbean, combining regular recurrence with unpredictability: the hurricane season comes to the Caribbean every autumn, but no one can predict until the last minute which particular islands will be hit (*L'Ile*, p. 15).

The hurricane, in other words, unlike a human opponent, can never be definitively defeated because it will always return. Resistance in this context must also be a continuous process, orientated towards survival rather than victory: people protecting themselves and their houses and animals, and then salvaging, mending and rebuilding. Thus Maximin addresses his heroine Marie-Gabriel in the final chapter: 'Je te quitte avec un pays dévasté, mais un pays retrouvé: île battue, île combattue, très belle, et bâtie. Habituée à édifier dès le lendemain du cyclone, à rebâtir sans attendre les surlendemains d'arrivée du prochain' (p. 154). Resistance requires the flexibility to bend to the wind rather than be broken by it: the frequency of the verb 'rebâtir' is almost equalled in the text by that of the verb 'plier' – as in 'l'île pliée sans rompre, battue ce soir heure par heure, à rebâtir demain' (p. 25); or in reference to the house, 'qui pour durer ne provoque pas l'éternité avec des pierres de taille et des ferrements bétonnés, mais qui saura plier pour nous survivre' (p. 29).[13] It is necessarily reactive and adaptive, a question of repairing what has been damaged rather than starting again from scratch; and it acquires an almost ethical value as Marie-Gabriel defiantly addresses the hurricane: 'Avec tes loques nous allons rebâtir nos cabanes, comme nous avons fabriqué avec des barils jetés nos tambours sacrés. Nous n'avons aucune envie ici de reconquérir le paradis: il sent autant le dégoût et la trahison, avec son oubli de tous les enfers des pays torturés' (p. 64). The point is not to create a perfect 'paradise', but to make the best of what has survived, and so to remain in solidarity with the suffering of the islands. Equally, the aim is not to control the hurricane, which would be not only impossible but also, perhaps, undesirable; in the comparable case of the volcano in *Soufrières*, Rosan writes in his notebook: 'Il faut tout faire pour maîtriser la catastrophe, et espérer qu'on ne le pourra pas complètement. Car si un jour un Etat se rend maître du volcan, c'est qu'il se sera déjà rendu maître de ses habitants' (p. 238). Ultimately, the hurricane and the volcano are not simply enemies: they have positive as well as negative connotations, and above all they have the logical necessity of natural phenomena – as the volcano in *Soufrières* points out, 'Seulement la nature n'est pas forcément un spectacle de bontés, et il n'est pas de lion sans antilope ni d'antilope sans lion, comme le proclame la sagesse des très vieux continents' (p. 152).

Opposition thus merges 'chaotically' into accommodation: defending oneself *against* the hurricane becomes almost indistinguishable from learning how to live *with* it ('vous surprenez le cyclone, à tenir sans rien lui demander, sinon de laisser vivre, vous comme lui', p. 40). The text nevertheless stresses throughout that this is indeed a form of resistance, involving real danger and requiring real courage and endurance. But it can have no definitive outcome: surviving one hurricane is no guarantee that one will survive the next one, that will inevitably come sooner or later. This distinguishes it from what Bongie defines as the modernist conception of resistance that is predicated on revolution and looks towards a better future; resistance in this case consists in a way of living in the present, and a non-teleological conception of time which informs the whole community. Indeed – and here again the difference from political resistance is striking – it looks to the past rather than the future; the old people know what to do better than the young, and '[des] vieilles dames se moquaient des jeunes et des étrangers qui charriaient des caddies de surgelés, sans se rendre compte que l'électricité sera coupée pour longtemps. Dix années sans cyclones altèrent l'héritage des gestes instinctifs de survie' (p. 13). Resisting the hurricane, in other words, relies upon traditional knowledge, collectively acquired and passed on within the community. This fund of socialized expertise is the basis for the community's confidence in its ability to cope; in *Soufrières*, the people can enjoy themselves drinking and dancing even as the electricity fails, because 'les bougies et les butagaz avaient été prévus, les événements ne pouvant prendre de court une population bien préparée à l'attente des cyclones chaque année à la même époque' (p. 233).

* * *

A prominent difference between *Soufrières* and *L'Ile et une nuit* is that the former is dominated by group scenes. In each chapter, the narrative moves between different locations, many of which are the homes of the various characters, who themselves are moving between their different houses and other meeting places. There are of course also passages where a character is alone, and solitude is an important theme here as throughout Maximin's work, but the main emphasis is on a *group* of friends circulating around a number of places, inviting each other for dinner, dropping in on each other, helping each other out, playing music, dancing, drinking, and so on. They rely on and support each other emotionally. They are all very politically and culturally active: the demonstration against Pinochet is an important event, they are stunned by the news of the Soweto massacre, Antoine and Inès are producing a play by Wole Soyinka adapted to a Guadeloupean context, Adrien and Ariel meet up at the jazz festival in Avignon, Marie-Gabriel is writing a novel, they all have lively political arguments, and generally behave according to the conventional ideal of 'a community'.

In *L'Ile et une nuit*, in contrast, Marie-Gabriel is alone throughout. Whereas the threat of a volcanic eruption results in evacuations which bring people together, physically as well as emotionally, the hurricane requires everyone to shelter in and protect their own house, and since Marie-Gabriel lives alone in Les Flamboyants, she remains alone for the duration of the narrative. But, paradoxically, it is in *L'Ile et une nuit* that we find the most explicit emphasis on collective solidarity – and this paradox forms the basis of Maximin's representation of community in the novel. The first chapter, in particular, repeatedly stresses the importance of 'nous' and 'ensemble': 'Nous allons chercher ensemble les mots [...] Ensemble, nous aurons très soif de paroles enracinées' (p. 11); and the combination of physical solitude and communal feeling: 'Nous savons bien que ce n'est pas facile *tout seul* de rester *entre nous*, pour tenter de vivre *ensemble* le danger qui nous attend ce soir. Et qui n'attendra pas que *chacun chez soi* vérifie bien que nous sommes tous *ensemble*' (p. 13, my italics). It emphatically rejects the idea that the individual can accomplish anything on his or her own: 'Qui marche seul n'avance pas. Qui meurt tout seul ne sème pas. Qui espère seul n'attend rien' (p. 12). The same theme returns in the final chapter, where the author reassures Marie-Gabriel: 'que tu n'as pas été seule pendant cette nuit d'horreur solitaire, que tu n'as pas triché quand tu disais: *nous*' (p. 158).

This *nous* is not fusional; it is formed on the basis of a common situation as opposed to social or psychological identity: everyone is alone, and so everyone is the same. It illustrates the basic logic which for Nancy refutes the very possibility of the absolute individual subject; as he puts it: 'to be absolutely alone, it is not enough that I be so; I must also be alone in being alone – and this of course is contradictory'. If being alone is something that we have in common, then it is itself a form of relation, and '[this] relation tears and forces open [...] the "without relation" from which the absolute would constitute itself' (IC, p. 4).[14] Since the similarity which links Marie-Gabriel to others is not a question of individual character but is based solely on a shared predicament – ultimately, a shared fear of death – it is an instance of Nancy's 'like-being', which 'bears the revelation of sharing: he or she does not resemble me as a portrait resembles an original […] The similitude of the like-being is made in the encounter of "beings toward the end" that this end, *their* end, in each case "mine" (or "yours") *assimilates and separates in the same limit*' (IC, p. 33).

Thus Marie-Gabriel in *L'Ile et une nuit* is not a lone individual subject; she is a singular being existing through her relations with other singular beings, or what Maximin calls 'le nous de chacun': 'Mais surtout, ce soir, il nous faut prendre bien garde à nous, à bien préserver le nous de chacun' (p. 12). This 'being-singular-plural' is, moreover, integral to the basic structure of the text, in terms of its positioning of narrative voice. There are seven chapters, each recounting one hour of the hurricane's passage over the island; in each one the narrative voice is different, and its relation to Marie-Gabriel also varies, so that she appears as either a first-, second-, or third-person pronoun. A pronoun expresses a relationship between one person and another (who may be the same, as in the case of 'je'); and therefore, as in Nancy's 'exposition', Marie-Gabriel is present in the text only as a shifting series of relationships to other 'voices'.[15]

The predominance of pronouns over nouns or proper names in the novel also means that these varying relations are not immediately obvious, with the result that none of the characters is established in advance of the discursive relations constructed by the text. In the first chapter the narrating subject is the plural 'nous', and the reader initially assumes that its referent is a group of people living in Les Flamboyants. This is partly because of the reiterated emphasis on being 'together', partly because a common-sense reading of sentences such as 'Nous avons juste eu le temps avant l'alerte numéro deux de faire provision d'eau et de conserves' (p. 13) suggests a number of people making preparations together. But gradually in the course of the chapter, the use of 'nous' becomes a little strange, putting its referent in question. For instance 'we' remember helping Rosan to build his house: 'Et les femmes y ont pris leur part. Gerty, Elisa, et nous' (p. 22) – why distinguish between some of the women by referring to them in the third person while amalgamating others into 'nous'? Then Siméa phones, and this leads to the name 'Marie-Gabriel' appearing for the first time in the text: Siméa 'a une envie folle de venir aux Flamboyants déguster les raisins de sa marraine Marie-Gabriel' (p. 24) – which would seem to place Marie-Gabriel unambiguously as *not* part of the 'nous'. But this is followed immediately by:

> Mais ce serait surtout pour *lui* faire raconter une dernière fois le conte des treize poussins […] Cette histoire, que *nous* lui avons contée pour son anniversaire, une histoire uniquement réservée aux soirs de doutes et de

renaissances et que Siméa demande à réentendre ce soir [...] Sur une dernière
silence de l'adolescente, *nous* avons raccroché. (pp. 24–25, my italics)

There is no way to read this coherently other than by identifying Marie-
Gabriel with 'nous'; she slides from third- to first-person pronoun,
culminating in the distinctly odd 'nous avons raccroché'. Marie-Gabriel,
in other words, becomes identifiable as the subject of enunciation only
via the detour of introducing herself into the text as an *other*. Equally,
the referent of the plural pronoun 'nous' turns out to be singular – prominently reiterated in the chapter's final words: 'tous nos miroirs l'un après
l'autre n'ont reflété qu'un seul regard' (p. 31). This use of 'nous' is a
simple but effective way of expressing Nancy's 'being-singular-plural'.

In the second chapter Marie-Gabriel is addressed, as 'vous', by a voice
which we eventually realize does not emanate from a human being, but
from the books which she has read and her own writings. In the third,
she is speaking on the telephone, as 'je' this time rather than 'nous', to a
'tu' which turns out to be her lover Adrien and who never replies; only
at the end of the chapter do we learn that the phone lines have been cut
by the hurricane and so this has been a purely imaginary contact. (Within
this chapter, also, the referent of 'tu' occasionally changes, since at times
she is talking to herself.[16]) The fourth chapter has an impersonal omnis-
cient narrator; the fifth, like the second, a non-human narrative voice –
this time, music, addressing her as 'tu'; the sixth chapter is the third-
person narration, using elements of Guadeloupean folk tales, of her
mythical survival and rebirth; and finally, in the seventh chapter, an
authorial voice emerges, addressing Marie-Gabriel both as his imagined
creature and as a woman he is in love with, and saying good-bye to her.

This complex play of pronouns has several functions. It constructs
Marie-Gabriel as a subject lacking any solid individual presence, existing
only in relation to others, and as consequently rather elusive: the ambiguities surrounding her textual existence have the effect of distancing the
reader from her slightly, preventing any straightforward identification.
In addition, the pronominal structures *separate* at the same time as they
relate: the initial 'nous' breaks down into a series of discrete, if unstable,
relations – a process repeated in miniature at the opening of the last
chapter: 'Nous: pronom aveugle impersonnel, parmi nous: Toi et nous.
Elle et moi. Toi et lui et moi. Toi et nous deux encore. Nous sans vous.
Nous sans toi. Toi sans nous?' (p. 151). In this way the discursive structure of the novel reinforces the 'spaced-out' conception of community
that is also imaged by the physical solitude of its protagonist. While being
alone in danger clearly intensifies the need for community and solidarity

with others – 'Vous faites la foule, si vous êtes seule. Vous inventez autrui toujours revenant' (p. 41) – it does not, in Maximin's case, produce a desire for fusional, essentialist community, but rather Nancy's 'spacing of the experience of the outside, of the outside-of-self. The crucial point of this experience was the exigency, reversing all nostalgia and all communal metaphysics, of a "clear consciousness" of separation' (IC, p. 19). Maximin's allusion to the plant that opens and shuts its leaves as the wind brushes it against other plants provides a nice image for this: the atmosphere in Les Flamboyants is 'un mélange de solitude et d'ouverture, comme le mouvement d'une Manzè-Marie, petit feuillage qui s'ouvre ou se referme au gré de ce que le vent lui donne à effleurer' (p. 84). Similarly, his way of taking his leave of Marie-Gabriel at the end of the novel is exemplary of the kind of relationship that has been evoked throughout, and that now includes also the reader (as 'Vous'): 'Je et Tu plus jamais en Nous. Je vais te quitter. Tu vas me laisser te quitter. Je vais te laisser me laisser te quitter. Et Vous, vous allez nous laisser la laisser me quitter' (p. 152).[17] The community is formed of fluid relationships between separate beings, relationships that are never possessive or exclusive, and that evolve in accordance with changing circumstances.

Marie-Gabriel is single, and an orphan; her relationships – and this is true of most of the other characters as well – are those of friendship, which can include love and sexual relations (with Antoine and Adrien), but are not socially organized in terms of kinship or marriage. Antoine and Adrien are close friends, and are not jealous of each other's relation with Marie-Gabriel; the three of them form, in her words, 'une trinité bien rare: une trinité sans troisième' (*Soufrières*, p. 223). *L'Ile et une nuit* further suggests at some points that this kind of emotional freedom is connected to a *rootlessness* of which the orphan Marie-Gabriel is the central image, but that also extends beyond her. In the fourth chapter, she reflects that '[être] orpheline, c'était être condamnée à vie à être vue par tous les autres comme un oiseau posé sur une branche nue en lieu et place d'une fleur enracinée' (p. 93); but this apparently negative characterization needs to be read in conjunction with a fragment in the first chapter: 'La Guadeloupe est plus qu'un arbre. Même sans racines elle peut fleurir. Notre île est une vraie case, édifiée par notre grande famille d'orphelins fiancés' (p. 12). In other words, the death of parents, like the uprooting of trees by the hurricane, does not preclude the 'flowering' of lateral relationships between 'orphans' who create their own family, and communities do not need to define themselves by their *origins*. It is not that Marie-Gabriel's parents are unimportant to her; the sentence on page

93, quoted above, leads on to 'Mais, pour ce soir, elle n'avait garde d'oublier la leçon d'espoir de ses deux parents morts qui avaient survécu par miracle au cyclone de 1928' (p. 93). But the refusal of teleological time that we have already seen at work in the novel also means that relations to others are not subject to a continuous one-way linear progression. 'Enracinement' or rootedness remains an important positive theme in the novel, but is stripped of its nostalgic and static connotations: roots have to be actively 'grown', from the present back into the past; the novel that Marie-Gabriel is writing is described at the end of *L'Ile et une nuit* as a work of 'reinvention' of her 'roots' (p. 163). The past is thus in effect created by the present. Bongie quotes Maximin's remark that 'the present always invents a past for itself out of its own desire', and comments 'the ancestral past and the identity that might once have accompanied it are for Maximin nothing more or less than inventions generated out of desire, a rhetorical *inventio*'.[18] The notion of origin, in other words, is not negated, but is reworked to become the paradoxical *result* of creative activity in the present.[19] As such, it is not 'outside' the world; Maximin's novels echo Nancy's argument that the origin of being cannot be outside being, because the originary plurality of being logically excludes the possibility of a single origin at a given point in time.[20]

* * *

The form of community-in-solitude at work in *L'Ile et une nuit* also includes *literature* and *music*. The 'being-with' that sustains Marie-Gabriel through the hurricane is also a matter of being with books and music; this is reflected in the fact that the narrative voice in the second hour belongs to the books she reads, and that of the fifth hour is the voice of music. In the second chapter, she keeps her spirits up by reading – even though this means using up the oil lamp – and the voice of literature describes the way in which it helps her:

> Vous résistez, sous le grand camouflage des vies livrées en pages ouvertes à vos visages et vos masques dans la chambre recluse. Vous tenez bon, délivrée des fuites inutiles face aux eaux de la mort, face à cet enfer enragé autour de tous vos intérieurs. La lampe à pétrole illumine la chambre à mèche déployée, prodiguant une petite heure de gaspillage d'éclats pour écouter les derniers échos de vos pages fraternelles. (p. 35)

But it does not actually name any authors or titles. Its presence is manifested in more subtle and anonymous fashion through the intertextual relations set up with other literary texts: with Suzanne Césaire's 'Le grand camouflage', Henri Michaux's *Face aux verrous*, and many others.[21]

Fragments of these appear in the text, but are not signalled in any way; it is up to the reader to recognize them – and to the extent that we are able to do this, we too are drawn into the intertextual 'community' created in this chapter, but also in the novel as a whole (and in Maximin's other novels): the text of *L'Ile et une nuit* is full of echoes of other texts, mainly literary, but including also some folk tales, and some jazz and blues lyrics.

The musical community is largely confined to the fifth chapter. By this time, the damage to the house is already such that Marie-Gabriel has been forced to retreat into the bathroom; alone in this confined space, she is comforted by the voice of music offering her a form of 'company' that can take her beyond the limits of her present physical situation. This whole chapter is characterized by its repetition of 'compagnie', 'compagnons' and, especially, 'accompagner' – in its double musical and personal sense. Marie-Gabriel takes with her into the bathroom seven audio cassettes; she cannot actually listen to them, because there is no electricity, but she lies in the bath 'playing' them by unwinding each tape and running it through her fingers as she remembers the music recorded on it. The music is thus independent of its material support (and she is in fact destroying the cassettes by unwinding the tapes); she is 'listening' to what is not there, the exact counterpart of Miles Davis's injunction quoted in the chapter: 'Ne jouez pas ce qui est là, jouez ce qui n'est pas là' (p. 104). But despite the extreme tenuousness of its presence, the music, like the books in the second chapter, has the power to help her resist the hurricane and to counteract her loneliness: 'mes neuf musiciens d'Afrique du Sud, d'Amérique et de ta Caraïbe vont initier pour toi seule la résistance aux violences de ton cyclone et de leurs propres ghettos' (p. 123).

The sense of community is particularly strong because all the music she 'plays' is black, and it enables her to draw on the support of the whole history of black people's suffering and struggle.[22] But within this common framework, the variety and diversity of different cultural traditions is emphasized: there are three cassettes of North American jazz, one of Haitian popular music, one Guadeloupean, one Cuban, and one of South African jazz. Moreover, each type of music creates links with the histories of the people it belongs to, so that we find, for instance, references to Mandela and Soweto in association with Dollar Brand Ibrahim (p. 123), and in conjunction with the Haitian cassette a fleeting allusion to the Haitian boat people whose fears of drowning echo Marie-Gabriel's own: 'Même le soleil est parti quand ton bateau a chaviré, sans une étoile pour éclairer l'exil, mais dans un archipel protégé par les desseins vaudou'

(p. 105). Music thus serves to weave together a network of connections with other communities across time and space, while preserving their differences. Maximin also stresses the hybridity of each contemporary form of music, whose African roots are combined with a range of other influences: Cuban music, for instance, is made up of '[les] accents déchirés d'un héritage des chants d'esclaves, traversé du désir d'Afrique et d'Arabie, *via* les jardins d'Andalousie, enraciné en blues afro-cubain' (p. 113) – and the Cuban singer Célia Cruz is described as a '[voix] de flamenco nègre, de blues créole et de soleil métis', and is further identified with the Haitian Amerindian queen Anacaona (p. 114). In this way Maximin counters the idea that each society should have its own 'authentic' music: music is about openness and exchange, as he comments:

> Le jazz de Harlem et la musique cubaine sont les musiques qui ont bercé notre enfance; il n'y a rien de seulement guadeloupéen, de seulement antillais. Notre plus grande ouverture a été la musique: c'est en elle qu'on a le plus pris du monde et c'est par elle qu'on a le plus donné. Elle ne peut être une clôture d'authenticité car elle change sans cesse de tradition: ses maîtres-mots sont inventer, faire du neuf, improviser. (*Trilogie*, p. 199)

Célia Cruz and Anacaona also form part of a series of female figures whose presence challenges the male dominance of traditional black music: Billie Holiday, evoked by a quotation from 'Strange Fruit' (p. 103), whose suffering is described in terms that echo Marie-Gabriel's feeling of being 'attacked' by the noise of the hurricane: 'un soir, la tempête de ses malheurs faisait un bruit si fort que, pour ne pas devenir sourde, elle s'est mise à chanter' (p. 103); the Haitian singers 'Mes Sœurs Toto, Mariann et Emilie' (p. 105); and the Guadeloupean group of women drummers, the 'Sœurs de l'Akadémiduka', and their 'transgression antillaise de l'universel interdit des tambours au féminin' (p. 106). Black music, in other words, not only expresses the fight against racial oppression, but also embodies the particular struggle of women for equality and recognition within the black community: 'Avec toi ici cette nuit, et partout ailleurs avec toute femme esclave libérée, mes paroles de blues, de songs, de tangos, de léwoz et de guajiras sont toutes pour appeler l'amour au secours des tendresses violées, et faire écouter aux hommes le tambour au ventre des mal-entendues' (pp. 106–107).

Each of the seven cassettes thus functions as the starting point for a series of associative links with other figures and other histories, situating Marie-Gabriel in a virtual community of solidarity and inspiration; as the music tells her, 'Avec moi tu ne seras plus seule pour ton blues et pour ton combat: tu vas te souvenir et je vais t'enchanter' (p. 99). But the memories evoked by the cassettes are also more personal: she remembers the people who gave them to her, or with whom she has listened to them in the past. Therefore, not only does music create its own network of associations, but Marie-Gabriel's relationships with her friends are also characterized by and mediated through music. In fact, particular pieces are seen as expressing the unique personalities and lives of particular individuals – she remembers how she and Adrien together chose the pieces that they would want to play at their friends' funerals (p. 117). Music is not self-contained, in other words, but informs Marie-Gabriel's relations with both other societies and other individual people.

This musical 'community' also, in parallel with literature in the second chapter of the novel, has an intertextual dimension which involves the active participation of the reader. The seven cassettes that provide its main structure are (unlike the books in Chapter 2) clearly identified; but this chapter also contains numerous allusions to other musicians, titles and lyrics which operate as it were independently of Marie-Gabriel's own memories. Some of them are named, but others appear as anonymous fragments of text, such as the implicit but fairly obvious reference to 'Strange Fruit' mentioned above. This, however, is immediately followed by a more complex and far more cryptic allusion: 'Souviens-toi encore de mon Frère pianiste emprisonné, qui avait dessiné le clavier de son piano sur le mur de sa cellule, et plaquait autour de minuit les accords d'une danse infidèle au silence de sa tête matraquée' (p. 103). The connection with Marie-Gabriel, who is also silently 'playing' music while 'imprisoned' in her bathroom, is not difficult to make. But guessing the identity of the pianist requires the reader to recognize that 'autour de minuit' and 'une danse infidèle' are in fact titles of jazz compositions – and, in the first case, also the title of a film. 'Round Midnight' is a Thelonious Monk number (Monk figures on the fourth of Marie-Gabriel's cassettes); but it is also the title of a film, made by Bertrand Tavernier in 1986, based substantially on the life of Bud Powell; and one of Powell's compositions was called 'The Dance of the Infidels'; and later in his life he was arrested and beaten up by police before being incarcerated in a mental hospital. The text returns to him at the end of the chapter. After describing how Marie-Gabriel runs a bath and submerges herself beneath the water, anticipating her mythical death and rebirth in the sea in the following chapter, it goes on: 'Alors en mon solo je repense au pianiste emprisonné, aux sons de liberté plaqués sur son piano dessiné au mur de toutes nos prisons' (p. 124); tells us that his last composition was called 'Un cercueil à la mer'; and then refers to something that he

wrote before his death in hospital. Powell did indeed write a poem entitled 'Eternity' just before he died, and I imagine that the line Maximin
quotes in large capital letters – 'THERE IS KNOW END...' (p. 125) – is
taken from it. But the name of Bud Powell is never mentioned; the reader
can only discover it by being alert to the textual allusions, and, of course,
knowing quite a lot about the history of jazz.[23] There is a slightly irri-
tating aspect to this: it is easy to feel that reading *L'Ile et une nuit* at times
becomes too much like trying to solve a crossword puzzle. On the positive side, however, it does transform the text into a radically relational
construct, constantly setting its own words in juxtaposition with the
words of others.

Despite the variety of kinds of black music evoked, there is a definite
preponderance of allusions to jazz: Billie Holiday, Bud Powell,
Thelonious Monk, Miles Davis, John Coltrane, Charlie Mingus, Clifford
Brown, Duke Ellington, Lester Young, the Art Ensemble of Chicago,
Dollar Brand/Abdullah Ibrahim, Lionel Hampton and Albert Ayler. I
want to suggest that this is because jazz, more than other forms of music,
exemplifies the kind of open-ended, mobile, 'spaced-out' community that
Maximin creates in *L'Ile et une nuit*.[24] Equally, and for the same reasons,
jazz can be seen as a privileged example of Nancy's 'literature' and of
what in *The Inoperative Community* he calls 'literary communism'.
Covering all forms of art, but in the specific sense of that which interrupts myth and unworks meaning, 'literature' is a manifestation of
sharing and being-in-common: literature 'makes for a being that *is* only
when shared *in common*' (IC, p. 64). Unlike myth, it does not create a
communal identity; rather, it reveals our shared but singular existence(s):
one writes always for others, but '[what] is shared therefore is [...] sharing
itself, and consequently everyone's nonidentity, each one's nonidentity
to himself and to others, and the nonidentity of the work to itself, and
finally the nonidentity of literature to literature itself' (IC, p. 66).

All popular music is collective in its evolution – the same tunes are re-
used and re-worked by different players – and frequently in its
performance, which more often involves a group than a single singer or
player. This is true of jazz; but jazz also differs from traditional folk
music, for instance, in two crucial ways: it attaches greater importance
to conscious *innovation*, and in each performance the relations between
the musicians are freer because they are based not on set procedures, but
on each of them in turn *improvising*: Miles Davis's musicians do not
rehearse but start immediately to 'improviser ensemble' (p. 104).
Therefore each performance 'dies' because it can never be exactly

repeated, but improvisation continues indefinitely – as the music tells Marie-Gabriel, 'Ma mort par improvisation chaque soir est loin d'être finie' (p. 105); jazz is a form of continual sharing which never congeals into a finished self-contained entity. Improvisation requires each player to be open to the others, and to the unpredictable; the text quotes Dollar Brand's comment, 'Jouer pour moi n'est pas un moyen de transmettre un message, mais de le recevoir' (p. 116). Charlie Mingus is similarly presented as 'celui qui sait prêter ses oreilles aux autres joueurs' (p. 110); and the description of his playing emphasizes the equality of all the members of the band, and the way in which improvisation allows each of them to preserve their own space and their own 'nonidentity' while relating to the others: 'Non pas accompagnateur, mais compagnon chef de sa bande, chacun poussé à son extrême altérité, à charge pour lui-même de souder les solitudes à la beauté de son thème et aux riffs d'unison' (p. 110). A group of jazz musicians, in other words, unlike the more organic and fusional community of a folk group, is an 'unworking' community of singular beings exposed to each other.

In *L'Ile et une nuit*, the 'voice' of music describes itself in terms which echo Nancy's emphasis on the breaks and spaces in literature and its unfinished quality: 'ma voix de déchirure, ma voix de méandres cassés, ma voix désarticulée entre désir et désespoir, mourante entre deux flics, ma voix de gorge raptée contre une rançon de couplets mal finis, de refrains sans début' (p. 100). But it is in the descriptions of jazz, specifically, that we find the clearest equivalent of literature's ability to 'interrupt'; for instance, the description of Mingus cited above also insists that he is the 'improvisateur de *ruptures* afin d'harmoniser toutes les ségrégations' (p. 110, my italics). A different kind of 'interruption', perhaps, is the 'huitième note inventée: la note du silence' (p. 108) – invented, according to Maximin, by Monk and Ellington: a hesitation inserted into the melody, which precisely echoes the quality of suspension associated with literature's interruption of myth. Thus Monk is imagined playing 'Round Midnight': 'il est tellement seul qu'il joue en m'écoutant, et qu'il attend l'accord de la note à venir, ma note innocente, entre la note prévisible et le vide à improviser, pour offrir à la liberté un premier pas vers sa libération' (p. 109). Nancy's image for interruption *per se* is a voice or music that suddenly stops, allowing 'something else' to be heard: 'in this something else one hears again the voice or the music that has become in a way the voice or music of its own interruption: a kind of echo, but one that does not repeat that of which it is the reverberation' (IC, p. 62) – and that is the voiceless voice of being-in-common, which one can perhaps equate here with the 'eighth note of silence'.

Maximin's description of jazz, like Nancy's evocation of literary communism, shows how its always unfinished quality goes together with its endless circulation between different musicians and listeners. Literature, according to Nancy, 'does not come to an end':

> Literature does not come to an end at the very place where it comes to an end: on its border, right on the dividing line [...] It does not come to an end at the place where the work passes from an author to a reader, and from this reader to another reader or another author. It does not come to an end at the place where the work passes on to another work by the same author or at the place where it passes into other works of other authors [...] It is unended and unending – in the active sense – in that it is literature. (IC, p. 65)

It is a nice coincidence, therefore, that Maximin chooses to end, precisely, the fifth chapter with the line taken from Bud Powell's poem: 'THERE IS KNOW END...' (p. 125).

The question of how far Nancy's literary communism is also relevant to the *literary* community represented in Maximin's writing is more ambiguous. Nancy distinguishes between literary communism and the 'myth of the literary community' (IC, p. 64), and in many respects, particularly in *Soufrières*, the self-conscious and rather precious attitude towards literature and writing evinced by the characters is closer to this: they quote poems to each other, give each other literary texts to read, write each other long letters in a very 'literary' style, and generally 'commune' with each other through literature. On the other hand, Marie-Gabriel's attitude towards the novel that she is writing in *Soufrières* also emphasizes the characteristics of 'endlessness' and sharing that are central to literary communism. Her novel (which becomes the narrative voice at this point) describes her reluctance to bring it to a close: 'elle quête encore chaque occasion d'une ultime dérive: une nouvelle donne d'histoires anciennes, un conte pour veiller, un appel de lectures, un envol de feuillets, un pourvoi de désirades, frêles esquives au risque du courant, afin de retarder la conclusion de mon fleuve au sein de sa mer' (p. 254). In fact, Marie-Gabriel thinks not so much of ending the novel as of simply 'leaving' it, like an empty house open to others: 'Moi, j'ai envie de quitter mon histoire en laissant toutes les fenêtres ouvertes et la clé sur la porte' (p. 180). As this resistance to closure goes together with a desire to open her text up to other participants, literature becomes an open-ended, never completed, conversation: 'J'aimerais tellement que l'écriture soit comme une autre façon de parler [...] à moi-même et à toi, à ton enfant futur et à mes parents morts, à tous les nous-mêmes nous-mêmes vivant entre les

deux [...] Mais c'est difficile de faire un livre avec tant de portes ouvertes'
(p. 46).

L'Ile et une nuit contains much less explicit comment on writing or
reading than *Soufrières* does. Both novels, however, display the very high
levels of intertextuality that I have already referred to, and Maximin has
made it clear how much importance he attaches to this incorporation of
other voices into his writing as the expression of a form of collectivity.[25]
Nancy himself does not accord any particular importance to the intertextual dimension of literature, and in fact the discussion of literary
communism in *The Inoperative Community* has nothing to say about it.
But one could argue that the essential features of literary communism are
exemplified with particular acuity in intertextuality; in the first place,
Nancy's insistence on literature's lack of homogeneity, on its interruption and spacing, is clearly fulfilled in a text made up of juxtaposed
fragments of many other texts. Intertextuality has the further effect of
disoriginating the text, in so far as it cannot be seen as emanating simply
from the single figure of the author: at any given point, the words we are
reading (may) 'belong' to someone else. It thus 'interrupts' also the myth
of the author (IC, p. 69). For Maximin, it is closely related to his 'refus
de poser l'auteur en héros principal ou en demiurge, c'est-à-dire en maître
du Je parce qu'il y a chez moi essentiellement le souci du nous' (*Trilogie*,
pp. 14–15), and his desire to 'donner la parole à d'autres "je"' (p. 16).
The experience of reading his novels is therefore one of responding to a
multiplicity of different subjects of enunciation. Equally, intertextuality
could be said to enhance the *suspension* of meaning that is essential to
literature in its difference from myth; precisely because they are quotations, the incorporated fragments of other texts cannot be read as direct
expressions of the author's own ideas or emotions, and thus do not have
the same status as evidence of what the author 'really means'. Above all,
however, intertextuality would seem to be a particularly concrete enact-
ment of Nancy's conception of literature as communication between
singular beings: each quoted fragment communicates with the other text
that it evokes, and, in thus opening out onto a multiplicity of other texts,
Maximin's novel counters the conventional view of a bounded, self-
contained work and promotes the endlessness of literature: as the voice
of literature tells Marie-Gabriel, 'Chaque livre en appelle un autre pour
offrir un lendemain à sa fin' (p. 48). In these various ways the intertextual dimension of *L'Ile et une nuit* contributes to the novel's unworking
of mythical aspects of literature.

It also unworks the traditional conception of community; the 'sense' of community that emerges from *L'Ile et une nuit* is one which re-situates the collective in relation to both time and space. Its confrontation with the natural, and therefore recurrent, phenomenon of the hurricane determines a non-linear temporality; and the physical isolation of its heroine throughout the novel allows it to explore forms of non-localized, 'virtual' community that include not only solidarity with equally isolated people facing a common danger, but also music and literature. In so far as these latter consist in fragmentary, relational *meanings*, the novel also makes a connection similar to that which Nancy makes between sense *and* community – and solitude: 'Sense does not take place for one alone. Because sense is "being-toward", it is also "being-toward-more-than-one", and this obtains even at the heart of solitude' (SW, p. 88).

CHAPTER 7

On Not Belonging: Surrogate Families and Marginalized Communities in Maryse Condé's *Desirada*

In the ten novels which precede *Desirada*, Condé introduces her readers to a large variety of characters and locations while returning constantly to certain recurrent themes: migration, rootlessness, loss of tradition, oppressive families, women trying to lead autonomous lives in a male-dominated world, secrets buried in family history, and misguided attempts to base a personal identity on ethnic or genealogical criteria. *Desirada* continues to explore these themes, but from a new angle: an opposition between the breakdown of the biological family unit and the contrastingly positive strength of relationships not based on biological kinship: friendship and *surrogate* parent–child relationships. This opposition is expanded into a contrast between traditional organic communities, of which the family is an essential component, and a far more fluid and amorphous kind of community of people who are, sometimes for economic or political reasons but often because of family breakdown, excluded from the former type – people who 'don't belong'.[1]

The central character of *Desirada* is Marie-Noëlle, daughter of Reynalda and grand-daughter of Nina. Reynalda became pregnant with her when she was fifteen and tried to drown herself, but was rescued by Ranélise; a few months after Marie-Noëlle's birth, Reynalda left Guadeloupe for Paris and broke off all contact with her until, twelve years later, she forces Ranélise to send her to Paris to live with her. Marie-Noëlle has never known who her father was; eventually, when she is an adult and married to Stanley, Reynalda tells her that she was raped by Gian Carlo Coppini, who employed and also had a sexual relation with Nina; but Marie-Noëlle eventually comes to the conclusion that this is probably not true, that her father is probably (although she is never certain) the Coppinis' priest, and that Reynalda, far from being raped, had probably been in love with him. The rape, in fact, had taken place one generation earlier: Marie-Noëlle discovers that Nina had been raped by her cousin Gabin, who is thus – although Reynalda herself never knows this – Reynalda's father. The whole question of paternity is thus fraught with issues of rape, incest, and child abuse; initially, however, for Marie-Noëlle it is simply a mystery, and the whole narrative of *Desirada* is driven by her quest to discover who her father was. As a child, '[elle] se jurait d'y mettre les années qu'il faudrait, mais un jour de déchiffrer l'indéchiffrable' (p. 34). As an adult, she still feels that not knowing her biological father's identity in effect deprives her of an identity, and hence of the possibility of becoming a writer: 'Comment pouvait-elle prendre la plume tant qu'elle ne saurait ni qui elle était ni d'où elle sortait? Bâtarde née de père inconnu. Belle identité que celle-là!' (p. 220).

But by the end of the novel she has realized the futility of this quest for an identity based on filiation, and in fact the aspect of her family that causes her more real suffering is not her fatherlessness but her mother's cold, withdrawn attitude towards her. Marie-Noëlle at first thinks this may be related to the circumstances of her birth – a child born of rape – but in fact Reynalda is equally unloving towards Garvey, the son she has with Ludovic (p. 232). The real reason is that Reynalda was not loved by *her* mother, Nina: as she says to Marie-Noëlle, 'je ne peux pas vous donner ce que je n'ai jamais reçu moi-même' (p. 101). Nina rejected Reynalda because she looked like Gabin (p. 190), thus initiating a pattern which persists over three generations. Biological maternity is no guarantee of maternal love – as Marie-Noëlle reflects, 'La Nature manque à ses obligations. Les femmes qui ont vécu l'expérience de Reynalda, de victimes se transforment en bourreaux' (p. 141). Marie-Noëlle herself has inherited the emotional coldness of her mother and grandmother: she is glad that she is unable to have children (p. 143), and she is unable to express her affection towards Ranélise or Nina. As far as Reynalda is concerned, her feelings are a violently ambivalent mixture of hatred and forlorn love.[2] Reynalda was born on La Désirade, the bleak remote island off the coast of Guadeloupe – 'Au bout du bout de la mer, c'est un rocher désolé' (p. 175) – that Marie-Noëlle has nightmares about; and it is tempting to interpret the 'Desirada' of the novel's title as the desired but unreachable mother.

There are also many other examples of unloved and mistreated children: Marie-Noëlle's schoolfriend Saran, Reynalda's childhood friend Fiorella (daughter of Gian Carlo), Nina herself, who after her mother's death was treated like a slave by her aunt (p. 186), and more generally, many of the unnamed children and adolescents whom Marie-Noëlle teaches (p. 81, p. 142). Ludovic sums up this generalized failure of parental love: 'Nos mythes ont la vie dure. Nous croyons que les liens de parenté sont les plus solides [...] Tous ces enfants torturés, maltraités, dépécés, tous ces fétus jetés dans les poubelles, mis à pourrir dans les grands bois ne les ont pas réduites au silence et nous sommes là à répéter, après elles, des choses que la réalité contredit' (p. 277). Another sign of the breakdown of 'family values' is the nature of most of the sexual relationships portrayed in the text: men are often exploitative and/or violent (Gian Carlo forces his wife to have sex with him (p. 69), does not care about Nina, and has also been in prison for bigamy, p. 192), while adolescent girls are simply promiscuous: Awa, Saran, Leïla and Araxie all regularly have sex with groups of boys or young men. The Catholic church, supposed guardian of the sanctity of marriage and the chastity of young girls, is shown as a major source of sexual abuse; the central example of Père Mondicelli's probable seduction of the fourteen-year-old Reynalda is echoed by other similarly lecherous priests: Nina's grandfather was – again, probably – a priest (p. 184), Nina herself was abused by Père Steiner, one of the priests working in the leper colony (p. 186) who, after she becomes pregnant by Gabin, wishes he had actually raped her himself ('J'ai bien vu qu'il regrettait ce qu'il n'avait pas fait', p. 189) – and, when she is given a job as housemaid to another group of priests, they want her to live in the presbytery 'pour m'avoir plus facilement, je crois' (p. 189).

The failure of the traditional family has repercussions on the larger scale of social relations in general. The kind of orthodox respectable community built on stable patriarchal family units and subscribing to conventional moral norms cannot accept or integrate individuals such as Reynalda, Marie-Noëlle, Ludovic, Garvey, Stanley and most of their friends.[3] Reynalda and Ludovic are not married, and Stanley, who 'avait horreur de ce qui se nommait famille, ayant laissé loin derrière lui son papa, sa maman, ses frères, ses sœurs' (p. 96), marries Marie-Noëlle purely to facilitate their immigration into the United States. Marie-Noëlle's dominant emotion is loneliness; she does not feel that she belongs anywhere. This is true in the first place on the level of the family: her sense that 'elle n'avait pas vraiment sa place dans le triangle d'affection que [Ludovic] formait avec Reynalda et Garvey' (p. 41) is exacerbated when Reynalda becomes pregnant again: 'Elle était déjà exclue du territoire familial. Cet enfant à naître allait occuper la place qui ne serait jamais la sienne' (p. 100). But she has exactly the same feeling of exclusion in relation to the wider community of respectable people who lead 'normal' lives. The well-dressed, confident, affectionate Parisians in the street almost seem to belong to a different species of humanity from her (p. 98) – and, watching them, her reaction is to go into a café 'simplement pour sentir la chaleur des autres humains' (p. 98) – but the only person who speaks to her is another shabbily dressed outsider: 'Qui se ressemble s'assemble: elle n'attirait que des paumés' (p. 98). Or, on a train going to Brussels, she feels the same alienation from the other passengers in her compartment: 'Rien qu'à leur tête on voyait que ces voyageurs-là étaient des gens sans histoire. Des gens normaux. Issus de familles normales' (p. 257).

But the most significant example of this feeling of exclusion from normal community occurs in relation to Claire-Alta, Ranélise's younger sister. When Marie-Noëlle goes back to Guadeloupe to attend Ranélise's funeral, she re-enters the community she had known as a child but which is now, she soon discovers, 'un monde auquel elle n'appartenait pas'(p. 148). Claire-Alta starts crying as Marie-Noëlle prepares to go back to Boston: 'Pourquoi pleurait-elle? Simplement parce qu'elle faisait partie de ces personnes normales qui pleurent à l'occasion des départs et des enterrements, qui se réjouissent aux cérémonies de fiançailles ou de noces et qui battent des mains lors des baptêmes' (p. 211). This kind of socially generated and socially endorsed emotion, conventional but sincere and straightforward, is something Marie-Noëlle cannot share. She is regarded with disapproval and mistrust by the mourners attending Ranélise's funeral, where she does not, in their eyes, behave properly (she does not show any emotion, and drinks too much, pp. 137–38). Thus her idyllic childhood memories of Guadeloupe are replaced by the disillusioned realization that she does not belong here either. In fact, it is more difficult to fit in here than in Europe or the United States, because Guadeloupe is still, despite its modernization and its tourist industry, a small and closed community, suspicious of outsiders. Marie-Noëlle inspires in her fellow mourners 'un sentiment qui ressemblait à la peur et qu'ils ne comprenaient pas. Ils sentaient qu'elle venait d'ailleurs, d'un ailleurs pour eux aussi profond, aussi mystérieux que la forêt dense' (p. 138) – and they are careful to keep their distance from her. Relationships here are based on kinship ('Tous les Guadeloupéens sont parents', p. 176), and people's lives follow known, predictable patterns: Nina tells Marie-Noëlle to go back to Boston because '[il] n'y a pas de place pour toi ici. [...] Ici, chacun depuis la naissance connaît le chemin dans lequel il doit marcher et la place où, à la fin, il faudra qu'il se couche' (p. 202).

This amounts to an implied critique of the representation, dominant in many Antillean novelists, of Guadeloupe and Martinique as ideal organic communities free from the alienation and depersonalization that afflicts Europe and North America. This, Condé suggests, is a sentimental anachronistic myth, a 'légende rabâchée, offerte à la consommation des grands et des petits pour apaiser leurs angoisses' (p. 162).[4] As though to make it clear that Marie-Noëlle's experience of return to the island is not simply a consequence of her individual psychological problems, the text introduces a Guadeloupean taxi-driver in Paris who has had a very similar reaction to going 'home':

> L'excès de beauté du pays l'avait intimidé, comme s'il se promenait sur une scène étrangère. Son univers à lui, c'étaient les banlieues tristes, les stades, les terrains de foot. Il ne s'était jamais senti à son aise. Il était de trop partout. […] Il n'avait retrouvé son souffle familier qu'à son retour à Paris. Et pourtant, il ne se prenait pas pour un Français. (p. 244)

In other words, he is a Guadeloupean who does not feel at home in Guadeloupe, but whose relationship to France is equally ambivalent: he does not identify with the French, but the only place where he does feel he belongs is in the margins of the French capital. Marie-Noëlle's reaction to his account both identifies herself with him and generalizes their common situation beyond any geographical or ethnic specificity: 'Combien étaient-ils à travers la planète Terre à partager la même malvie? Assez pour former une autre race, assez pour peupler un autre monde' (p. 244). In this negative sense, she begins to conceive the outlines of an alternative community – that of those who do not belong straightforwardly to a particular place or established social group, and who have in common solely the fact of not belonging.

It is this kind of marginalized, heterogeneous grouping that *Desirada* presents as the relatively positive alternative to the traditional familybased community of 'normal' people. It is important to emphasize that the opposition is not – as it has been in most earlier Caribbean literature of immigration – between the Caribbean on the one hand and Europe and North America on the other. That is, it is not between one geographically based culture and another, but between 'respectable', homogeneous, rooted communities anywhere in the world, and that formed by the people who are excluded from them. These do not necessarily speak the same language, live in the same place or belong to the same race; all they have in common is their marginal situation and the emotions it generates. Thus when Marie-Noëlle, returning to Paris as an adult, remembers her first arrival at the airport as a bewildered child, she finds herself identifying with the other frightened little girls of different nationalities whom she now sees around her: 'Elle la retrouvait partout, cette petite fille. […] Dans cette petite Indienne, cette petite Chinoise, cette petite Américaine aux longs cheveux blonds. Ce qui compte, c'est la détresse' (p. 238).

In so far as this community has any territory, it is the poor, racially mixed suburbs of cities in Europe and the United States. The Paris that Marie-Noëlle comes to live in has become 'capitale de la couleur, Paris des Deuxièmes Générations, des négropolitains, des harkis et des beurs' (p. 166);[5] in Nice, too, Marie-Noëlle and her friends from the sanatorium socialize with 'une bande de jeunes chômeurs, arabes, antillais, turcs, en tout cas métèques comme elles-mêmes, sans famille fixe' (p. 76). When she and Stanley go to Boston, they find a flat in a similar area inhabited by African-Americans and immigrants. Her husband is a Trinidadian Londoner, and her friends come from Guinea, Guadeloupe, Haiti, Tunisia, Armenia and Argentina, but none of them are white Americans or French. When Anthea Jackson's colleagues – middle-class black academics – warn Marie-Noëlle against racial prejudice in America, she cannot see how it affects her:

> Et puis, où était-il ce monde des Blancs, des Caucasiens qu'on voulait qu'elle redoute? Peu vraisemblable. Irréel comme celui des loups-garous. Elle allait et venait dans un tout autre monde. Parmi des Noirs, des basanés, des métis, des métèques, des exilés, des transplantés, des déracinés. La majorité de ceux qu'elle cotôyait savaient à peine l'américain, ne lisaient pas les journaux, ne regardaient que les programmes de télévision en langue étrangère. (p. 112)

In this 'other world', relationships are formed not on the basis of socially recognized ties or common interests, but on a combination of chance encounters and emotional needs.[6] A strikingly large number of them take the form of surrogate parent–child relations, presented in systematic counterpoint to the loveless relations between parents and their biological children.[7] Thus it is pure chance that Ranélise notices Reynalda drowning in the harbour, but she takes her in, looks after her and, because of her longing for a baby of her own, is overjoyed when Reynalda abandons Marie-Noëlle with her. Marie-Noëlle's early childhood is idyllic; Ranélise is so devoted to her that she gradually forgets that she is not her real mother (p. 21), is devastated when she is summoned to Paris, and dies, never having seen her again, with Marie-Noëlle's name on her lips (p. 136). Once in France, Marie-Noëlle no longer has a loving mother; she does, however, acquire a surrogate father in the shape of Ludovic, who in fact performs all the maternal roles as well. Reynalda's apathy towards her daughter is contrasted with the attitude of Natasha, mother of Marie-Noëlle's friend Awa: she wants to adopt Marie-Noëlle and take her back to Africa, but Reynalda, to Marie-Noëlle's great distress, refuses to let her go (p. 55). Then Marie-Noëlle finds another friend and surrogate mother in Mme Esmondas, their neighbour in the appartment block – 'maternelle comme sa mère ne l'était pas' (p. 49) – who also longs for a child. Later, in Boston, she is employed to teach French to Anthea's daughter Molara, and finds yet another surrogate mother in Anthea, who initiates her into the academic world and reacts like a proud parent when she is awarded her doctorate (p. 223). Molara herself is adopted, and Anthea lavishes her affection and money on her.[8] Conversely, Marie-Noëlle comes to treat Molara, her precociously intelligent pupil, as her own surrogate daughter (p. 142). Thus the advantages of surrogate relationships are not only that they are freely chosen – Marie-Noëlle thinks of Molara as 'cette enfant-là qu'elle s'était choisie' (p. 143) – but also that they are more flexible and multivalent than biological relations: Marie-Noëlle can simultanously be Anthea's daughter and Molara's mother. She is also Molara's teacher and, informally, Anthea's student, and the novel provides other examples of the teacher–student relationship as a quasi-parental one: Reynalda was cared for and protected by one of her teachers, Madame Lépervier (pp. 85–86), and Marie-Noëlle is more concerned to provide emotional understanding and support for her students than to teach the books on the syllabus (p. 81, p. 142). Conversely, Marie-Noëlle feels that her students at Roxbury are 'ses seuls amis, ceux qui lui avaient permis de supporter les pires moments de sa vie en Amérique' (p. 219).

Anthea is of course Marie-Noëlle's *friend* as well, and friendship in general is also presented as filling the gap opened up by the failure of biological families. The relationships Marie-Noëlle forms with other girls and women give her far more emotional sustenance than she receives either from Reynalda or from her sexual relationships with men. When Awa comes to stay with them in Savigny-sur-Orge the two girls immediately become intimate, inseparable friends, and this lasts until they are adult. The narrative very explicitly privileges friendship over family when Awa runs away from her parents in Africa and comes to 'rejoindre, à Boston, Marie-Noëlle, la seule personne qui se souciait d'elle sur la terre' (p. 121). Similarly when Saran, Marie-Noëlle's schoolfriend, plans to run away from her father and stepmother and go to America, she wants Marie-Noëlle to come with her, and Marie-Noëlle 'aurait donné n'importe quoi pour laisser Savigny-sur-Orge loin, loin derrière elle' (p. 59). Later, in the sanatorium, she is happy because she makes friends with Leïla and Araxie, and does not miss the lack of family contact at all (p. 75).

Most of these friends are people who are significantly different from Marie-Noëlle herself. Some of them – Mme Esmondas, Arelis – are much older. Anthea is also older, but differs more strikingly in her social position as a successful middle-class academic, which allows Marie-Noëlle to 'partager une existence tellement différente de la sienne' (p. 116). Above all, they are of many different nationalities.[9] Condé has made clear how much importance she attaches to friendships that do not require a basis in ethnic similarity:

> D'une certaine facon tous ces repères, la famille, la biologie, les rapports noués sur la proximité du sang, disparaissent au fur et à mesure. On se trouve amené à se choisir, soit une famille, une communauté, qui n'est pas forcément composée de gens de la même origine que soi. Finalement, on se trouve amené à avoir des amis américains, des gens des différents pays. Je trouve cela un enrichissement.[10]

The differences are not just of age, class, nationality or ethnic origin, but also of temperament and views. Marie-Noëlle is sceptical of Mme Esmondas's powers as a medium, and scornful of her gullible clients, but '[malgré] cela, les moments avec Mme Esmondas lui paraissaient bénis' (p. 48). Similarly, she forgives Anthea her obsessions and her over-intellectualism because she is grateful for the way in which Anthea has transformed her life (p. 123). As Condé comments, 'Par exemple, Marie-Noëlle devient l'amie d'une Africaine-Américaine, Anthea. Pour moi, c'est l'exemple parfait de ce genre de relation nouvelle. Des gens qui ne pensent pas comme vous. Pas du tout. Des gens dont la vie est différente – mais avec qui on peut quand même nouer des rapports d'affectivité.'[11] These surrogate parental relations and friendships thus form the basis for a 'community of those who have nothing in common'[12] – nothing, that is, except accidental contiguity and a need for company and affection.

The novel's treatment of them is determinedly egalitarian, in the sense that minor characters and short-lived relationships are accorded as much detailed attention as those which prove to have more permanent significance in the narrative. Saran, for instance, soon disappears from Marie-Noëlle's life when she is expelled from school, while Awa is present in the novel right up to the end. But the two girls are introduced and described in comparable detail. The sequence of events which has brought Saran to France from Guinea, leaving her mother behind, her unhappy relationship with her father's other wife and her habit of having sex with boys at the school for money (pp. 57–58), appear at the time – both to the reader and to Marie-Noëlle – to be as important as the lives of any of the other characters. Similarly, one whole short chapter is devoted to Mme Esmondas (pp. 45–49); she gets to know Marie-Noëlle through meeting her on the stairs, becomes her friend, gives her cocoa and biscuits in between seeing clients and tells her the story of her life, before suffering a heart attack and disappearing while Marie-Noëlle is away on holiday. But despite its brevity this is a close and intense relationship, and Marie-Noëlle is distraught at the loss of her friend and surrogate mother.

The text thus emphasizes the importance of temporary relationships in the mobile and insecure existences of the characters. But beyond this, it also goes into what might seem an unnecessary amount of detail in the information it gives on minor characters; for instance, it does not merely communicate the *fact* of Mme Esmondas's telling Marie-Noëlle at length about her past – which would be sufficient to establish their closeness – but, using the free indirect speech which is so prominent throughout, in effect tells the reader her story as well (pp. 47–48). Thus even minor characters, whose ostensible function in the narrative is to provide parallels or contrasts to Marie-Noëlle, or to supply information in her quest to discover her father's identity, are never introduced without the reader learning about their own predicament and their own thoughts and emotions, *from their own point of view*. Fiorella, for instance, is spoilt by her parents but remains depressed and tearful: 'Aussi il lui semblait que sa jeunesse poussait entre des deuils comme l'herbe entre les dalles des tombeaux' (p. 90); Arelis mourns the death of her drug-dealer son Anthony, murdered by unknown fellow-gangsters, and hates living in the United States (pp. 126–28); and the three and a half pages of Claire-Alta's free indirect speech (pp. 149–53) revolve around her own problems with her husband as well as her reactions to Marie-Noëlle. These and other similar passages form digressions from the central story of Marie-Noëlle, and make it impossible for the reader to focus exclusively on her. Indeed, the profusion of episodic characters whose complicated past histories and present emotions are described in unrelenting detail sometimes becomes confusing (and the confusion is compounded by the fact that, conversely, figures who play more central and permanent roles in Marie-Noëlle's life are not always clearly recognizable as major characters: the significance of Père Mondicelli for the lives of both Reynalda and Marie-Noëlle, for instance, is never clearly stated). But by presenting minor characters as subjects of enunciation, expressing not only their emotions but their vision of events – by allowing them temporarily to take over the narration, in other words – *Desirada* refuses to comply with conventional criteria of narrative coherence and puts in their place a deliberately unhierarchized representation of a multiple, decentred network of interacting but separate characters and narrative incidents.[13] For Condé here as for Nancy, 'Being' is communication and circulation; it is '*our* web or "us" as web or network, an *us* that is reticulated and spread out, with its extension for an essence and its spacing for a structure' (BSP, p. 28).

The community that is thus evoked is characterized by its lack of boundaries. Unlike the communities to be found in the other novels studied here, it is not located in one specific place.[14] The Guadeloupean community is, as we have seen, criticized for its narrow-minded fear of the outside world, and the communities formed by settled indigenous French or American individuals are simply inaccessible to Condé's characters. They, in contrast, belong – in so far as they belong anywhere – to a 'community' whose defining feature is that it cannot be defined. Caribbean, African-American and Latin American novels frequently have very large numbers of characters, who often migrate far from their birthplaces, but they are almost always linked in some predetermined way. This is often genealogical: the novel that recounts the history of a family over several generations has become a staple of the genre, and Condé herself has contributed *La Vie scélérate* to this category.[15] What is new and very striking about *Desirada* is that it introduces us to more than sixty characters who are not organized into family structures, or according to any other principle such as place, ethnicity or professional milieu. (Most of them are socially marginal, but not all: Anthea is an established academic, Claire-Alta is firmly embedded in her working-class but upwardly mobile Guadeloupean community.) Thus not only is the emphasis placed on the heterogeneity of this 'community', but the differences between people are shown to be *uncategorizable* – far more random than the culturally determined differences that actually serve to constitute and consolidate more traditional visions of 'minority' communities. While the predominance of migration in the novel does result in its principal locations being racially mixed, with people of different backgrounds living side by side, *Desirada* is strangely unconcerned with the idea of cultural difference; there are no examples of it posing an obstacle to personal relationships, for instance (as there were in Condé's earlier novels *Heremakhonon* and *Une Saison à Rihata*[16]). There is not even any mention of language differences, and the problems these might be expected to have caused Marie-Noëlle in her new English-speaking environment in Boston; nor is racism a prominent issue in the novel. Thus when Condé states that '[ce] qui m'intéresse, c'est la rencontre des cultures, les conflits, les modifications qui en résultent',[17] this is not to be interpreted according to the standard conventions of liberal discourse on cultural difference; it is rather, I think, an appreciation of the existence of large numbers of people across the world who do not have a 'cultural background' in the normal sense, and of the consequences of this state of affairs. As Nancy comments in the 'People are Strange' section of *Being Singular Plural* (pp. 5–10),

> Not only are all people different but they are also all different from each other. They do not differ from an archetype or a generality. The typical traits (ethnic, cultural, social, generational, and so forth), whose particular patterns constitute another level of singularity, do not abolish singular differences; instead, they bring them into relief. (p. 8)

The 'members' of *Desirada*'s 'community' – and this precisely makes both terms extremely problematic – are simply *people*, in the sense which Nancy develops in 'People are Strange'.[18]

Since the fundamental characteristic of this community is its unbounded, indefinable nature, it cannot consist entirely of migrants (which would in itself be a definition). Thus Ranélise, Nina and Claire-Alta never leave Guadeloupe, and Anthea, despite her visits to Africa, is solidly based in the US. But it is true, and significant, that the majority of the characters do move between continents and make their lives in a succession of different cities.[19] Their movements are also far more varied than the classic trajectory of immigration, from the Antilles to France and/or North America. Ludovic, for example, has travelled from Haiti to Cuba, then to the United States, Canada, Mali, Mozambique, Germany and Belgium before arriving in Paris. His friend Rodrigue went from Haiti to Cuba, from there to study in Moscow where he married Natasha, and from there to Guinea where Awa was born. Gian Carlo Coppini's family were originally Polish Jews who emigrated to Italy; forced to leave Milan when he got his employer's daughter pregnant, Gian Carlo took her to Guadeloupe – simply because of a travel advertisement in an Italian newspaper which convinced him that the Caribbean climate was better than that of the United States – thus reversing the usual immigration route from the Caribbean to Europe.

Desirada is not the only novel by Condé to accord such central importance to the phenomenon of migration.[20] But it is the first which refuses to grant any privileged status to an individual's or a family's place of origin; because there is no 'home' to return to, as Marie-Noëlle discovers when she does return to La Pointe, there is no contrasting sense of exile either; her reaction to the idea of leaving France and emigrating to America, for instance, is just a bleak equation of the two places: 'Est-ce que je vais simplement troquer le désert de Nice pour le désert de Boston?' (p. 95). With *Desirada* Condé thus moves away from the problematic of diaspora to that of decentred migration.[21] Ludovic, for example, is never sure what to say when asked where he comes from (p. 38), and does not feel that he belongs to any country: 'Moi qui n'ai jamais eu de pays à moi, est-ce que c'est Haïti? Ou bien Cuba? Ou bien le Canada? Ou bien les Etats-Unis d'Amérique?' (p. 272). This kind of rootlessness is not seen as negative, but nor is it celebrated in *Desirada* as simplistically positive.[22] In Marie-Noëlle's case at least, it is not the result of her own volition: she is brought to Paris by her mother, she goes to Boston because Stanley wants to go there, and she continues to live in America simply because she cannot see any point in going anywhere else: 'Elle n'avait aucune détermination à y finir son existence. Pourtant, elle ne se voyait pas vivre ailleurs' (p. 163). The lack of attachment she feels for all the places she has lived in produces a strange kind of discontinuity in her life, because as soon as she has moved on somewhere else, the place she has just left begins to seem unreal and dream-like. When she is in the sanatorium in the south of France, 'elle pouvait s'imaginer que ces années à Savigny-sur-Orge n'avaient pas de place dans la réalité' (p. 74); when she goes to Guadeloupe, '[il] lui semblait qu'elle avait rêvé Boston, son récent calvaire et tous les mois de deuil qu'elle venait de connaître. Son cœur se demandait s'il avait vraiment ressenti toute cette douleur' (p. 160); and when she comes back from Guadeloupe, '[elle] avait souvent l'impression qu'elle avait rêvé tout cela [...] De retour à Roxbury, ce qui venait de lui arriver à la Guadeloupe perdait toute vraisemblance' (p. 217).

At the same time, however – and this is less a contradiction than an effect of the generalized mobility of the novel's characters – the various places she and her friends live in are also very similar. Despite the constant movements, there is a sense of staying within the same mobile community of marginalized multi-racial groups in poor districts on the edge of big cities. Thus as she gets used to living in Camden Town, a suburb of Boston, she realizes that '[à] la vérité, Camden Town ressemblait à Savigny-sur-Orge' (p. 105) – not because it seems French, but because '[il] était habité par des Africains-Americains, des Africains, des immigrés venus de toutes les îles de la Caraïbe ou des pays de l'Amérique latine' (p. 105).[23] Conversely, the suburbs of Paris remind her of Boston (p. 238), as does the party Garvey gives to celebrate her arrival (p. 241). Ludovic's new flat in Brussels is very similar to the one they lived in in Savigny-sur-Orge (p. 265); and even Guadeloupe is similarly characterized by 'pauvreté, laideur. [...] Sans le soleil qui mettait son éclat généreux là-dessus, ce décor aurait été aussi désolé que celui de Camden Town' (p. 139). Thus a combination of urban poverty and migration creates series of places which replicate themselves on both sides of the Atlantic, and people like Marie-Noëlle, Ludovic and Stanley move around from one to the other without ever feeling either fully at home or completely out of place. In fact, as in the case of the Guadeloupean taxi driver in Paris, these are the only places in which they do feel at ease, and in which, in a constrained and transitory fashion, they make some kind of home. Despite the dirt, ugliness and violence of Camden Town, Marie-Noëlle becomes attached to it (p. 105) and decides to stay there after Stanley's death: 'elle n'avait pas eu le cœur de quitter Camden Town, cher et familier dans sa laideur et son désordre comme la figure d'une bonne parent disgraciée' (p. 143). The very dehumanization and anonymity of this America – its lack of community, in traditional terms – make it the right sort of place for someone like her: 'Les Etats-Unis d'Amérique étaient faits pour ceux de son espèce, les vaincus, ceux qui ne possèdent plus rien, ni pays d'origine, ni religion, peut-être une race et qui se coulent, anonymes, dans ses vastes coins d'ombre' (p. 163).

Significantly, however, '[elle] *ne savait pas* […] *expliquer* son attachement pour un pays qu'elle avait abordé par hasard comme ses illustres prédécesseurs, mais qui la retenait fermement' (p. 162, my italics). In other words, just as the amorphous openness of this marginal community makes it impossible to define its boundaries, so it is also lacking in the self-conscious representation of its collective identity that Nancy associates with common being. In this it is contrasted in the text with several far more explicit ideals of community that generate a rhetoric which the text treats with varying degrees of irony. The attempts of the African-American churches to instil moral values into their 'communauté noire [qui] avait oublié Dieu' (p. 130) are unambiguously ridiculed, by juxtaposing fragments of their rhetoric ('Il fallait que cela cesse. Comment? Grâce à un effort de purification générale', p. 130) with Awa's sarcastic commentary. Anthea's vision of the black community, in contrast, is secular and revolves around her goal of 'revalorizing' the African race. There is implicit criticism of the way in which her political aims override her relations with individuals; bringing up Molara is a question of developing her talents so that everyone is forced to 'saluer sa perfection noire' (p. 110) and so the mother–child relationship is exactly parallel to the ideological project: 'élever sa fille, sa petite Molara, et, par son travail, revaloriser sa Race' (p. 110). In the same way, the award of Marie-Noëlle's PhD is interpreted by Anthea as her own achievement, done for the sake of 'la Race' (p. 223). But Anthea is shown overall to be a generous, understanding person, and is not caricatured to the same extent as the Christian version of black community.[24]

Ludovic's vision of community is presented even more ambivalently.

He is the founder, in France, of 'Muntu', a sect originally created by Paulius Polydor, an Antillean civil servant working in the Ivory Coast, who after having a vision of a black God declares himself a prophet.[25] According to Ludovic, 'Muntu' has a miraculous effect on the juvenile delinquents he works with: 'Guidés par ses principes, les braqueurs ne braquaient plus, les voleurs faisaient la charité et les plus rétifs devenaient doux comme des agneaux' (p. 41). But the Marxist Rodrigue ridicules it, and the two friends engage in long heated discussions over these two competing theories of society – both of which the text treats with a laconic detachment: 'discussions passionnées. Sur la révolution cubaine. Fidel Castro était-il vraiment le Lider Maximo que d'aucuns adoraient? Sur le marxisme dont Ludovic prévoyait les limites. Sur Muntu dont les principes faisaient rire Rodrigue' (pp. 55–56). And by the time Marie-Noëlle returns to Paris neither Muntu nor anti-colonialist Marxism is of any interest to Ludovic's young delinquents, 'qui n'avaient en tête que les filles et la frime [...] L'Afrique, Cuba, Fidel Castro, Sékou Touré les intéressaient beaucoup moins que Stevie Wonder ou Marvin Gaye' (p. 100). But, despite the ironic tone in which Muntu's effect on the black and 'beur' community of the Parisian suburbs is recounted, it is made clear that it has indeed been of some efficacy, and Ludovic distinguishes pragmatically between the extravagant hallucinations of its founder and its usefulness in his own work with young criminals.[26]

The final example of a self-conscious promotion of a community is Stanley's 'Symphonie du Nouveau Monde', which he composes in celebration of America's multi-racial migrant communities and their supposedly regenerating effect on America as a whole (p. 107). The symphony is not well-received by its audiences, and Stanley's insistence on introducing it with a long oration on the same theme is greeted with boredom and derision (p. 117). But after his death, Marie-Noëlle comes to believe that perhaps he was after all a real musical genius, ignored and misunderstood by his contemporaries: Garvey admires him (p. 231), and the trombonist at the Soho club reveres him as superior to Jimi Hendrix and Bob Marley (p. 259).

Thus although the black Christian ideal of community is unequivocally satirized, the other versions of communitarian rhetoric are associated with characters whom we respect, and are described with an unemphatic mixture of irony and sympathy. The text does not reject them, but it does not endorse them either; and this attitude is in itself part of *Desirada*'s refusal to formulate its own general conception of what 'community' might mean. By implication, though, this very refusal means that it is *not* the conscious self-representation of community as imma-nence and work; the 'community' of the novel's characters does not 'play back to itself' images of its identity, and nor does the author.

But the text's non-committal stance extends more widely than the explicit question of types of community. The narrative rarely moves away from a quasi-factual level; it relates or describes events and characters' reactions to them, but without *interpreting* them to the reader. It oper-ates through an accumulation of detail which is left to stand on its own, without drawing any generalizing conclusion. While very different from an impersonal discourse – the tone is conversational, with a lot of small throwaway ironic comments – it assumes a kind of down-to-earth, commonsensical posture which excludes any explicit theorization or, indeed, any substantial authorial comment. It is interesting that Condé herself distinguishes between the generalizing statements of essayists and the hesitant 'nuances' of fiction: 'Je pense que nous autres romanciers, nous avons le sens de la nuance [...] tandis que ceux qui font des essais, qui ont des thèses à démontrer, ils sont trop entiers dans ce qu'ils disent. Il leur manque la fiction – la fiction introduit une sorte de doute, de ques-tionnement, que eux n'ont pas'.[27] Although *Desirada* does not have any of the literary features of the avant-garde texts that one would normally associate with Nancy's conception of literature as suspending and unworking meaning – it can be read perfectly well as a conventional realist novel, with none of the overtly transgressive elements of Placoly's *L'Eau-de-mort guildive*, for instance – it illustrates perfectly both the subtle infiltration of 'doubt' and 'questioning' that undermines general affirmations, and fiction's preference, which Condé herself takes to extremes, for the concrete and the particular. In this way it recalls not so much Nancy's comments on literature as his articulation of *sense* as nothing over and above the relations between singular existences.

This, together with the novel's determination, discussed earlier, not to hierarchize its elements, means that it is therefore left to the reader to pick out significant patterns from this opaque mass of information. We come to realize, for instance, that Marie-Noëlle's view of Reynalda is distorted by the resentment she feels towards her mother, and that in fact the two women are extremely similar in their emotional inhibition, their intelligence and desire to study, and their habit of using men for their own ends. The work of interpretation is done by the reader, through selecting and putting together specific concrete details that are dispersed in the text and finding parallels, repetitions and reversals (as I have been trying to do in this chapter). Reading *Desirada* is in some respects like reading a detective novel – and thus seems a similar endeavour, at least superficially, to Marie-Noëlle's attempt to find the identity of her father and clarify the circumstances surrounding her birth. But her project is ultimately shown to be not only fruitless, but pointless and even harmful – a distraction from the business of living her life in the present – and in reality both her aims and her methods are significantly different from the activity of reading the novel. Whereas the reader is confronted with too much information, Marie-Noëlle never has enough; rather than *selecting* relevant from irrelevant facts, she, unlike the reader, proceeds by *building* imaginary reconstructions of the past on the inadequate basis of the incomplete, unreliable and conflicting testimonies of other people. Several long sections of the novel consist of these reconstructions, which all have a quality of fantasy rather than logical deduction: the first is introduced by 'Parfois la nuit en attendant Stanley, Marie-Noëlle *rêvait* sa mère' (p. 83, my italics) – followed by nine pages of narrative concerning Reynalda's childhood in La Pointe, and including details that Marie-Noëlle is unlikely to have been told (the bathroom in the Coppini house, Reynalda's route to school, etc.). She becomes so absorbed in this imaginary narrative – these 'rêveries' (p. 91) – that on Stanley's return she momentarily wonders who he is. But the novel even opens with an account of her birth told *as she 'remembered' it*:

> Ranélise lui avait tant de fois raconté sa naissance qu'elle croyait y avoir tenu un rôle; non pas celui d'un bébé terrorisé et passif que Mme Fleurette, la sage-femme, extirpait difficilement d'entre les cuisses ensanglantées de sa mère; mais celui d'un témoin lucide; d'un acteur essentiel, voire de sa mère, l'accouchée, Reynalda elle-même.[28] (p. 13)

– and this false memory, in which she is cast not as the baby but in the two alternative roles of witness and mother (an uncharacteristic and significant *identification* with Reynalda), alerts the reader to the imaginary basis of her subsequent reconstructions and 'souvenirs imaginaires' (p. 17) as well.[29] As the narrative progresses, she discovers how different the reality of the past was from her reconstruction of it, not just on the central issues – Nina was not exploited by Gian Carlo but was passionately in love with him, it was Ludovic rather than Reynalda who had insisted on bringing Marie-Noëlle to Paris, and so on – but also on minor details such as the appearance of Mme Duparc, who employed Reynalda when the latter first arrived in Paris: Marie-Noëlle imagines her as '[élégante], voire un peu évaporée' (p. 247) but she is in reality far more sensibly and austerely dressed. Mme Duparc's appearance has no bearing on her usefulness as a witness to Reynalda's years in Paris, and the fact that Marie-Noëlle has created for herself a vivid if clichéd image of her reinforces our feeling that she is perhaps less interested in uncovering the factual truth than in day-dreaming about her mother's life. However horrific the version of her birth that she has come to believe in – the rape of the fourteen-year-old Reynalda by Gian Carlo – she has become perversely attached to it, as to a phantasy, and Nina's demolition of it causes her more pain than relief. As Nina says, 'Tu as l'air déçue, toute chagrinée. Ce n'est pas cette histoire-là que tu avais envie d'entendre, pas vré? Tu avais rêvé. Tu avais envisagé des tas d'autres choses dans ta tête et tu étais venue jusqu'ici [...] pour trouver un fondement à tes imaginations' (p. 202).

Marie-Noëlle's obsession with identifying her father is motivated by her lack of a sense of her own identity; in other words, her notion of identity is based on filiation and origin. This not only contrasts with the novel's privileging of surrogate family relations over biological paternity, but it also has implications which extend to the more general conception of *meaning* that governs her quest. She feels that her life is meaningless, and blames Reynalda for this.[30] By implication, meaning has to be sought in the *past* – it is a question of finding the meaning of her present life in terms of Reynalda's past life[31] – but it is also of necessity holistic: the secret that lies buried in the past will, once uncovered, explain *all* the diverse aspects of her present existence. It is these two features of meaning – its orientation towards the past, and its totalizing character – that the text of *Desirada*, in its typically unobtrusive fashion, contests. It does so not by leaving the mystery unsolved, but far more radically by suggesting that the identity of Marie-Noëlle's biological father was never what she was really searching for. The father's identity is never definitely proved, but nor is it exactly left as a complete mystery; it is fairly clear by the end of the novel, after she has visited Mme Duparc, that her father was in fact Père Mondicelli (p. 256). Also, Claire-Alta's memory of Reynalda treasuring an expensive prayer-book and refusing to say where it has come from, and writing a mysterious letter and receiving a reply just before announcing her departure to Paris, strongly suggests that Reynalda remained secretly in contact with him after being rescued by Ranélise, and therefore that she was probably in love with him, and so had been seduced rather than raped.

If the mystery that has dominated the novel had been definitely and triumphantly solved as in a detective story, *or* if it had been left intact as a haunting insoluble enigma as in a fantastic novel, its status as the principal issue of the narrative would also have remained intact. But a *probable* answer has the effect of devaluing the original question, because it is a distinctly unsatisfactory resolution to the problematic that the novel has set up. It is, in other words, a way of sidelining this whole aspect of the plot, and directing our attention elsewhere. And, right at the end of the novel, Marie-Noëlle makes what is in fact a far more important discovery (although the text presents it with its usual lack of emphasis): that she has all along been unconsciously in love with Ludovic. She reacts with surprise when Awa points out how attractive he is ('Elle n'avait jamais pensé à Ludovic comme à un bel homme. Elle n'avait souvenir que de son vaste cœur qui lui avait offert refuge', p. 222); but when Garvey hints that he and Reynalda are on the verge of separating, she greets the news with 'jubilation' and is forced to admit to herself 'combien elle jalousait sa mère et combien elle convoitait ce qu'elle possédait' (p. 236). It is only during her final trip to Paris, however, that she gradually becomes fully aware of her feelings for Ludovic; she is disappointed to be met only by Garvey and his friend and realizes 'combien elle avait espéré quelqu'un d'autre à l'attendre' (p. 237); and this makes her begin to wonder whether the real motive for her visit is not to interview Mme Duparc, but something else: 'elle avait la conviction qu'elle venait chercher quelque chose qu'elle avait toujours désiré, quelque chose qui s'était toujours dérobé , et qu'à présent elle avait assez d'audace pour vouloir la posséder' (p. 237). Then – ironically, while she is on her way to Mme Duparc's flat – she realizes that she had in fact come to Paris solely to see Ludovic, and wonders: 'Pourquoi est-ce qu'elle avait si longtemps méconnu la vérité?' (p. 244).

Moreover, he is the real reason why she has not been able to fall in love with any other man: 'En fait toute sa vie, elle n'avait fait que chercher Ludovic à travers une quantité d'autres hommes et, à chaque fois, elle avait été flouée' (p. 244); the 'meaninglessness' of her life has thus not been Reynalda's fault so much as the consequence of her own Oedipal jealousy of Reynalda. She has indeed been trapped in the past, but not only – not even primarily – the past that has ostensibly dominated her actions up until now: not the past of her search for her biological father, but that of the sexual love, originating in her childhood, for her surrogate father. When she finally meets up with Ludovic in Belgium, he gently refuses to sleep with her because, he says, 'Tu t'es mis dans l'idée que tu veux de moi. Mais, en réalité, tu ne veux que te venger de ta mère. Je ne ferai pas l'amour avec toi. Ce serait trop facile, méprisable pour nous deux' (p. 278). By claiming her as his daughter – 'Tu ne seras jamais que ma fille, la première-née. Celle que je ne savais pas que j'avais' (p. 278) – he does more than prove the superiority of surrogate over biological fatherhood: he releases her simultaneously from her fatherlessness and from her unconscious hopes of an Oedipal sexual relationship with her surrogate father. It is only when both these conditions are fulfilled that she can concentrate on moving forward into the future – as he says, 'Il y a devant toi une place faite pour le bonheur que tu rempliras quand tu cesseras d'épier par-dessus ton épaule' (p. 277). The fact that the short final chapter following this is, unlike the rest of the novel, narrated by Marie-Noëlle in the first person, strongly suggests that – as Ronnie Scharfman observes ('Au sujet d'héroïnes', p. 148) – she has now acquired a truer sense of her place in the world.

In other words, the development of the narrative subtly demonstrates the fallacy of focusing all one's attention on one issue in the expectation that it will prove to hold the key to the *whole* meaning of one's existence. This implicit critique of a totalizing conception of meaning also involves the reading process, and, ultimately, the nature of the community that the novel puts in place. As I have argued, the reader of *Desirada* to some extent acts like a detective, selecting out relevant 'clues' from a prolifer-ation of characters and incidents. Some of the things that we thereby notice (and that Marie-Noëlle does not appear to notice) are indeed rele-vant to the issue of Marie-Noëlle's father's identity.[32] But there are also many other indications, whose significance relates to other aspects of her life or the lives of the people she meets. Our activity of interpreting the text is far more widely based than Marie-Noëlle's search for clues to her father's identity, and does not result in a single 'answer' or 'message'. The meanings that the process produces are derived, as I have argued above, from specific concrete details of information; but equally, they are themselves diverse and small-scale, still embedded in particular situations and relationships. They do not build into generalized conclusions but are, to use Nancy's term, *singular*. Equally, to the extent that they emerge out of juxtapositions of parallel or contrasting events and characters, they are relational or 'plural'. Nancy's argument that meaning does not form a superstructure of abstract generalizations, but can exist only on the level of existence itself, as relation and circulation between singular beings – 'we are meaning in the sense that we are the element in which significations can be produced and circulate' (BSP, p. 2) – is exemplarily demonstrated by Condé's novel . It never summarizes or explains itself – and is therefore also very difficult for the reader to summarize. Another way of putting this would be to say that 'its' meaning cannot be *extracted from* it, because its meaning is not something that it 'has' but something that it 'is', to quote Nancy's distinction (BSP, p. 1).[33] Rather than being a discrete and distinct end-product that the text *works* to produce, meaning constitutes itself solely within the *space* of the text, in the 'originary spatiality of sense' that Nancy describes in *The Sense of the World* (p. 14), and solely as sharing: *'meaning itself is the sharing of Being'* (BSP, p. 2). It is this conception of meaning that is at work in *Desirada*, and that is congruent with its refusal to define the paradoxical unbounded 'community' – or, better, 'being-singular-plural' – that it nevertheless represents. Marie-Noëlle moves from a frustrated desire to belong – to a family or an orthodox community – to an acceptance of her singular existence amongst an undefined multiplicity of other singular existences; she relinquishes the myth of community for the reality of being-singular-plural.

Conclusion

Each of the preceding chapters has been devoted to a different novel's representation of community; I would like to conclude by exploring some of the differences and similarities between them. Do they share a common sense of community, or do they have nothing in common? Is the sense of community merely a matter of common sense, in both senses, or is it a problematic, fragile and conflictual construct?

Nancy defines community in general as *resistance*: 'The community resists: in a sense, as I have said, it is resistance itself' (IC, p. 58). By this he means specifically resistance to the immanence of common being; and by no means all the novels studied here understand community or resistance in this way. But resistance in its broader conventional meaning does seem to form the most obvious starting point for the search for a common sense of community, in that all of the communities represented in these novels are shown to be struggling against something. What that is, however, varies greatly – and, to the extent that they are shaped by the forces that they are opposing, produces very different types of community.

One might have expected, for instance, that the most widespread form of struggle would be that against poverty. But while it is true that poverty is an almost universal condition of the lives depicted in these novels, it never forms the explicit central theme of the novel; it is more usually seen as the consequence of some other lack or some other hostile force, which needs to be overcome before the material standard of living can be improved. These other forces can be social or natural; they can be external or internal (or internalized); and they can be extremely local or more general. Also, they may overlap and interact with each other: they are not exclusive categories. The hostile social forces sometimes take the form of the repressive apparatuses of the state – the very concrete, specific clashes with the police, the army, the prison system and the criminal courts that we find in *Gouverneurs de la rosée*, *Texaco* and *L'Eau-de-mort guildive*, for instance. *Le Quatrième Siècle*, although it does contain numerous instances of this kind of repression, sees its main enemy in more general terms as the continuing lack of political power that afflicts the slaves' and maroons' descendants even in the twentieth century:

success, in this perspective, would involve dismantling the neo-colonial status of the island as a whole, not just winning a particular local battle as in *Texaco*. In other novels such as *Desirada*, the enemy is not the state as such, but exclusion from 'normal', conventional society; and in *Pluie et vent sur Télumée Miracle* it is principally the internalized racism which is seen as the psychological aftermath of slavery. In *L'Ile et une nuit*, finally, the main enemy is not a social phenomenon at all, but the natural force of the hurricane – and, as we have seen, natural disaster in the form of drought plays an important if ambiguous role in *Gouverneurs de la rosée* as well.

One could also attempt a different kind of classification of types of resistance: not according to their object (social, natural, etc.), but according to whether their aim is to achieve *change* or simply ensure *survival* within an environment that is not seen as susceptible of change. In the case of natural enemies such as the hurricane, survival rather than change is of course the only possible strategy, and *L'Ile et une nuit* explores all the implications of this situation. But where the forces in play are social, different communities adopt very different attitudes towards the possibility of change (for instance, large-scale social change requires *collective* action, whereas planning for survival can be either collective or individual, and one might differentiate between *L'Ile et une nuit* and *Pluie et vent sur Télumée Miracle* on this basis). The criticism directed at *Pluie et vent sur Télumée Miracle* to which I have referred in Chapter 3 is in effect accusing it of opting for survival over the possibility of change, and conversely Schwarz-Bart's defenders argued for the merits of an ethics of survival as against the histrionic self-destructiveness of revolutionary movements.

But this debate also has the effect of polarizing the two concepts excessively: survival and change do not necessarily constitute a clear-cut binary opposition, and this is revealingly illustrated in some of the other novels discussed here. *Le Quatrième Siècle*, for instance, is overall quite unambiguously committed to the necessity of change, on the scale of the society as a whole, and hence to the importance of building a new, hitherto non-existent political consciousness within the society. There is no sense in this novel that continuing to live with the *status quo* is a possible option. But at the same time the novel laments the inability of the maroon community to *survive* in modern Antillean society, and seems to claim that for change to be possible, some elements at least of the old maroon consciousness need to be integrated into the new political consciousness: survival and change, in other words, work together in this instance. In

Texaco they are even more closely imbricated, so that there is no indication at all, as there is in *Le Quatrième Siècle*, of tension between the two. The squatters inhabiting Texaco are first and foremost concerned to ensure their immediate survival rather than bring about large-scale social change; but their achievement in securing their existence through the official legitimization of Texaco is presented as a definite, irreversible victory (very different from the on-going, indeed never-ending process of survival in *Pluie et vent sur Télumée Miracle* and *L'Ile et une nuit*) that does constitute a real change as far as this particular, very local situation is concerned. Beyond this, also, the existence of all the Quartiers is equally shown in *Texaco* to be a force for change on a wider scale, as they import their rural practices and values into the towns and thus create a new and better 'ecology' of urban living. Finally, the riots which dominate *L'Eau-de-mort guildive* arguably *negate* the concepts of *both* change and survival: they endanger the survival of the inhabitants but without entertaining any illusions that they will succeed in bringing about permanent change; they simply enact a spontaneous collective refusal to accept the conditions of life imposed on them by the authorities.

* * *

Another important factor is the question of *leadership*. This affects the type of struggle that is possible – leadership can impose an organization and discipline, and inspire a confidence, that would otherwise be lacking – but also, perhaps more fundamentally, is itself possible only within a certain type of community and on the basis of a certain conception of individual subjectivity. The two most clear-cut and striking examples of leadership in the novels I have been considering are Manuel in *Gouverneurs de la rosée* and Marie-Sophie in *Texaco*. Both of these figures lead active campaigns to improve the material conditions of life for their respective communities, and both succeed. They inspire trust and devotion in their followers and identify completely with the struggle they are leading; and without them, the victories would never have been won. Télumée, in *Pluie et vent sur Télumée Miracle*, does not actively lead a collective struggle, but exemplifies the different kind of leadership associated with the role-model. This is not a question of 'doing' so much as of 'being' – in other words, being an inspiring example for others to emulate – and as such it is even more clearly associated with a certain conception of the subject than the more practical forms of leadership practised by Manuel and Marie-Sophie. In fact, however, these two figures are role-models *as well as* practical leaders: Manuel inspires his community by his own example of courage and self-sacrifice as much as by his persuasion, and Marie-Sophie at times acts as a role-model in a way that is strikingly similar to Télumée. By her example and her exhortation she gives the other women courage: as she says, 'Il me suffisait d'avoir l'air de savoir, de ne pas écarquiller les yeux devant les macaqueries de leur destin. Et le peu que je leur disais suffisait à les porter (pour un moment encore) dans le courage de vivre' (p. 436). Like Télumée also – and this must surely be a conscious allusion – she sees herself as a 'coq de combat' (p. 380). The others look up to her, as their counterparts do to Manuel and Télumée, as an exemplary, powerful and charismatic individual.

The leader and/or role-model thus presupposes an individual subject who has all the characteristics of Nancy's 'immanence': sovereign autonomy, self-sufficiency and self-consciousness. The maroon community of *Le Quatrième Siècle* provides an interesting example of this: leaders such as the first Longoué and Melchior present all the characteristics of the immanent individual; as I have argued in Chapter 2, their autonomy turns out to be largely an illusion, but for as long as the illusion is sustained they are able to function as effective leaders. This (appearance of) immanence also seems to be linked to stereotypical representations of gender. Manuel is a perfect example of idealized masculine heroism, adored by women as well as emulated by men, and Longoué and Melchior are archetypal patriarchs. Conversely Télumée and Marie-Sophie embody the two main variants of the stereotypical strong, independent, long-suffering Caribbean woman: in Télumée's case the emphasis is on the ability to endure and to be strengthened by suffering, and on an almost maternal attitude to men, whereas Marie-Sophie is the aggressive 'femme de guerre créole' who refuses to be bullied by men and competes with them on equal terms, even in physical combat. Even Délira in *Gouverneurs de la rosée*, who takes control of the situation after her son's death in order to ensure the transition between his leadership and that of Larivoire (another wise, courageous patriarch), conforms to the traditional image of the maternal creole woman who protects her community even while apparently deferring to male authority.

The leadership represented in *Texaco* and *Gouverneurs de la rosée* operates on a local level: the village of Fonds-Rouge, the 'Quartier' of Texaco. Télumée's influence is similarly restricted to the people with whom she comes into direct personal contact. Their achievements are equally local and circumscribed. On one level this is just a requirement of fictional verisimilitude: a novelist working in a predominantly realist tradition cannot simply invent, with any credibility, a fictional leader of a major social or political movement (a better alternative is to base one's novel on a real historical figure, and there are a number of French Caribbean examples of this). But the communities of Fonds-Rouge and Texaco and the maroon community in *Le Quatrième Siècle* are also characterized, in their very different ways, by their *closure* to the external world, and as this suggests there is a strong correlation between leadership and the closed immanent community. Thus in *Le Quatrième Siècle*, the maroon community has leaders, but the unbounded community of modern creolized society does not: neither papa Longoué nor Mathieu acts as a leader.

In *Le Quatrième Siècle*, also, the collective struggle is, as I have said, on a much larger scale, involving the island of Martinique as a whole, its political status and the social effects of its relationship to metropolitan France. This struggle does not have a single leader, but it does nevertheless ultimately rely on a conception of collective political consciousness and agency which presupposes the same sovereign subject that underpins leadership. In Chapter 2 I have analysed the rather convoluted dynamic of this novel's positing, undermining, and then ambiguously reinstating the existence of this politically knowing and freely acting subject; but the conclusion that Glissant sees it as a necessary and possible project, if not an already realized phenomenon, is quite clear. In its emphasizing of the dangers of *illusory* autonomy, however, *Le Quatrième Siècle* is far more cautious in this regard than *Texaco* is. It is revealing also that the internal migration from the countryside to the towns is presented by *Texaco* as a willed quest for freedom – 'conquering the town' – whereas exactly the same historical phenomenon is in *Le Quatrième Siècle* seen as economically determined , chaotic and far from wholly positive in its results.

Leadership, then, presupposes a bounded community; unbounded communities cannot have leaders. Thus the issue of leadership is entirely irrelevant to *Desirada*. *L'Eau-de-mort guildive* provides an even more extreme contrast: here, the only form of collective political action that is seen as possible is *essentially* leaderless, in that the rioters' only strength lies in their lack of organization, their anonymous elusiveness and the authorities' inability to contain them. This phenomenon (it is hardly a strategy) of non-containability thus takes the unbounded community and makes its very unboundedness into a political force of resistance – thus coming close to Nancy's equation of community with resistance to immanence and closure.

* * *

All of the above considerations – the nature of the community's 'enemies', the distinction between the aim of change and that of survival, and the possibility or otherwise of leadership – interact with the different conceptions of *time* that are at work in the novels, which vary significantly in their presentation of the relationships between the present, the past and the future. The goal of change presupposes a teleological view of time orientated towards a better future – as in *Gouverneurs de la rosée, Le Quatrième Siècle*, and *Texaco* – whereas the time-scale of survival is non-teleological: the static 'frozen' time of *Pluie et vent sur Télumée Miracle* or the cyclical time of *L'Ile et une nuit*. Benítes-Rojo's opposition between 'apocalyptic' and 'chaotic' time is very relevant here, not only to *L'Ile et une nuit* as previously discussed, but also to *Pluie et vent sur Télumée Miracle* and *Desirada*. In the first case, Télumée's view of life is quintessentially anti-apocalyptic, since she believes that everything that can happen to her is ultimately survivable, and the uncontrollable but repetitive ups and downs of her life are also a good example of 'chaos'. As for *Desirada*, the novel's shift away from the totalizing and highly dramatized quest for biological filiation (which, Marie-Noëlle at first believes, will *change* her life) towards the realization of existence as an unhierarchized and heterogeneous plurality of singular meanings could also be described as a rejection of the apocalyptic in favour of chaos.

But survival, although it is primarily focused on the present, also often draws on the past. The past can either represent a source of the practical knowledge that survival in the present requires (in *L'Ile et une nuit* the traditional expertise in coping with hurricanes is at risk of being lost, and as a result the community is more vulnerable than it used to be; in *Texaco* the inhabitants of the new urban slums survive thanks to their traditional rural knowledge), or it can act as the basis for an identity which will also protect people in their present situation: Télumée draws strength from rooting herself in the lineage of the Lougandor women, Marie-Sophie's position is derived from her status as the original founder of Texaco, supported by the traditional authority of the Mentô. Conversely, in these novels in which survival rather than change is prominent, the *future* is characteristically regarded with apprehension or even dread: *Pluie et vent sur Télumée Miracle* is the clearest example of this, but it also runs through *L'Eau-de-mort guildive*, and both contrast strikingly with the confidence in the future that informs the teleological view of time that defines *Gouverneurs de la rosée* and *Le Quatrième Siècle*.

L'Eau-de-mort guildive is not of course unambiguously dedicated to survival, as the outbreak of rioting and consequent deaths makes clear. It is, however, entirely non-teleological in its representation of time; there is no chance that the riots will result in a better future, or indeed in anything other than continued repression. *Desirada* is similarly non-teleological in its vision of community. It is also the only one of the novels I have discussed in which the past is seen as actively negative; it is extremely critical of the nostalgia for the traditional organic community that Guadeloupe is sometimes seen to represent (as in *Pluie et vent sur Télumée Miracle*, arguably), and it also demonstrates the damaging effects of the attempt to base one's identity on filiation, and hence on the past – Marie-Noëlle's futile search for the identity of her biological father is shown to be responsible for her isolation and unhappiness. This search is itself a response to her feeling of exclusion, from both family and society, but as the novel progresses her struggle against exclusion gives way to the realization that neither exclusion nor inclusion is a relevant concept in the contemporary experience of unbounded community. Liberation, in her case, is above all liberation from the past.

The 'teleological' novels show communities working purposefully towards a future that will be at least in part their own creation. What is perhaps more surprising is the positive value that they also invest in the past. That is, the contrast is not between a bad past and a better future, but between a bad *present* and a future which, to a significant degree, is better *because* it re-establishes a contact with the past that the present has lost. To create the future, one has first to reintegrate the past with the present. This position has been most explicitly formulated by Glissant, but it equally forms the basis for the narrative structure of *Gouverneurs de la rosée* and *Texaco*. I have described the circularity of Roumain's narrative, in which the desired future is in fact a return to the village's past life before the feud and the drought, and shown how *Texaco* rejects the 'modernity' of contemporary urban Martinique in favour of the values associated with the island's rural past. The present is characterized very negatively in all three novels: drought and dissension in *Gouverneurs de la rosée*, soulless European-inspired architectural and social order in *Texaco*, and the alienation and abjection of twentieth-century urban Martinique in *Le Quatrième Siècle*. And all three novels also proclaim the necessity of restoring the link with the past in order to move out of the present into the future – to move 'back to the future', in effect. In the case of *Gouverneurs de la rosée*, the present constitutes merely an unfortunate hiatus between past and future; that is, the future is superimposed exactly on the past. Glissant and Chamoiseau both recognize the impossibility of this simple replication, and both stress the necessary complexity of any new synthesis of past and future. *Texaco* projects an ideal of the future city as incorporating the humanizing values of traditional rural society to produce a completely new urban ecology; and the double forward-and-back movement of *Le Quatrième Siècle* that I have outlined in Chapter 2 combines a positive stress on change and a new openness and inclusiveness in the creolized community with an insistence that an understanding of the past is an essential ingredient in the process of change. Looking back to the past in these cases is not nostalgic, but holds the key to the future; the past for the Antilleans, as Glissant puts it, is 'prophetic': 'Cette exploration [du passé] ne revient donc ni à une mise en schémas ni à un pleur nostalgique. C'est à démêler un sens douloureux du temps et à le projeter à tout coup dans notre futur [...] C'est ce que j'appelle *une vision prophétique du passé*' (*Discours*, p. 132).

   L'Ile et une nuit contributes a different element to this valorization of the past. Alongside its dominant cyclical view of time, it also offers the perception that the past is created, retroactively, out of the desire of the present. On one level this is in agreement with the views of Chamoiseau and Glissant, but Maximin's emphasis on the subjective nature of this creation, with its implication that the relevant past is not an objective reality but a strategic projection back in accordance with the needs of the present, could also be seen as a critique of Chamoiseau's and Glissant's reliance on the importance of *knowledge* of the past (although Glissant also recognizes that Antillean history is to a large extent an imaginary construct: 'l'essentiel de l'histoire de la Martinique, histoire raturée, se lit par hypothèse créatrice', *Discours*, p. 161). In any case, what all four authors imply very strongly is that the creation of a better future can never be achieved by a simple linear movement forwards; it is always a question of doubling back to the past in order to overcome the limitations of the present. Conversely, as we have seen, the only novels that are uninterested in the past or imply that it should simply be left behind – *L'Eau-de-mort guildive* and *Desirada* – are those which have no project for the future at all.

*   *   *

From the localized, rooted, closed village of *Gouverneurs de la rosée* to the mobile, rootless, unbounded groupings of *Desirada*, the representations of community in these seven novels would seem to offer more differences than similarities. There does not appear to be a great deal in common between the emphasis on unity of purpose, collective work and strong immanent individuals willing social change (*Gouverneurs de la rosée, Texaco*), and the ambivalent acceptance of historical change in *Le Quatrième Siècle*, or the stoical accommodation to an existing reality which is seen as permanent or cyclical (*Pluie et vent sur Télumée Miracle, L'Ile et une nuit*), or chaotic, disorganized and doomed rebellion (*L'Eau-de-mort guildive*), or release from the myths of belonging and filiation (*Desirada*). It is nevertheless worth noting that none of the communities represented in these novels is entirely closed. Fonds-Rouge fails to conform wholly to the self-sufficiency associated with the ideal of the organic community in so far as it requires the external intervention of Manuel's experience in Cuba in order to achieve its aims. A similar contradiction undermines the maroon community in *Le Quatrième Siècle*, whose self-sufficiency is also shown to be illusory. The specular closure of the community reflecting its role-model in *Pluie et vent sur Télumée Miracle* is broken open by the very different relationship in which Télumée finds herself with Médard at the end of the novel. The simultaneously real and mythical status of the narrative of the founding of Texaco – its foundational-fictional potency – comes apart to some extent through the contradictions inherent in the role of the 'marqueur de paroles'.

There are also more particular moments of unexpected similarities between very different communities. For instance, Télumée's feeling of non-entitlement, of 'living by mistake', is echoed in Marie-Noëlle's perception that she does not 'belong' anywhere. The sustaining and politicizing role of black music in *L'Ile et une nuit* recurs in Stanley's 'Symphony for a New World' in *Desirada*, while Maximin's use of proverbs and folklore has a similar function in *Pluie et vent sur Télumée Miracle*. One of the most important victories of the Texaco squatters is the securing of a reliable supply of running water, a less lyrical version of the discovery of the spring in *Gouverneurs de la rosée*. One could cite also the slave uprisings in *Le Quatrième Siècle*, as unplanned and as hopeless as the riots in *L'Eau-de-mort guildive*; the impression of inescapable doom that permeates *Pluie et vent sur Télumée Miracle* is also to be found in the assumed omnipresence of death in *L'Eau-de-mort guildive*; while the characters of *L'Ile et une nuit* draw on rural vernacular traditions of survival in a very similar fashion to their counterparts in *Texaco*.

In other words, to answer the question I posed at the beginning of this brief concluding chapter, the various communities I have been discussing do not have any *one* thing in common; but nor can they be neatly pigeonholed into a number of separate categories. The relationship between them could even, perhaps, be characterized in terms of the simultaneous sharing/separation of Nancy's 'partage'. They certainly suggest that the question of community – as lack, as myth, as political project, as basic ground of survival and necessary condition for change, or simply as inescapable reality of our existence in the world – has remained central to French Caribbean literature for the last fifty years. It is these very diverse but interconnected manifestations of a *sense* of community that I have tried to explore in this book.

Notes

Introduction

1 Thus Edouard Glissant, for instance, identifies the various historical, geographical and economic factors that have 'fragilisé le travail d'émergence de l'identité du peuple martiniquais' (*Le Discours antillais* (Paris: Editions du Seuil, 1981), p. 189).

2 Glissant, *Discours*, p. 15.

3 Frantz Fanon, *Peau noire, masques blancs* (Paris: Editions du Seuil, 1952).

4 Maryse Condé's *Desirada* (Paris: Robert Laffont, 1997) reflects this sense of the geographical and cultural unboundedness of the Caribbean community in the late twentieth century. Comments she has made elsewhere reiterate her belief in the impossibility of defining it, and indeed the undesirability of attempting to do so. In her article 'Chercher nos vérités' (in Maryse Condé and Madeleine Cottenet-Hage (eds.), *Penser la créolité* (Paris: Karthala, 1995), pp. 305–10) she argues 'Que sont les Antilles d'aujourd'hui? Un lieu sans contours définis, poreux à tous les bruits lointains, traversé par toutes les influences contradictoires' (p. 309). In the same way her reply to a question from Françoise Pfaff as to how she defines the Antillean identity is simply, 'Justement, je ne la définis pas; ce n'est pas une recette de cuisine' (Pfaff, *Entretiens avec Maryse Condé* (Paris: Karthala, 1993), p. 113).

5 I discuss 'créolité' in more detail in Chapter 5.

6 'Chercher nos vérités', p. 309. In her interview with Pfaff she formulates the writer's 'duty' as follows: 'Je pense que notre peuple est victime depuis quatre siècles d'une domination politique, culturelle et économique. En conséquence, il est en passe de perdre totalement sa parole. Il est menacé. Peut-être que le devoir des artistes et des créateurs est d'écouter avant qu'il ne soit trop tard. Et, ce faisant, de redonner au peuple une fierté qu'il est en passe de perdre aussi, de reconstituer sa parole et d'imaginer ce qu'elle pourra être demain' (Pfaff, *Entretiens*, p. 45).

7 'Interview accordé à R. Toumson', in GEREC (Groupe d'Etudes et de Recherches en Espace Créolophone) (ed.), *Sur Pluie et vent sur Télumée Miracle de Simone Schwarz-Bart (Textes, Etudes et Documents, 2)* (Paris: Editions Caribbéennes, 1979), pp. 15–23, p. 22; Simone Schwarz-Bart, *Pluie et vent sur Télumée Miracle* (Paris: Editions du Seuil, 1972).

8 In an interview reproduced in Christiane Chaulet-Achour's *La Trilogie caribéenne de Daniel Maximin* (Paris: Karthala, 2000), p. 59.

9 For Roumain, the writer's art 'doit être une arme de première ligne au service du peuple' ('La poésie, arme de combat', *Cahiers d'Haïti*, II.4 (1944), pp. 39–42, p. 40). Placoly formulates the theory of art and literature of his 'Groupe Révolution Socialiste' as 'En art comme en littérature, doit pouvoir transparaître clairement la volonté révolutionnaire de chacun' ('Contre le misérabilisme en littérature', reprinted in the special number of the group's journal *Tranchées* dedicated to him after his death (January 1993), pp. 67–68, p. 68). On Chamoiseau's view of the relationship between writer and community, see Chapter 5.

10 Jacques Roumain, *Gouverneurs de la rosée* (Paris: Editions Messidor, 1991); originally published by Les Editeurs Français Réunis, 1946.

11 Edouard Glissant, *Le Quatrième Siècle* (Paris: Gallimard, Collection

'Imaginaire', 1990); originally published by Editions du Seuil, 1964); Vincent Placoly, *L'Eau-de-mort guildive* (Paris: Denoël, 1973).

12 Patrick Chamoiseau, *Texaco* (Paris: Gallimard, 1992).

13 This is a dominant theme in *Le Discours antillais*, in which he writes, for instance: 'Le passé, notre passé subi, qui n'est pas encore histoire pour nous, est pourtant là (ici) qui nous lancine. La tâche de l'écrivain est d'explorer ce lancinement, de le "révéler" de manière continue dans le présent et l'actuel' (p. 132); and again, on the following page: 'Parce que la mémoire historique fut trop souvent raturée, l'écrivain antillais doit "fouiller" cette mémoire, à partir de traces parfois latentes qu'il a repérées dans le réel' (p. 133).

14 Daniel Maximin, *L'Île et une nuit* (Paris: Editions du Seuil, 1995).

15 Together with Philippe Lacoue-Labarthe, Nancy organized a conference in 1980 on the subjet of Derrida and politics; in the same year they set up the 'Centre de recherches philosophiques sur le politique' to promote further work on this theme.

16 'Of Being-in-Common', in Miami Theory Collective (ed.), *Community at Loose Ends* (Minneapolis: University of Minnesota Press, 1991), pp. 1–12, p. 6.

17 *The Inoperative Community* (Minneapolis: University of Minnesota Press, 1991), p. xxxvii. Subsequent references to this text will be marked 'IC'.

18 'But it is here that we should become suspicious of the retrospective consciousness of the lost community and its identity [...] because it seems to have accompanied the Western world from its very beginnings: at every moment in its history, the Occident has given itself over to the nostalgia for a more archaic community that has disappeared, and to deploring a loss of familiarity, fraternity and conviviality' (IC, p. 10).

19 B. C. Hutchens, *Jean-Luc Nancy and the Future of Philosophy* (London: Acumen, 2005), p. 34.

20 *Being Singular Plural* (Stanford, CA: Stanford University Press, 2000), p. 35. Subsequent references to this text will be marked 'BSP'.

21 'Of Being-in-Common', p. 7.

22 'Of Being-in-Common', p. 4.

23 *The Sense of the World* (Minneapolis: University of Minnesota Press, 1997), pp. 73–74. Subsequent references to this text will be marked 'SW'.

24 'In the work, the properly "common" character of community disappears, giving way to a unicity and a substantiality[...] The community that becomes *a single thing* (body, mind, fatherland, Leader...) necessarily loses the *in* of being-*in*-common' (IC, p. xxxix).

25 Georges van den Abbeele glosses this as '[Community] is not the product of any work or project [...] not an *œuvre* but what is unworked, *désœuvré*. It *is* what is given and what happens to "singular beings", the exhibiting or presenting of their singularity, which is to say, the copresenting of their *finitude* as the very basis or condition for their commonality' ('Introduction' to *Community at Loose Ends*, p. xiv).

26 Christopher Fynsk, in his foreword to *The Inoperative Community*, gives a useful elucidation of this connection, and also of the ways in which Nancy reorientates Heidegger's thought ('Experiences of Finitude', Foreword to Jean-Luc Nancy, *The Inoperative Community*, pp. vii–xxxv).

27 Myth is thus synonymous with collective identity: 'Not only does myth identify, it identifies itself above all: it is the infinite presupposition of its own identity and authenticity' (BSP, pp. 157–58). It is also a central element in totalitarianism, which in *The Sense of the World* Nancy describes as 'the immediate being-there or immanence of myth' (SW, p. 89).

28 Nancy explores this further in 'Art, a Fragment' in *The Sense of the World*.

29 Van den Abbeele provides a definition of the relation between myth and literature in his introduction to *Community at Loose Ends*: myth 'must be "interrupted", that is, disabled and displayed in its finitude as incomplete, exposed not as *œuvre* but as *désœuvré*. Such an interruption of myth is what Nancy calls "literature", by which he understands less some canon of aesthetically prized works of writing than all that which is communication in the *comparution* of singular beings' (p. xv).

30 In so far as being-in-common is also seen as the basis for any kind of progressive politics (I will discuss this later in this introduction), Nancy is here vulnerable to the criticisms that have been directed at other theoretical attempts to define all avant-garde literary texts that disrupt or suspend meaning as *automatically* progressive or revolutionary in political terms. See for instance the critique by S. Burniston and C. Weedon of Julia Kristeva's *La Révolution du langage poétique*, whose notions of the 'semiotic' and the 'chora' are not all that different from Nancy's 'literature' (S. Burniston and C. Weedon, 'Ideology, Subjectivity and the Artistic Text', in Centre for Contemporary Cultural Studies (ed.), *On Ideology* (London: Hutchinson, 1978), pp. 216–22; Julia Kristeva, *La Révolution du langage poétique: l'avant-garde à la fin du XIXe siècle, Lautréamont et Mallarmé* (Paris: Editions du Seuil, 1974). There is also an important debate on this question within postcolonial theory, notably between Homi Bhabha, in his 'Representation and the Colonial Text: A Critical Exploration of Some Forms of Mimeticism' (in Frank Gloversmith (ed.), *The Theory of Reading* (Brighton: Harvester Press, 1984), pp. 93–122) and Aijaz Ahmad, *In Theory – Classes, Nations, Literatures* (London: Verso, 2000).

31 Although he later abandons this term as being unhelpfully ambiguous: in 'Of Being-in-Common' he writes 'I recently used that expression [literary communism]: its equivocal character makes me reject it now. I am not speaking here of a community of letters' (p. 10).

32 The myth *of the writer* is also interrupted by literature: 'a certain scene, an attitude, and a creativity pertaining to the writer are no longer possible' (IC, p. 69).

33 '[Writing] is the act that obeys the sole necessity of exposing the limit: not the limit of communication, *but the limit upon which communication takes place*' (IC, p. 67).

34 Nancy's terms could be seen as not dissimilar to the distinction Roland Barthes makes between the 'writerly' and the 'readerly' text in *S/Z* (Paris: Editions du Seuil, 1970).

35 The French 'sens' is rendered as either 'sense' or 'meaning' in the English translations of Nancy's books.

36 '[The] only chance for sense and its only possible sense reside either this side of or beyond the appropriation of signifieds and the presentation of signifiers, in the very opening of the abandonment of sense, as the opening of the world' (SW, p. 3).

37 Hutchens formulates this as 'a finite thinking of a singular "sense" circulating in a multiplicity of singularities or a thinking that is not a general thought subsumed under universals and available to reflective immanence [...] Rather than permit the determination of singularities within a pre-conceived "Being", Nancy struggles to elucidate a social reality that just consists in *relations*' (*Jean-Luc Nancy*, p. 36).

38 The relationality of sense distinguishes it from signification: 'it is as relation that sense configures itself – it configures the *toward* that it is (whereas signification figures itself as identity [...]' (SW, p. 118).

39 Jean-Luc Nancy and Philippe Lacoue-Labarthe, *Retreating the Political* (London: Routledge, 1997).

40 Cf. Hutchens: 'Nancy suggests that we strive to discover a condition of the "refusal of domination" in the very spacing of community itself. One might say, then, that sovereignty is not a domination of any kind in the relation between politics and

the spacing of community, but the very resistance to such domination' (*Jean-Luc Nancy*, p. 129).

1   Restoring Lost Unity in Jacques Roumain's *Gouverneurs de la rosée*

1 J. Michael Dash, *The Other America: Caribbean Literature in a New World Context* (Charlottesville and London: University Press of Virginia, 1998), p. 18 and pp. 79–80.

2 A prominent feature of the whole text is the constant metaphorical linking of features of the landscape with the human body. Eric Sellin comments: 'the interpenetration of countryside and human being is found throughout the work, on virtually every page' ('Pastoralism and Nostalgia in Jacques Roumain's *Gouverneurs de la rosée*', in R. Antoine (ed.), *Carrefours de culture: mélanges offerts à J. Leiner* (Tübingen: Gunter Narr Verlag, 1993), pp. 473–80, p. 478).

3 '[This] something, which would be the fulfilled infinite identity of community, is what I call its "work" [...] The work itself, in fact, should not be understood primarily as the exteriority of a product, but as the interiority of the subject's operation' (IC, p. xxxix).

4 Roger Dorsinville, for instance, writes: 'A planer haut on invite le martyre. Malheur aux généreux. Manuel trouve l'eau, mais au moment de l'offrir en gage de réconciliation, il est crucifié. C'est le mythe du Christ' (*Jacques Roumain* (Paris: Présence africaine, 1981), p. 90).

5 To take just one example, its influence on the Senegalese writer Sembene Ousmane's novel *O pays mon beau peuple* (Paris: Buchet-Chastel, 1957) is very evident: the latter's plot is virtually identical to that of *Gouverneurs de la rosée*.

6 Jacques André, *Caraïbales* (Paris: Editions Caribéennes, 1981).

7 Detailed analyses of the imagery of the novel are given in André, *Caraïbales*; Sellin, 'Pastoralism and Nostalgia'; Beverley Ormerod, *An Introduction to the French Caribbean Novel* (London: Heinemann, 1983); and Ernest Pépin, 'Proposition pour une lecture de *Gouverneurs de la rosée*', in GEREC (ed.) *Sur Gouverneurs de la rosée de Jacques Roumain (Textes, Etudes et Documents, 1)* (Paris: Editions Caribéennes, 1978), pp. 30–40.

8 Léon-François Hoffmann describes the interplay between the authorial voice and the voices of the characters in the context of his analysis of the influence of creole on Roumain's writing: 'L'intéressant est que ces deux voix se recoupent à chaque instant. De manière que les habitants peuvent très bien emprunter la voix de l'auteur, son vocabulaire, sa syntaxe, pour devenir au sens propre ses *porte-parole*. [...] De même, l'auteur est fort capable d'abandonner son "français-français" pour parler au nom de ses protagonistes, et dans leur langue [...] On en arrive à ne plus très bien savoir quel est l'auteur. Parfois c'est un témoin impassible qui se borne à camper le décor et à décrire l'action. Mais parfois il intervient, il se solidarise explicitement avec les habitants; il lui arrive de passer brusquement de la troisième personne du pluriel à la première' ('Langages et rhétorique dans *Gouverneurs de la rosée* de Jacques Roumain', in Hoffmann, *Haïti: lettres et l'être* (Toronto: Editions du GREF, 1992), pp. 167–86 [pp. 183–84]).

9 Cf. André: 'la conquête de l'avenir est simultanément un retour aux sources, une manière de renouer avec l'origine' (*Caraïbales*, p. 49).

10 Roger Dorsinville points out that another motivation for Manuel's death is that it allows the novel to evade the confrontation with the town that would be the logical next step after the irrigation of the land: 'Roumain [a] escamoté, avec la mort de Manuel, le combat inévitable entre la ville, gestionnaire global, et le village réveillé' (*Jacques Roumain*, p. 80).

11 Mary Gallagher's *Soundings in French Caribbean Writing since 1950: The Shock of Space and Time* (Oxford: Oxford University Press, 2002) emphasizes the strength of the association between the Caribbean and *mobility*: 'The Caribbean is held to be unthinkable, then, as a static, demarcated area. Part of the Atlantic continuum, it is first and foremost fluid and, as such, comprises currents, flow, passage, and displacement' (p. 2).

12 'C'est pourtant de la bonne terre, pensait Manuel. Le morne est perdu, c'est vrai, mais la plaine peut encore donner sa bonne mesure de maïs, de petit-mil, et tous genres de vivres. Ce qu'il faudrait, c'est l'arrosage' (p. 46).

13 Beverley Ormerod, in her *Introduction to the French Caribbean Novel*, significantly titles the chapter on Roumain 'Fall and Redemption in Jacques Roumain's *Masters of the Dew*', and gives further indications of the biblical resonances surrounding Manuel.

14 Sellin, for instance, merely states that '[the] novel is a parable whose main character, Manuel, is a blend of a Christ-like saviour and the modern Marxist hero. His martyrdom and the light which seems to emanate from his face suggest the former, and his optimism for a new society in which all are equal and which is to be achieved through hard labor and resistance against resignation suggests the latter' ('Pastoralism and Nostalgia', p. 475). Ormerod argues that Manuel's Cuban experience works on two levels – literally, it is the moment at which he becomes a Marxist, but symbolically, it corresponds to his 'mystical initiation' as a mythical hero (*Introduction*, p. 24) – but without commenting on the contradiction between these two levels; she merely draws our attention to 'an elaborate system of thematic cross-references within the novel which link Communist ideals with the immediate realities of rural life, as well as with a plane of symbolic action which [...] echoes both the Christian tradition and that of older vegetation cults' (pp. 24–25).

15 Michel Serres, 'Le Christ noir', *Critique*, 29 (1973), pp. 3–25, p. 17.

16 'Nothing indicates more clearly what the logic of this being of togetherness can imply than the role of *Gemeinschaft*, of community, in Nazi ideology' (IC, p. xxxix). It is perhaps not irrelevant to note that the indigenist movement in Haiti, although not Roumain himself, was strongly attracted to at least some aspects of fascism; see Dash, *The Other America*, pp. 75–76.

17 Similar vocabulary is used in the description of the singing at the vodou ceremony, too: 'l'appel sourd du tambour retentit, précipitant le chant dans un nouvel élan, les voix des femmes fusèrent très haut, fêlant l'épaisse masse chorale' (p. 66).

2 Past, Future and the Maroon Community in Edouard Glissant's *Le Quatrième Siècle*

1 Edouard Glissant, *Poétique de la relation* (Paris: Gallimard, 1990).

2 See Nancy's 'Eulogy for the mêlée', in BSP, pp. 145–58.

3 '[The] indefinitely repeated and indefinitely suspended gesture of touching the limit, of indicating it and inscribing it,but without crossing it, without abolishing it in the fiction of a common body' (IC, p. 67).

4 As Nancy formulates it: 'Others "in general" are neither other "me's" (since there is no "me" and "you" except on the basis of alterity in general), nor the non-me (for the same reason). Others "in general" are neither the Same nor the Other. They are one-another, or of-one-another, a primordial plurality that co-appears' (BSP, p. 67).

5 J. Michael Dash, *Edouard Glissant* (Cambridge: Cambridge University Press, 1995), p. 14. Romuald Fonkoua provides a useful description of the work of the

Institut Martiniquais d'Etudes in his *Essai sur une mesure du monde au XXe siècle: Edouard Glissant* (Paris: Honoré Champion, 2002), pp. 146–63.

6 'Edouard Glissant between the Singular and the Specific', *Yale Journal of Criticism*, 11.2 (1998), pp. 441–64, p. 443 and pp. 443–44.

7 See for instance *L'Intention poétique* (Paris: Gallimard, 1997), originally published in 1969, where Glissant writes: 'Ma nation dans sa durée, son épaisseur, sa science et sa saveur est à bâtir, ainsi que sa parole [...] Nous appelons la nation future, et déjà ne pouvons respirer qu'avec elle. Car elle n'est pas seulement Etat, elle est pour nous Poétique de l'être qui se trouve' (p. 50).

8 Nancy, as we have seen, argues against this assumption in his critique of the politics of 'self-sufficiency' in *The Sense of the World*.

9 Jacques André in *Caraïbales* describes a similar movement from the foundation of the myth to its undermining, and in attributing the latter to the anti-realist quality of some of Glissant's writing produces an account which is much closer to Nancy's idea of literature's interruption of myth: 'Mais cette défaite du Marron est une victoire de l'écriture: c'est quand le texte rompt avec la pensée édifiante, changeant le mot, balançant la syntaxe qu'il balbutie au lecteur surpris "la première osée nue du langage neuf" (*Malemort*, p. 18)' (*Caraïbales*, p. 150). In fact, in what seems an implicit acknowledgement of the influence of Blanchot – an important figure for Nancy – on his analysis, André calls the two contrasting sides of Glissant's fiction 'L'ouvrage' (p. 116) and 'Désœuvrer' (p. 149). But he finds this 'new language' only in Glissant's subsequent novel, *Malemort* (Paris: Editions du Seuil, 1975); his reading of *Le Quatrième Siècle* is almost entirely negative, seeing the contradictory views of the maroons as an unintentional sign of the novel's 'failure' to make its myth credible (p. 150); whereas I would argue that they signal a more lucid awareness of the ambiguous, compromised status of the maroons.

10 Although some critics imply that it does; Richard Burton, for instance, stating simply that '[the] underlying theme of *Le Quatrième Siècle* is the progressive formation of this cultural unity-in-diversity', seems to me to underplay the problematic nature of the process (Richard Burton, 'Comment peut-on être martiniquais? The Recent Works of Edouard Glissant', *Modern Languages Review*, 79.2 (1984), pp. 301–12, p. 305).

11 A brief comment which Glissant makes on the novel in his later collection of essays, *Introduction à une poétique du divers* (Paris: Gallimard, 1996) runs counter to this view, suggesting that it is the descendants of the slave Béluse who triumph in the end: 'Les fiers Longoué, personnages d'un de mes romans, *Le Quatrième Siècle*, n'y venaient pas à bout des tenaces Béluse' (p. 70). But I would argue that this over-simplifies the novel, and is more revealing of the evolution in Glissant's thought between 1964 and 1996 than of the positions implied in *Le Quatrième Siècle*.

12 'Nommée "vertige", "ivresse" (*Le Q.S.*, p. 276), l'union à ce passé introuvable et trahi, liée à la protestation d'une condition d'exploité, reste pour l'homme et l'artiste la seule aventure, ce que le texte essaie de dire' (*Conquérants de la nuit nue: Edouard Glissant et l'H(h)istoire antillaise* (Tübingen: Gunter Narr Verlag, 1988), p. 136).

13 One could perhaps argue that the ambiguity resulting from the double movement, or double structure of interruptions, does ultimately produce a suspension of meaning that is comparable to Nancy's schema of literature interrupting myth.

14 'Culture et identité', in *Introduction à une poétique du divers*, pp. 59–79, p. 62. In *Le Discours antillais*, Glissant makes the point that not all societies produce myths that attempt to explain their origin; the significance of the Zulu myth of Shaka is that it recounts, not the founding of a people, but the moment in their history at which they first came into contact with the white man. Myths like these, he argues,

commemorate Relation rather than origin: 'Ce ne sont pas là des épopées fondatrices, de grands "livres" initiateurs, comme *L'Iliade* et *L'Odyssée*, l'Ancien Testament, les saga ou les chansons de geste. Ce sont les mémoires de la Relation, ce qu'on rassemble de l'unanimité d'un peuple avant que le grand dispersement de la colonisation soit intervenu' (p. 247).

15 In a slightly later article, André places even more emphasis on the mythical, and indeed phantasmatic, nature of the maroon community: '"Longoué", le Marron du "Quatrième siècle", c'est précisément *la mémoire de ce qui n'a jamais été*: le rejet sans le moindre compromis de l'ordre servile; mais aussi la paternité revendiquée, la responsabilité éponyme, l'héritage de liberté à transmettre, le désir de la filiation. Mémoire ou nostalgie? S'il fallait définir le désir de l'œuvre c'est comme désir du désir de filiation qu'il faudrait l'entendre' ('Le Renversement de Senglis: histoires et filiations', *CARE* (Centre Antillais de Recherches et d'Etudes, Paris), 10 (April 1983), pp. 32–51, p. 36).

16 The 'enracinement' metaphor carries over into the whole process of filiation; as Bernadette Cailler points out, the family tree of the Longoués is several times imaged as a real tree, rooted in the ground of the forest and growing into a number of different 'branches' of the family (*Conquérants*, p. 124).

17 It is 'unnatural' also in that it is dominated by women – Marie-Natalie dominates her husband Senglis, and the female slaves are dominant simply because there are almost no male slaves. Sexual life on the plantation is therefore profoundly abnormal, even by the standards of slavery: male slaves are hired from elsewhere to mate with the women, and the few men that do live on the plantation are therefore not only dehumanized by their status as slaves, but also deprived of even the male animal's role of sexual reproduction (p. 70).

18 A fuller description of the slave revolts and their place in the narrative as a whole is given in my *Edouard Glissant and Postcolonial Theory: Strategies of Language and Resistance* (Charlottesville and London: University Press of Virginia, 1999), pp. 61–66.

19 Bernadette Cailler comments that 'as noticed by a number of critics, from Glissant's early pages on, the figure of the Negator (Black Maroon, Indian Rebel, Militant, Storyteller) does not function merely, or even essentially, in opposition to that of the Conqueror (Colonizer, Plantation Owner, Administrator, *Béké*), but, more essentially, it functions in relation to the "non-heroic" characters of the Antillean population, the plantation slaves, and later on, the peasants, townsfolk, workers, soldiers, police, and even *bourgeoisie de couleur*' ('Edouard Glissant: A Creative Critic', *World Literature Today*, 63.4 (1989), pp. 589–92, p. 590).

20 In *Le Discours antillais* Glissant writes of the Name that 'sa force vient d'être choisi et non pas imposé. Ce n'est pas le nom parental, c'est le nom conquis. Peu importe que je m'appelle X ou Glissant; l'important est que je ne subisse pas mon nom, que je l'assume avec et dans ma communauté' (p. 285). See also Priska Degras, 'Se nommer soi-même', *Carbet*, 10 (1990), pp. 57–64.

21 '[The] "communities" and "fraternities" that constitute our image of primitive life (the construction of which has, in general, shown itself to be fantastical)' (BSP, p. 49).

22 Louise's first response to her freedom is to try to persuade Longoué to escape to St-Domingue; papa Longoué recognizes that his son's 'seul et intense désir de partir [...] de nager dans l'espace au delà de l'horizon' (p. 239) is not a new phenomenon, but one already shared by his father, who also felt that 'cette terre n'était pas pour eux, pas encore pour eux' (p. 239), and that all of the family '[au] fond d'eux, [...] couvaient l'ardent souhait de connaître un ailleurs où ne plus être des objets, où voir et toucher à leur tour' (p. 239).

23 In his essay on the plantation system in *Poétique de la relation*, 'Lieu clos, parole ouverte', Glissant in fact describes the system as a whole as trapped in this delusional independence, unaware of the fragility of its economic dependence on the world outside: a 'contradiction [qui] oppose la volonté d'autarcie de la Plantation à sa réelle dépendance par rapport au monde extérieur' (p. 81).

24 'The phrase "myth is a myth" harbors *simultaneously* and *in the same thought* a disabused irony ("foundation is a fiction") and an onto-poetico-logical affirmation ("fiction is a foundation"). That is why myth is interrupted. It is interrupted by its myth' (IC, p. 55).

25 See Denise Gellini, 'Sur les traces du vent: une lecture du *Quatrième Siècle*', in Yves-Alain Favre (ed.), *Horizons d'Edouard Glissant* (Pau: J. & D. Editeurs, 1992), pp. 303–18. She writes: 'Les destins des deux lignées [...] se croisent et se répondent dans d'étranges jeux de miroir. Ainsi Melchior subit le charme de Stéfanise, fille d'Anne Béluse, qui lui renvoie l'image sauvage et guerrière de la jeune Louise, sa mère, telle qu'il ne l'a jamais connue. Papa Longoué adopte pour fils Mathieu Béluse dont il croise le regard dans la glace du coiffeur [...] Ainsi, entre le morne libre et la plaine servile, les unions et les haines trament les liens' (p. 314).

26 See for instance Cailler (*Conquérants*), Dash (*Edouard Glissant*), and Burton ('Comment peut-on être martiniquais?').

27 In an interview with me, Glissant stresses the importance of Martinicans' contribution to the Second World War – and, more ambiguously, the nominal ending of Martinique's colonial status as it became an Overseas Department – in creating this sense of a new openness to the world in 1946: 'Donc il y a eu des participations de gens des colonies, qui ont fait qu'on a commencé à comprendre qu'on existait dans le monde, qu'il y avait quelque chose qui se passait. Et cette ouverture au monde, c'est ça. La départementalisation a été plutôt une déception – pas pour tout le monde, mais pour moi et quelques autres. Une énorme déception, énorme. Mais, bon, ça s'est passé comme ça. Mais c'est surtout l'ouverture au monde qui était important' ('Souvenirs des années 40: interview avec Edouard Glissant', *Esprit créateur*, Spring 2007, pp. 96–104 [p. 103]).

28 Michael Dash, for instance: 'Papa Longoué's story is one of mutual interdependence and the emergence of a composite, creole, culture' (*Edouard Glissant*, p. 84).

29 See for instance the essay 'Créolisations dans la Caraïbe et les Amériques' in *Introduction à une poétique du divers* (pp. 11–32).

30 As Cailler comments, 'Papa Longoué représente le dernier lien avec un passé que, désespérément, Mathieu et quelques autres avaient cherché à connaître pour pouvoir naître à l'acte, au futur' (*Conquérants*, p. 113).

31 The text also at one point equates historical knowledge with the act of choosing a name that signals autonomous identity: 'Celui qui porte un nom est comme celui qui apprend à lire [...] Il quitte le trou béant des jours et des nuits, il entre dans le temps qui lui réfléchit un passé, le force vers un futur' (p. 180).

32 Interestingly, in the much later article on the plantations in *Poétique de la Relation*, Glissant states that the concern with recovering history as a basis for identity springs from conditions on the plantation rather than the maroons: 'C'est dans les prolongements de la Plantation [...] que c'est imposé pour nous la recherche de l'historicité, cette conjonction de la passion de se définir et de l'obsession du temps' (p. 89).

33 See 'Les Ecarts déterminants', in *Poétique de la relation* (pp. 155–71), for the distinction Glissant makes between 'l'identité-racine' and 'l'identité-relation'.

3 Living by Mistake: Individual and Community in Simone Schwarz-Bart's *Pluie et vent sur Télumée Miracle*

1 See for instance Caroline Oudin-Bastide, '*Pluie et vent sur Télumée Miracle*: fatalisme et aliénation', *CARE*, 2 (June 1974), pp. 83–97.

2 Mireille Rosello, '*Pluie et vent sur Télumée Miracle*', *Présence francophone*, 36 (1990), pp. 73–90.

3 'Les gens montaient à ma case […] Je les regardais venir avec ennui, lassitude, encore prisonnière de mon propre chagrin' (p. 226).

4 Maryse Condé, *La Parole des femmes: essai sur les romancières des Antilles de langue française* (Paris: L'Harmattan, 1979), p. 16. Kathleen Gyssels makes the further point that 'le passage sans transition d'un état d'âme à son contraire rend la narration ambivalente et entraîne des lectures opposées. De fait, pour d'aucuns, *Pluie et vent sur Télumée Miracle* est un roman fataliste, un roman de l'aliénation et de la misère, alors que pour d'autres, il prône au contraire l'optimisme et la victoire sur l'aliénation' (*Filles de Solitude. Essai sur l'identité antillaise dans les (auto-) biographies fictives de Simone et André Schwarz-Bart* (Paris: L'Harmattan, 1997), p. 30).

5 Roger Toumson comments that '[la] folie a pour forme, très exactement, la déchirure, et pour contenu, la discontinuité ontologique' ('*Pluie et vent sur Télumée Miracle*: une rêverie encyclopédique: sa structure, son projet idéologique', in GEREC (ed.), *Sur Pluie et vent sur Télumée Miracle de Simone Schwarz-Bart (Textes, Etudes et Documents, 2)* (Paris: Editions Caribéennes, 1979), pp. 25–73, p. 61.

6 Kathleen Gyssels defines it as a 'complexe d'inexistence qui affecte à la fois l'individu et la communauté noire' (*Filles de Solitude*, p. 56). Priska Degras links it explictly to the legacy of slavery: 'La question fondamentale qui se trouve enclose dans cette obsession de l'esclavage […] est, ainsi que l'exprime, à plusieurs reprises, Télumée et d'autres personnages, celle de l'humanité du Nègre et de la légitimité de sa présence non seulement sur la terre des Antilles mais aussi, d'une façon plus générale, de sa présence au monde' ('*Pluie et vent sur Télumée Miracle* de Simone Schwarz-Bart: l'impossibilité du nom et l'absence du patronyme', in M. Condé (ed.), *L'Héritage de Caliban* (Pointe-à-Pitre: Editions Jasor, 1992), pp. 85–101, p. 99).

7 There is an echo here of Fanon's claim that all mental illness in colonized societies is a result of colonialism rather than any individual pathology. See the 'Introduction' to his *Peau noire, masques blancs*.

8 These repetitions have been analysed in detail by Ernest Pépin in 'Le jeu des figures répétitives dans l'œuvre', in GEREC (ed.), *Sur Pluie et vent sur Télumée Miracle de Simone Schwarz-Bart (Textes, Etudes et Documents, 2)* (Paris: Editions Caribéennes, 1979), pp. 79–102.

9 Gyssels explains the theme of magical metamorphosis into an animal in similar terms, but gives a different interpretation of animality as a fantasy of escape from the slave-owner: 'l'esclave est ravalé au rang de bête si bien qu'il s'imagine être cet animal; il fait appel au "devenir-animal" pour fuir le persécuteur' (*Filles de Solitude*, p. 243).

10 Pépin, 'Le jeu des figures', p. 93. He analyses this theme in terms of René Girard's work on the cathartic function of myth, in *La Violence et le sacré* (Paris: Grasset, 1972).

11 'Télumée aurait pu être Reine Sans Nom vieillissante. Ce sont les mêmes personnages, ils ont le même rayonnement, la même force. Elle a tenu le flambeau, c'est la digne fille' ('Interview accordé à R. Toumson', p. 15).

12 As Kathleen Gyssels comments, 'en situation d'abject humiliation le sujet cherche à se protéger par la désertion de son corps' (*Filles de Solitude*, p. 323).

13 Floating in the air or 'flying' is also associated with the Lougandors' sense of

superiority over others: 'Les Lougandor ont toujours aimé survoler, ils s'accrochaient des ailes et ils se hissaient' (p. 32).

14 'Interview accordé à R. Toumson', p. 20.

15 Gyssels' analysis of the community's ambivalence towards Télumée (*Filles de Solitude*, pp. 310–15) concentrates more narrowly on its effect on the couple: 'ce qui assomme le couple est ce qui le constitue inextricablement: le voisinage protège autant qu'il enferme et tue' (p. 314).

16 Toumson thus sees him as the most extreme example of 'folie antillaise': 'Son "crâne fendu", sa "cervelle qui danse" le font identique aux autres humains. Exemplairement dissocié, dédoublé, il a simplement pour fonction de porter, à son point de crise, la folie regnante' (*Pluie et vent sur Télumée Miracle*, p. 62).

4   Singular Beings and Political Disorganization in Vincent Placoly's *L'Eau-de-mort guildive*

1 The novels are: *La Vie et la mort de Marcel Gonstran* (Paris: Denoël, 1971); *L'Eau-de-mort guildive* (Paris: Denoël, 1973); *Frères volcans* (Montreuil: Editions La Brèche, 1983). Most of the shorter pieces are collected in the volume *Une journée torride. Essais, nouvelles* (Montreuil: Éditions La Brèche, 1991). Placoly also wrote a large number of plays that were performed in Martinique, but few of which have been published. 'Adieu Frère Volcan', the special number of the Groupe Révolution Socialiste's review *Tranchées* that was published in 1993 to commemorate his death, contains a number of other texts by Placoly, as well as tributes by his friends and colleagues.

2 Placoly himself comments: 'Je serais d'ailleurs impuissant à reconstruire quoi que ce soit, une scène qui ait la logique élémentaire du narré, un épisode qui ait la logique réconfortante du vécu'. Quoted in Roland Suvélor, 'Vincent Placoly ou le parcours inachevé', *Tranchées Spécial Vincent Placoly* (January 1993), pp. 14–17, p. 14.

3 While at the Sorbonne in the 1960s he became involved in the politics of the anti-Stalinist left and the events of 1968; on returning to Martinique in 1969 he helped to found the 'Groupe Révolution Socialiste', a Trotskyist group which split from the Martinican Communist Party; he wrote a regular column for its newspaper and led numerous local campaigns. In Martinique today, he is remembered as much for his political activity as for his literary works.

4 'Vincent Placoly s'en va: adieu, frère volcan', *Justice*, 2 (9 January 1992); reprinted in *Tranchées Spécial Vincent Placoly* (January 1993), pp. 11–12.

5 Jean-Luc Nancy, 'You ask me what it means today…', *Paragraph*, 16.2 (1992), pp. 108–10, p. 109.

6 See Introduction, note 29.

7 Although it is absolutely characteristic of Glissant's *Malemort* (Paris: Editions du Seuil, 1975), also set largely in Fort-de-France and published two years later than *L'Eau-de-mort guildive*.

8 As Christopher Fynsk comments in his foreword to *The Inoperative Community*, 'there is a point at which death exposes a radical meaninglessness that cannot be subsumed. And when death presents itself as *not ours*, the very impossibility of representing its meaning suspends or breaches the possibility of self-presentation and exposes us to our finitude' ('Experiences of Finitude', IC, p. xvi).

9 Chapter 1 is an exception, perhaps to make it easier for the reader to gain a foothold in the narrative.

10 'The "ground" is itself, through itself and as such, *already* the finitude of singu-larities [...] it is made up only of the network, the interweaving, and the sharing of singularities' (IC, p. 27).

11 Placoly has questioned the importance of identity in these terms: 'Aujourd'hui, je pense que nous sommes un peu trop obsédés par la recherche de ce qui nous appar-tient en propre. Qu'est-ce-qui nous appartient en propre, en fait?' ('Interview avec A. Brossat et D. Maragnès', in Alain Brossat and Daniel Maragnès (eds.), *Les Antilles dans l'impasse? Des intellectuels antillais s'expliquent* (Paris: Editions Caribéennes, 1981), pp. 30–36, p. 33).

12 Barthes' description of a text that is 'comme un échange chatoyant de voix multiples, posées sur des ondes différents et saisies par moments d'un *fading* brusque, dont la trouée permet à l'énonciation de migrer d'un point de vue à un autre, sans prévenir' (*S/Z*, p. 49), is an excellent description of *L'Eau-de-mort guildive*.

13 In his Foreword to *The Inoperative Community*, Christopher Fynsk elucidates the link in Nancy's thought between the subject and the order of signification: 'Nancy is attempting to expose what still speaks in a term like "community" when we assume the closure of the metaphysics of subjectivity – any communion of the subject with itself, any accomplished self-presence – and with it the closure of representation or signification (a signifying order assured by and for a subject)' (IC, p. xi).

14 With one exception: the 'enfant de la nature' whose solitary life is described (pp. 60–62) before her meeting with Valdes's troop. But she is exceptional in other ways as well, a magic being who speaks in bird-language and has her origins in a folk tale.

15 Sometimes this interstitial positioning of the narrative point of view is effected purely by small syntactic details. In a fragment already quoted, the way in which the owner of the cow stolen by Ignigni is introduced into the text ('Celui qui vient de déboucher sur la place [...]', p. 29) is subtly but significantly different from a formula such as 'Un homme vient de déboucher sur la place [...]'. The latter could be cate-gorized as an externally focalized narrative presenting the scene to the reader; but 'Celui qui' implies that the reader can already 'see' the man and is therefore posi-tioned as part of the scene, but not identified with any particular character. The narrative point of view, in other words, is that of one of the crowd.

16 For instance, the outcome of the trial is not clear; there is no indication that the four workers succeeded in proving their innocence, but on the other hand they seem to have been released from prison. When Giap is arrested again later on, the guard warns him: 'Une fois, contre vous, la justice n'a pas frappé. Mais ne la prenez pas pour maman!' (p. 171).

17 In his *Les Damnés de la terre* (Paris: Maspéro, 1961) Fanon argues that the colonized subject can liberate himself or herself only through the violent struggle of decolonization: 'Au niveau des individus, la violence désintoxique. Elle débarrasse le colonisé de son complexe d'infériorité, de ses attitudes contemplatives ou désespérées. Elle le rend intrépide, le réhabilite à ses propres yeux' (p. 127).

5   Conquering the Town: Stories and Myth in Patrick Chamoiseau's *Texaco*

1 'Marqueur de paroles' is the term which Chamoiseau gives to his own persona *qua* narrator in the novels. It designates a figure who listens to and writes down the oral narratives of the character(s) involved in the novel, rather than being a narrator in his own right. For an extended discussion of the 'marqueur de paroles', see

Dominique Chancé, *L'Auteur en souffrance: essai sur la position et la représentation de l'auteur dans le roman antillais contemporain (1981–1992)* (Paris: Presses Universitaires Françaises, 2000).

2 This vision of the Quartiers as a fruitful combination of old and new, rural and urban, may seem rather idealized, but is not purely a figment of Chamoiseau's imagination; it is corroborated by the Martinican sociologist André Lucrèce, who analyses the co-existence of the two 'systems', which 'interpénètrent sans se confondre' (*Société et modernité: essai d'interprétation de la société martiniquaise* (Case Pilote: Edition de l'autre mer, 1994), p. 16). Lucrèce argues that the norms of the 'archaic' society still protect people living in the semi-rural fringes of the towns, but not in the 'milieu urbain, producteur de misère, où la modernité a battu en brèche le système régulateur issu de la société archaïque' (p. 86), thus endorsing Chamoiseau's view that what enables the marginalized poor to cope with the rigours of urban life is in fact the old rural society, and in particular its communitarian traditions: 'De ce point de vue, la société archaïque martiniquaise apporte la leçon suivante: l'éthique vraie est forcément compréhensive et non réductible au *moi* dont elle conteste la sédimentation, parfois irrévocable, face à l'autre' (p. 153). Serge Letchimy makes similar points in his *De l'habitat précaire à la ville: l'exemple martiniquais* (Paris: L'Harmattan, 1992), commenting that the way in which the Quartiers are constructed 'établit un réseau de communications, support d'un réseau communautaire plus large' (pp. 17–18), and that 'la tolérance se combinant à l'entraide, les conditions tacites d'occupation de l'espace structurent des règles communautaires, basées sur la permissivité mutuelle et la solidarité' (p. 23).

3 Thus Lorna Milne describes 'l'espace du quartier' as 'apparemment chaotique, mais régi par des relations subtiles fondées sur la solidarité' (*Patrick Chamoiseau: espaces d'une écriture antillaise* (Amsterdam: Rodopi, 2006), p. 53.

4 Richard Burton describes it as 'les tresses d'histoires – trop obliques, trop disparates, trop entortillées, en un mot trop *créoles* pour être résumées ici – de cet investissement de l'espace urbain qui s'entrelaçent pour former l'immense tapisserie de la vie martiniquaise qu'est *Texaco*' (*Le Roman marron: études sur la littérature martiniquaise contemporaine* (Paris: L'Harmattan, 1997), p. 187).

5 Maeve McCusker, 'Telling Stories/Creating History: Patrick Chamoiseau's *Texaco*', *ASCALF Year Book*, 3 (1998), pp. 23–33, p. 23 and pp. 31–32. One could cite as another typical postmodern feature of the novel its use of parody: the nick-naming of the town planner as 'le Christ' parodies the Bible, as do the novel's section titles: 'Annonciation', 'Le Sermon de Marie-Sophie Laborieux (pas sur la montagne mais devant un rhum vieux)', 'Résurrection'; and the subtitles accompanying the latter (e.g., 'où l'urbaniste qui vient pour raser l'insalubre quartier Texaco tombe dans un cirque créole et affronte la parole d'une femme-matador') parody the old-fashioned chapter headings of pre-twentieth-century novels. More generally, the tone of the narrative is often humorous and irreverent; the battles with the police are described with a kind of mock-heroic grandeur, for instance.

6 Dominique Chancé recognizes this aspiration towards unity and sees it as the author's response to the diversity of the creole community: 'C'est la réponse spécifique du roman à la multiplicité d'un univers désordonné où s'expriment des voix diverses, et c'est par là qu'il recherche une cohérence, dans la tentative renouvelée de tisser une "tresse" unique d'histoires avec tant de couleurs variées. Il représente la tentative de refonder l'unité d'une collectivité diverse' (*L'Auteur en souffrance*, p. 35).

7 Burton contrasts this unicity unfavourably with the multiple viewpoints of Chamoiseau's first novel, *Chronique des sept misères*: 'A la richesse hétéroglottique de son premier roman, et à la multiplicité de ses points de vue, *Texaco* substitue l'uni-

vocité d'une seule narratrice dont l'optique tend à se confondre avec celle de l'auteur' (*Le Roman marron*, p. 199).

8 Christine Chivallon, in her 'Eloge de la spatialité: conceptions des relations à l'espace et identité créole chez Patrick Chamoiseau' (*ASCALF Year Book*, 1 (1996), pp. 24–45) analyses *Texaco* in a way which offers interesting parallels with my account above. She sees it as containing three different conceptions of identity based on different relations to place and space: one characterized by 'unité et cohérence' (p. 27), which is contested by an 'identité mobile: éloge du désordre et du multiple' (p. 31), and, finally, the synthesis of these two in an 'identité rhizome: unité et multi- plicité' (p. 35). Despite the symmetry of this schema, she does seem to me to recognize the ultimate priority of unity over disorder – writing for instance: 'L'unité du peuple y est en effet bien trop présente pour faire disparaître toute idée d'ordre, de lignes fédératrices ou de cohésion. La trame du roman vient d'ailleurs pallier la difficulté majeure à faire l'éloge du chaos en même temps que de montrer des cohérences, des équilibres, fussent-ils secrets. […] l'écrivain s'est ménagé un espace d'écriture où il peut à loisir faire l'éloge du désordre. Mais on peut se demander ce que deviendrait cet éloge sans que se profile la conception de l'identité-racine, ressource que le romancier utilise de façon singulière à l'état de désir ou d'aspiration collective, pour révéler ce peuple dont le risque serait en définitive de disparaître dans un abandon sans concession au paradigme du désordre' (p. 40). In somewhat similar fashion Burton sees *Texaco* as ultimately oversimplifying the relations between Texaco and 'L'En-ville' by reducing everything to a series of binary oppositions (*Le Roman marron*, pp. 193–200), concluding that 'le paradoxe fondamental de *Texaco*' is that 'cet éloge de la créolité urbaine est on ne peut plus "français" dans la logique bina- riste qui le sous-tend' (p. 200).

9 'L'intervention d'une sorte de mythe de fondation investit en effet d'ores et déjà le lieu d'une mémoire, celle de l'origine, mémoire qui […] s'annonce comme sacrée puisque le Mentô est celui qui connaît les mystères de la lointaine Afrique. Autour du récit fondateur s'accomplit aussi la fonction réunificatrice du mythe: celle qui permet de situer en une même origine (un même lieu) les liens tissés entre les hommes et les femmes d'un même peuple' ('Eloge', p. 28).

10 Milne argues that one of *Texaco*'s main themes is 'la lutte de Marie-Sophie pour devenir le sujet de ces trois verbes fondamentaux – habiter, aimer, écrire' (*Patrick Chamoiseau*, p. 113) – in other words, her progress towards full, autonomous subjecthood.

11 'Je sentais aussi (comme mon Esternome me l'avait fait sentir) qu'il fallait face à l'En-ville organiser un vrai Quartier de mornes' (p. 350).

12 See for instance the repetition of 'C'est moi qui…' on page 437.

13 '[The] fulfilled infinite identity of community is what I call its "work"' (IC, p. xxxix).

14 Patrick Chamoiseau, Raphaël Confiant and Jean Bernabé, *Eloge de la créolité* (Paris: Gallimard, 1989).

15 David Dabydeen, 'A nation built of stories', *The Times* (13 March 1997), p. 28.

16 Although not in the 'Noutéka des mornes': 'C'était bâtir le pays (pas le pays mulâtre, pas le pays béké, pas le pays kouli, pas le pays kongo: le pays des nèg-terre)', pp. 166–67.

17 Richard and Sally Price claim that the characters in the 'romans de la créolité' 'foster an illusion of diversity by peopling the island with a reified set of categories drawn from crosscutting kinds of schemata (class, "race", national origin, etc.)' ('Shadow-Boxing in the Mangrove', *Cultural Anthropology*, 12.1 (1997), pp. 3–36, p.10).

18 'En outre, le quartier Texaco semble confirmer par ses qualités mêmes la force triomphale de cette culture, car sa configuration et son atmosphère reflètent parfaitement la culture créole elle-même' (Milne, *Patrick Chamoiseau*, p. 108).

19 Michel Giraud criticizes the 'créolistes' in precisely these terms, while also accusing them of a totalitarian capture of the whole cultural field in an attempt to promote their own literary and intellectual careers. Their conception of cultural identity, he argues, is based on 'la problématique fautive de l'origine [...] Leurs discours et leurs actes tendent en effet à réduire – précisément sous les espèces de la créolité – les *identités* antillaises à un patrimoine, qui est certes vu comme le produit d'une histoire complexe, mais d'une histoire cristallisée en une tradition à laquelle ils veulent qu'on reste fidèle alors qu'ils l'idéalisent largement et, donc, la reconstruisent en fonction de leurs exigences présentes et de l'avenir auquel ils aspirent' ('La créolité: une rupture en trompe-l'œil', *Cahiers d'Etudes Africaines*, 148 (1997), pp. 795–812, p. 800).

20 From an interview with me, New York, 13 March 2001.

21 Chivallon notes the prominence of the metaphor of the 'corde', which, she argues, 'donne sens à une sorte d'unité qui transcende la dispersion. Dans l'agglomérat d'éléments fragmentés, des liens ou des connections se révèlent saillantes [sic] et solides' ('Eloge', p. 35).

22 See note 2 above.

23 Chamoiseau's gesture of thanking the real inhabitants of Texaco 'qui ont bien voulu satisfaire mes impossibles curiosités' at the end of the book reinforces this display of authenticity. The intermixing of fictional events and characters with real historical ones (the abolition of slavery, the destruction of Saint-Pierre, De Gaulle's visit to Martinique, the riots of 1959, etc.) could also be seen as serving the same realist purpose.

24 In her emphasis on the immediacy of the scene of oral story-telling, the face-to-face contact between the *conteur* and his audience (p. 25), Chancé echoes Nancy's evocation of the (mythical) scene of someone recounting a myth to his community – and, in so doing, bringing them together into a communal unity: 'We know the scene: there is a gathering, and someone is telling a story. We do not yet know whether these people gathered together form an assembly, if they are a horde or a tribe. But we call them brothers and sisters because they are gathered together and because they are listening to the same story' (IC, p. 43). In very similar terms, Chancé writes: 'En effet, le conteur parle à la communauté qu'il suscite réellement, dans l'instance de sa parole [...] La scène de l'oraliture est une scène sociale. Comme dans les tragédies grecques, un peuple, une communauté s'y fonde' (p. 25).

25 The 'marqueur de paroles' thus in fact places himself *outside* her community, contrary to Chancé's claim that he creates a world in which he is fully integrated. In this respect, *Texaco* differs significantly from Chamoiseau's previous novel *Solibo magnifique*, where the equivalent figure plays a full part in the events of the narrative.

26 Milne makes the further point that this 'archive' of written texts also reinforces the supposed reality of the 'marqueur de paroles' himself: 'Tout cet appareil apocryphe sous-tendant l'authenticité apparente de l'*histoire* de Texaco [...] ne fait en réalité qu'épaissir le tissu fictionnel du roman et en particulier de ce narrateur homodiégétique qui prétend avoir cueilli et raconté le *récit* de Marie-Sophie' (*Patrick Chamoiseau*, p. 135).

27 H. Adlai Murdoch's analysis of Chamoiseau's *Solibo magnifique* provides an interesting comparison here; he interprets this novel's 'critical interplay between writing and orality – and the impossibility of the former to represent the latter' (*Creole Identity in the French Caribbean Novel* (Gainesville: University Press of Florida,

2001), p. 228) in a very different way, as a deconstructive technique pointing to the unrepresentability of Solibo's life and, by extension, creole reality in general: 'both the plot that seeks to re-cover the trace of the absent, since deceased Solibo and the discursive re-presentation of this paradoxically secondary story-in-reverse are ultimately governed by a logic of absence and lack that figures the cycle of displacement and deferral that encapsulates the unrepresentability of a creolized difference' (p. 229). But despite the apparent similarity of the oral–written relationship in the two novels, a crucial difference is that the story-teller Solibo is not presented as the original narrator of the particular story *that we are reading*; it is the fact that Marie-Sophie does perform this role in *Texaco* that, I would argue, makes it difficult for the reader to see her 'absent' oral narrative as a deliberate aporia in the text.

28 Chancé formulates the position very trenchantly: 'Ainsi, le "marqueur de paroles" est pris dans une duplicité que l'on peut résumer ainsi: il ne fait que montrer ce qui existe, mais ce qu'il montre n'existe pas ailleurs que dans sa vision prophétique. Il ne fait qu'entendre une parole, un discours qu'il rapporte, mais cette parole n'existe que parce qu'il la recueille' (*L'Auteur en souffrance*, pp. 99–100).

6 Community, Nature and Solitude in Daniel Maximin's *L'Ile et une nuit*

1 *L'Isolé soleil* (Paris: Editions du Seuil, Collection Points, 1981); *Soufrières* (Paris: Editions du Seuil, Collection Points, 1987); *L'Ile et une nuit* (Paris: Editions du Seuil, 1995).

2 See for instance Mireille Rosello's analysis of Césaire's poetry in her *Littérature et identité aux Antilles* (Paris: Karthala, 1992).

3 Bongie, 'The (Un)exploded Volcano: Daniel Maximin's *Soufrières* and the Apocalypse of Narrative', in his *Islands and Exiles: The Creole Identities of Post/Colonial Literature* (Stanford, CA: Stanford University Press, 1998), pp. 348–401. Nesbitt writes: 'from a comprehensible historical process, the French colonization of the Antilles becomes instead an uncontrollable, sublime force of nature that devastates the island' (*Voicing Memory: History and Subjectivity in French Caribbean Literature* (Charlottesville and London: University of Virginia Press, 2003), p. 164).

4 Roumain's *Gouverneurs de la rosée*, as I have discussed in Chapter 1, is criticized by Michel Serres precisely for confusing the two levels, and attempting to superimpose a struggle against political oppression onto a battle with the weather.

5 There is some similarity here with the non-human elements of the community in *L'Eau-de-mort guildive*.

6 'In his use of the volcano as the central focus of *Soufrières*, a novel that takes place in 1976 and chronicles the reactions of various Guadeloupeans to an anticipated explosion of *la Soufrière*, Maximin […] is interrogating, and commemorating, the (im)possibility of an explosive identity politics of the sort posited by such modernist thinkers as Césaire, Fanon, and the leaders of the Black Power movement' (Bongie, '(Un)exploded Volcano', pp. 362–63).

7 All the chapter titles of *Soufrières* are taken from the titles of paintings by the Cuban artist Wifredo Lam.

8 'This second apostrophe marks out an intermediary space of difference that troubles, at the same time as it joins together, the emphatically alliterative invocation of beginnings that the two alphas of the chapter titles also suggest. As such, this apostrophe can be read as standing for the "relation" between Maximin's first and

second novels: each is connected to the other in a way that deprives it of a separate identity' ('(Un)exploded Volcano', p. 365).

9 'Dans *Soufrières*, le malheur prédit, attendu, n'était pas venu; mais dans *L'Ile et une nuit*, on constate que lorsque le malheur arrive, on est suffisamment fort pour lui résister' (Maximin, in one of a series of interviews with Christiane Chaulet-Achour, reproduced in her *La Trilogie caribéenne de Daniel Maximin*, p. 55. Subsequent quotations from these interviews will be referenced as *Trilogie*).

10 See the section entitled 'From the Apocalypse to Chaos' in Benítes-Rojo's *The Repeating Island: The Caribbean and the Postmodern Perspective* (Durham, NC: Duke University Press, 1992), pp. 10–16.

11 I discuss this aspect of the novel more fully in 'The (De)construction of Subjectivity in Daniel Maximin's *L'Ile et une nuit*', *Paragraph*, 24.3 (2001), pp. 44–58.

12 In the same vein, the old schoolmistress in *Soufrières* remarks: 'Alors, même sur notre misère, il faut tenir la position et montrer que nous savons vivre au-dessus de la mort. Simplement, à l'inverse des autres peuples, nous sommes partis de la mort pour aller vers la vie' (p. 187).

13 See my 'The (De)construction of Subjectivity' for a more detailed discussion of this conception of resistance.

14 Thus Nesbitt's claim that '[in] its retreat into the most inward recesses of subjective experience, *L'Ile et une nuit* seeks to recover for the Antillean subject the possibility of an autonomous understanding by reducing experience to the most basic of sense data and to then master this nature through a poetic and musical quasi-logic in its struggle for self-preservation' (*Voicing Memory*, p. 168) does not adequately recognize the centrality of the collective or 'plural' dimension to Marie-Gabriel's subjectivity.

15 In his interview with Chaulet-Achour, Maximin comments: 'Dans mon "je", c'est la relation aux autres qui m'intéresse' (*Trilogie*, p. 15). Clarisse Zimra's comment on *L'Isolé soleil* is equally illuminating in relation to *L'Ile et une nuit*: 'Maximin's characters share a determined refusal to be penned within strict definitional boundaries of any sort, an insistence that the self is always situational, provisional, and relational' ('Daughters of Mayotte, Sons of Frantz: The Unrequited Self in Caribbean Literature', in Sam Haigh (ed.), *An Introduction to Caribbean Francophone Writing: Guadeloupe and Martinique* (Oxford: Berg, 1999), pp. 177–94, p.192).

16 In the sentence 'Tu vois comment, par une nuit de cyclone, il n'y a peut-être plus d'espoir, mais il reste de la vie' (p. 66), 'tu' clearly refers to Adrien; this is followed by a sentence beginning 'Alors, toi-même, tu te rends compte [...]' which we at first also read as addressing him; but the next sentence retrospectively makes it ambiguous, since here she is definitely talking to herself: 'Tu as bouché depuis une heure tes oreilles au fracas d'ici-dans' (p. 66).

17 In *Soufrières*, too, the relationship between Marie-Gabriel and Adrien privileges separation, in this sense, over fusion: 'ta lune et ton soleil qui tournent chacun autour de l'autre en redoutant leur fusion dans l'éclipse qui leur ferait perdre leur éclat particulier' (p. 260).

18 Bongie, '(Un)exploded Volcano', p. 358. The quotation from Maximin is taken from Clarisse Zimra's introduction to the English translation of *L'Isolé soleil*, pp. xi–lix, p. xxvii (Daniel Maximin, *Lone Sun*, trans C. Zimra (Charlottesville and London: University Press of Virginia, 1989)).

19 Thus in her diary Siméa envisages the possibility that her as yet unborn child will 're-create' her: 'Mon enfant se recréera une mère en moi comme une nouvelle source remodèle la mer à son débouché' (*L'Ile*, p. 80).

20 'If the world does not "have" an origin "outside of itself", if the world is its own origin or the origin "itself", then the origin of the world occurs at each moment of the world. It is the *each time* of Being, and its realm is the *being-with* of each time with every [other] time' (BSP, p. 83).

21 Suzanne Césaire, 'Le grand camouflage', *Tropiques*, 12 (1945), pp. 267–73; Henri Michaux, *Face aux verrous* (Paris: Gallimard, 1954). I do not intend to analyse these allusions in detail, partly for reasons of space and partly because I doubt that I have recognized all of them. For more extended studies of intertextuality in Maximin's novels see Chaulet-Achour, *Trilogie*; Lydie Moudileno, *L'écrivain antillais au miroir de sa littérature* (Paris: Karthala, 1997), Chapter 6; Ronnie Scharfmann, 'Rewriting the Césaires: Daniel Maximin's Caribbean Discourse', in Maryse Condé (ed.), *L'héritage de Caliban* (Pointe-à-Pitre: Editions Jasor, 1992); Clarisse Zimra, 'Tracées césairiennes dans *L'Isolé soleil*', in J. Leiner (ed.), *L'Athanor d'un alchimiste: Colloque international sur l'œuvre d'Aimé Césaire* (Paris: Editions Caribéennes, 1987), pp. 347–67.

22 Nesbitt stresses the cultural significance of music as an expression of collective struggle in black communities (*Voicing Memory*, pp. 151–53). He then gives a detailed analysis of the formal parallels between jazz – specifically Coleman Hawkins and John Coltrane – and the writing of *L'Isolé soleil* and *L'Ile et une nuit* respectively.

23 Or knowing someone who does: I am grateful to Mervyn Poley for his help in identifying these allusions.

24 'Si l'écriture de Daniel Maximin tend vers la musique, [...] c'est qu'à travers elle se cherche une liberté créatrice, dont le jazz, parce qu'il est l'art de l'improvisation, offrirait un modèle' (Chancé, *L'Auteur en souffrance*, p. 147).

25 '[Le] désir principal est de retrouver le "nous", de retrouver les paroles antérieures qui ont déjà été dites, et pas seulement par les écrivains' (*Trilogie*, p. 59).

7 On Not Belonging: Surrogate Families and Marginalized Communities in Maryse Condé's *Desirada*

1 The theme of community in Condé's work has been discussed mainly in relation to the very different type of community to be found in her *Traversée de la Mangrove* (Paris: Mercure de France, 1989). See Patrick ffrench, 'Community in Maryse Condé's *Traversée de la Mangrove*', *French Forum*, 22.1 (1997), pp. 93–105; and Jean-Xavier Ridon, 'Maryse Condé et le fantôme d'une communauté inopérante', in Christiane Albert (ed.), *Francophonie et identités culturelles* (Paris: Karthala, 1999), pp. 213–26.

2 'L'amour qu'elle avait éprouvé pour Reynalda et qu'elle avait enfoui à l'intérieur d'elle-même, puisqu'il ne servait à rien, avait laissé une place aride et pierreuse à l'endroit de son cœur. C'était à cause de Reynalda si elle n'avait de goût pour rien, pour personne, si elle dérivait sans but dans l'existence' (p. 96).

3 For Céleste, for instance, it has become simply meaningless. She says: 'De nos jours, le mot de famille n'avait plus de signification. Ni celui de tribu. Ni celui de village. Ni celui de communauté' (p. 263).

4 The books by francophone authors that Marie-Noëlle teaches with her students in Boston reinforce the myths that they have about Guadeloupe, and serve to 'construire une mythologie qui convient à tous' (p. 219). In the interview which Condé granted me (New York, 13 March 2001), she stressed the nostalgic nature of the ideal of the traditional Guadeloupean community: 'L'idée de communauté est

devenue un fantasme. Les gens ont voulu se conformer à des récits que leurs parents ont tenus [...] A l'origine il a dû y avoir une communauté, mais elle s'est modifiée; elle s'est tellement modifiée, tellement transformée, qu'on ne peut plus la définir'.

5 The allusion to Paul Eluard's *Capitale de la douleur* (Paris: Gallimard, 1926) suggests that this is not an entirely painless development.

6 Garvey, who suffers from the same habitual loneliness as his sister, likes big cities because '[d'une] certaine manière, on n'était jamais perdu puisqu'on trouvait toujours un esseulé comme soi-même à qui raconter sa misère' (p. 242).

7 Ronnie Scharfman comments that 'les thèmes du double, de la répétition, de l'écho et du miroir qui structurent le roman renvoient tous, me semble-t-il, au besoin du personnage de combler le vide dans l'impossible désir de se fondre et de s'identifier à une mère aimante' ('Au sujet d'héroïnes péripatétiques et peu sympathiques', in Madeleine Cottenet-Hage et Lydie Moudileno (ed.), *Maryse Condé: une nomade inconvenante* (Pointe-à-Pitre: Ibis Rouge Editions, 2002), pp. 141–48, p. 143). This is a perceptive observation, but I would argue that Scharfman's approach underestimates the positive values ascribed by the novel to these surrogate relationships, which provide genuine emotional support in their own right.

8 '[Anthea] avait arraché Molara à l'indifférence d'un père et d'une mère qui végétaient dans la misère d'un bidonville africain' (p. 110). This is a rather more ambivalent version of the biological/surrogate tension: the violence of 'arraché' and the widespread use of free indirect speech throughout the novel make the reader suspect that the original parents' 'indifférence' is Anthea's own biased judgement .

9 While this is simply taken for granted in Marie-Noëlle's case, Reynalda's earlier friendship with Fiorella in Guadeloupe was unusual enough to generate some bewilderment; Nina recounts how '[depuis] notre premier jour à La Pointe, Fiorella et Reynalda étaient devenues des inséparables. Pourquoi? En vérité, cela paraissait tellement bizarre. Une noire, l'autre blanche. Une laide comme le péché, l'autre, pareille à un enfant du bon Dieu' (p. 193).

10 Interview, 13 March 2001.

11 Interview, 13 March 2001.

12 Cf. Alphonso Lingis, *The Community of Those Who Have Nothing in Common* (Bloomington: Indiana University Press, 1994).

13 I have discussed a rather similar promotion of irrelevance in 'Breaking the Rules: Irrelevance/Irreverence in Maryse Condé's *Traversée de la Mangrove*', *French Cultural Studies*, 15.1 (2004), pp. 35–47.

14 In Condé's view, even the 'Caribbean' community is not localized geographically. In her interview with me, she quotes a student who had been reading *Desirada* and asked her 'Mais pour vous, où commence, où finit la Caraïbe?' – and comments 'Et j'ai trouvé que c'est une excellente question'. Elsewhere she herself asks: 'Que sont les Antilles d'aujourd'hui? Un lieu sans contours définis, poreux à tous les bruits lointains, traversé par toutes les influences contradictoires' ('Chercher nos verités', p. 309).

15 *La Vie scélérate* (Paris: Seghers, 1987).

16 *Heremakhonon* (Paris: Union générale d'éditions, 1976); *Une Saison à Rihata* (Paris: Robert Laffont, 1981).

17 In Pfaff, *Entretiens*, p. 47.

18 '"People" clearly states that we are all precisely *people*, that is, indistinctly persons, humans, all of a common "kind", but of a kind that has its existence only as numerous, dispersed, and indeterminate in its generality. This existence can only be grasped in the paradoxical simultaneity of togetherness (anonymous, confused, and indeed massive) and disseminated singularity (these or those "people(s)", or "a guy", "a girl", "a kid") (BSP, p. 7).

19 Even the archetypally traditional French Duparc family has a relative who becomes bishop of Guadeloupe.

20 Mary Gallagher claims that '[indeed], the most concerted representation of mobility across the Americas is to be found in the writing of this prolific author' (*Soundings in French Caribbean Writing*, p. 257).

21 Dominique Licops analyses this progression in her comparison of *Desirada* with Condé's earlier novel *La Vie scélérate*, 'Expériences diasporiques et migratoires des villes dans *La Vie scélérate* et *Desirada* de Maryse Condé', *Nottingham French Studies*, 39.1 (2000), pp.110–20. In *La Vie scélérate*, Licops argues, '[l'expérience] urbaine des personnages s'inscrit dès lors dans des trajectoires qui présupposent une origine commune, des mouvements de dispersion et de retour basés sur la possibilité de retracer une généalogie et de transmettre une mémoire familiale. Par contre, dans *Desirada*, le mouvement vers les métropoles européennes et américaines et l'installation des personnages dans celles-ci, s'accompagnent d'une re-connaissance de la part inconnaissable de l'origine, d'une perte de mémoire' (pp. 110–11).

22 Although elsewhere Condé has characterized it in more lyrical terms: 'Je crois maintenant que c'est l'errance qui amène la créativité. L'enracinement est très mauvais au fond. Il faut absolument être errant, multiple, au-dehors et au-dedans' (Pfaff, *Entretiens*, p. 46).

23 Similarly Roxbury, where she teaches, is 'un quartier aussi misérable que Camden Town, peuplé comme lui presque uniquement de Noirs et de Latinos' (p. 141).

24 Nor is she presented with such aggressive irony as Debbie, an otherwise similar figure in Condé's earlier novel, *Les Derniers Rois mages* (Paris: Mercure de France, 1992).

25 The concept of 'Muntu' was in fact popularized by the German Africanist Jahnheinz Jahn, in his book *Muntu: An Outline of New African Culture* (New York: Grove Press, 1961), originally published in German in 1958.

26 'Il nous racontait comment, chaque nuit, il bavardait avec Jésus, Jésus nègre noir, un python enroulé en collier autour de son cou. Je n'y croyais pas à toutes ces bêtises. Quand même, j'admirais le travail que Muntu réalisait au sein de nos communautés' (p. 275).

27 Interview, 13 March 2001.

28 Birth, together with death, is as we have seen Nancy's prime example of a phenomenon that escapes the consciousness of its subject and so exposes us to our finitude (IC, p. 15). Marie-Noëlle's fantasy of remembering her birth could thus be interpreted as a rather poignant sign of her desire to establish herself through biological filiation as an immanent subject.

29 Lydie Moudileno emphasizes the unreliability of Marie-Noëlle's memories, and the difficulties these pose for the reader's interpretation of her experience, in her 'Le Rire de la grand-mère: insolence et sérénité dans *Desirada* de Maryse Condé' (*The French Review*, 76.6 (2003), pp. 1151–60). She writes: 'En même temps qu'elle présente l'anamnèse comme un procès essentiel, la voix narrative insiste dès le début sur la nécessité de considérer les réminiscences de Marie-Noëlle comme "souvenirs imaginaires" […] On retrouve au long du roman cette oscillation entre une invitation à prendre les souvenirs au sérieux, et une mise en garde contre le caractère sélectif et lacunaire de la mémoire' (pp. 1153–54).

30 'Reynalda qui était peut-être la raison première de cette impossibilité à donner une bonne direction à son existence' (p. 206).

31 Reynalda herself encourages her in this project. Having recounted her own version of Marie-Noëlle's origins, she concludes: 'C'est tout ce que je peux te donner. La vérité. Dans l'espoir que tu comprendras et que de cette manière, tu commenceras

à vivre ta vie' (p. 102).

32 For instance, the hints of Père Mondicello's guilt (e.g., the fact that he left La Pointe to work in the leper colony, p. 158) that emerge long before she begins to suspect him; or the discrepancies in Reynalda's story that might indicate that she is lying: the first time Reynalda describes Nina's and Gian Carlo's lovemaking, Nina remains silent like 'un objet passif' (p. 70), but in a subsequent version '[ma] maman couinait comme un rat ou gueulait comme un cochon qu'on égorge' (p. 208).

33 Rather ironically in view of Condé's self-proclaimed 'prosaic' temperament (she tells Françoise Pfaff '[la] poésie ne m'a jamais paru me convenir. Je suis trop moqueuse et caustique. Pas lyrique pour deux sous', Pfaff, *Entretiens*, p. 62), this definition of meaning is more usually associated with poetry than with prose.

Bibliography

Ahmad, Aijaz, *In Theory – Classes, Nations, Literatures* (London: Verso, 2000).

André, Jacques, *Caraïbales* (Paris: Editions Caribéennes, 1981).

— 'Le Renversement de Senglis: histoires et filiations', *CARE*, 10 (1983), pp. 32–51.

Barthes, Roland, *S/Z* (Paris: Seuil, 1970).

Benítes-Rojo, Antonio, *The Repeating Island: The Caribbean and the Postmodern Perspective* (Durham, NC: Duke University Press, 1992).

Bhabha, Homi, 'Representation and the Colonial Text: A Critical Exploration of Some Forms of Mimeticism', in Frank Gloversmith (ed.), *The Theory of Reading* (Brighton: Harvester Press, 1984), pp. 93–122.

Bongie, Chris, 'The (Un)exploded Volcano: Daniel Maximin's *Soufrières* and the Apocalypse of Narrative', in his *Islands and Exiles: The Creole Identities of Post/Colonial Literature* (Stanford, CA: Stanford University Press, 1998), pp. 348–401.

Britton, Celia, *Edouard Glissant and Postcolonial Theory: Strategies of Language and Resistance* (Charlottesville and London: University Press of Virginia, 1999).

— 'The (De)construction of Subjectivity in Daniel Maximin's *L'Ile et une nuit*', *Paragraph*, 24.3 (2001), pp. 44–58.

— 'Breaking the Rules: Irrelevance/Irreverence in Maryse Condé's *Traversée de la Mangrove*', *French Cultural Studies*, 15.1 (2004), pp. 35–47.

Burniston, S., and C. Weedon, 'Ideology, Subjectivity and the Artistic Text', in Centre for Contemporary Cultural Studies (ed.), *On Ideology* (London: Hutchinson, 1978), pp. 216–22.

Burton, Richard, 'Comment peut-on être martiniquais? The Recent Works of Edouard Glissant', *Modern Languages Review*, 79.2 (1984), pp. 301–12.

— *Le Roman marron: études sur la littérature martiniquaise contemporaine* (Paris: L'Harmattan, 1997).

Cailler, Bernadette, *Conquérants de la nuit nue: Edouard Glissant et l'H(h)istoire antillaise* (Tübingen: Gunter Narr Verlag, 1988).

— 'Edouard Glissant: A Creative Critic', *World Literature Today*, 63.4 (1989), pp. 589–92.

Césaire, Suzanne, 'Le grand camouflage', *Tropiques*, 12 (1945), pp. 267–73.

Chamoiseau, Patrick, *Solibo magnifique* (Paris: Folio, 1988).

— *Texaco* (Paris: Gallimard, 1992).

Chamoiseau, Patrick, Raphaël Confiant and Jean Bernabé, *Eloge de la créolité* (Paris: Gallimard, 1989).

Chancé, Dominique, *L'Auteur en souffrance: essai sur la position et la représentation de l'auteur dans le roman antillais contemporain (1981–1992)* (Paris: Presses Universitaires Françaises, 2000).

Chaulet-Achour, Christiane, *La Trilogie caribéenne de Daniel Maximin* (Paris: Karthala, 2000).

Chivallon, Christine, 'Eloge de la spatialité: conceptions des relations à l'espace et identité créole chez Patrick Chamoiseau', *ASCALF Year Book*, 1 (1996), pp. 24–45.

Condé, Maryse, *Heremakhonon* (Paris: Union générale d'éditions, 1976).

— *La Parole des femmes: essai sur les romancières des Antilles de langue française* (Paris: L'Harmattan, 1979).

— *Une Saison à Rihata* (Paris: Robert Laffont, 1981).

— *La Vie scélérate* (Paris: Seghers, 1987).

— *Traversée de la Mangrove* (Paris: Mercure de France, 1989).

— *Les Derniers Rois mages* (Paris: Mercure de France, 1992).

— 'Chercher nos vérités', in Maryse Condé and Madeleine Cottenet-Hage (eds.), *Penser la créolité* (Paris: Karthala, 1995), pp. 305–10.

— *Desirada* (Paris: Robert Laffont, 1997).

Dabydeen, David, 'A nation built of stories', *The Times* (13 March 1997), p. 28.

Dash, J. Michael, *Edouard Glissant* (Cambridge: Cambridge University Press, 1995).

— *The Other America: Caribbean Literature in a New World Context* (Charlottesville and London: University Press of Virginia, 1998).

Degras, Priska, 'Se nommer soi-même', *Carbet*, 10 (1990), pp. 57–64.

— '*Pluie et vent sur Télumée Miracle* de Simone Schwarz-Bart: l'impossibilité du nom et l'absence du patronyme', in M. Condé (ed.), *L'Héritage de Caliban* (Pointe-à-Pitre: Editions Jasor, 1992), pp. 85–101.

Dorsinville, Roger, *Jacques Roumain* (Paris: Présence africaine, 1981).

Eluard, Paul, *Capitale de la douleur* (Paris: Gallimard, 1926).

Fanon, Frantz, *Peau noire, masques blancs* (Paris: Editions du Seuil, 1952).

— *Les Damnés de la terre* (Paris: Maspéro, 1961).

ffrench, Patrick, 'Community in Maryse Condé's *Traversée de la Mangrove*', *French Forum*, 22.1 (1997), pp. 93–105.

Fonkoua, Romuald, *Essai sur une mesure du monde au XXe siècle: Edouard Glissant* (Paris: Honoré Champion, 2002).

Fynsk, Christopher, 'Experiences of Finitude', Foreword to Jean-Luc Nancy, *The Inoperative Community*, pp. vii–xxxv.

Gallagher, Mary, *Soundings in French Caribbean Writing since 1950: The Shock of Space and Time* (Oxford: Oxford University Press, 2002).

Gellini, Denise, 'Sur les traces du vent: une lecture du *Quatrième Siècle*', in Yves-Alain Favre (ed.), *Horizons d'Edouard Glissant* (Pau: J. & D.

Editeurs, 1992), pp. 303–18.

Girard, René, *La Violence et le sacré* (Paris: Grasset, 1972).

Giraud, Michel, 'La créolité: une rupture en trompe-l'œil', *Cahiers d'Etudes Africaines*, 148 (1997), pp. 795–812.

Glissant, Edouard, *Le Quatrième Siècle* (Paris: Editions du Seuil, 1964). Reprinted by Gallimard, Collection 'Imaginaire', 1990.

— *L'Intention poétique* (Paris: Editions du Seuil, 1969). Reprinted by Gallimard, 1997.

— *Malemort* (Paris: Editions du Seuil, 1975).

— *Le Discours antillais* (Paris: Editions du Seuil, 1981).

— *Poétique de la Relation* (Paris: Gallimard, 1990).

— *Introduction à une poétique du divers* (Paris: Gallimard, 1996).

— 'Souvenirs des années 40: interview avec Edouard Glissant', *Esprit créateur*, Spring 2007, pp. 96–104.

Gyssels, Kathleen, *Filles de Solitude. Essai sur l'identité antillaise dans les (auto-) biographies fictives de Simone et André Schwarz-Bart* (Paris: L'Harmattan, 1997).

Hallward, Peter, 'Edouard Glissant between the Singular and the Specific', *Yale Journal of Criticism*, 11.2 (1998), pp. 441–64.

Heidegger, Martin, *Being and Time*, trans. John Macquarrie and Edward Robinson (Oxford: Basil Blackwell, 1973).

Hoffmann, Léon-François, 'Langages et rhétorique dans *Gouverneurs de la rosée* de Jacques Roumain', in his *Haïti: lettres et l'être* (Toronto: Editions du GREF, 1992), pp. 167–86.

Hutchens, B. C., *Jean-Luc Nancy and the Future of Philosophy* (London: Acumen, 2005).

Jahn, Jahnheinz, *Muntu: An Outline of New African Culture* (New York: Grove Press, 1961, originally published in German in 1958).

Kristeva, Julia, *La Révolution du langage poétique. L'avant-garde à la fin du XIXe siècle, Lautréamont et Mallarmé* (Paris: Editions du Seuil, 1974).

Letchimy, Serge, *De l'habitat précaire à la ville: l'exemple martiniquais* (Paris: L'Harmattan, 1992).

Licops, Dominique, 'Expériences diasporiques et migratoires des villes dans *La Vie scélérate* et *Desirada* de Maryse Condé', *Nottingham French Studies*, 39.1 (2000), pp. 110–20.

Lingis, Alphonso, *The Community of Those Who Have Nothing in Common* (Bloomington: Indiana University Press, 1994).

Lucrèce, André, *Société et modernité: essai d'interprétation de la société martiniquaise* (Case Pilote: Edition de l'autre mer, 1994).

Maximin, Daniel, *L'Isolé soleil* (Paris: Editions du Seuil, Collection Points, 1981).

— *Soufrières* (Paris: Editions du Seuil, Collection Points, 1987).

— *L'Ile et une nuit* (Paris: Editions du Seuil, 1995).

McCusker, Maeve, 'Telling Stories/Creating History: Patrick Chamoiseau's

Texaco', *ASCALF Year Book*, 3 (1998), pp. 23–33.

Ménil, René, 'Vincent Placoly s'en va: adieu, frère volcan', *Justice*, 2 (9 January 1992); reprinted in *Tranchées* (January 1993), pp. 11–12.

Michaux, Henri, *Face aux verrous* (Paris: Gallimard, 1954).

Milne, Lorna, *Patrick Chamoiseau: espaces d'une écriture antillaise*(Amsterdam: Rodopi, 2006).

Moudileno, Lydie, *L'écrivain antillais au miroir de sa littérature* (Paris: Karthala, 1997).

— 'Le Rire de la grand-mère: insolence et sérénité dans *Desirada* de Maryse Condé', *The French Review*, 76.6 (2003), pp. 1151–60.

Murdoch, H. Adlai, *Creole Identity in the French Caribbean Novel* (Gainesville: University Press of Florida, 2001).

Nancy, Jean-Luc, *The Inoperative Community* (Minneapolis: University of Minnesota Press, 1991).

— 'Of Being-in-Common', in Miami Theory Collective (ed.), *Community at Loose Ends* (Minneapolis: University of Minnesota Press, 1991), pp. 1–12.

— 'You ask me what it means today...', *Paragraph*, 16.2 (1992), pp. 108–10.

— *The Sense of the World* (Minneapolis: University of Minnesota Press, 1997).

— *Being Singular Plural* (Stanford, CA: Stanford University Press, 2000).

Nancy, Jean-Luc, and Philippe Lacoue-Labarthe, *Retreating the Political* (London: Routledge, 1997).

Nesbitt, Nick, *Voicing Memory: History and Subjectivity in French Caribbean Literature* (Charlottesville and London: University of Virginia Press, 2003).

Ormerod, Beverley, *An Introduction to the French Caribbean Novel* (London: Heinemann, 1983).

Oudin-Bastide, Caroline, '*Pluie et vent sur Télumée Miracle*: fatalisme et aliénation', *CARE*, 2 (1974), pp. 83–97.

Ousmane, Sembene, *O pays mon beau peuple* (Paris: Buchet-Chastel, 1957).

Pépin, Ernest, 'Proposition pour une lecture de *Gouverneurs de la rosée*', in GEREC (ed.), *Sur Gouverneurs de la rosée de Jacques Roumain (Textes, Etudes et Documents, 1)* (Paris: Editions Caribéennes, 1978), pp. 30–40.

— 'Le jeu des figures répétitives dans l'œuvre', in GEREC (ed.), *Sur Pluie et vent sur Télumée Miracle de Simone Schwarz-Bart (Textes, Etudes et Documents, 2)* (Paris: Editions Caribéennes, 1979), pp. 79–102.

Pfaff, Françoise, *Entretiens avec Maryse Condé* (Paris: Karthala, 1993).

Placoly, Vincent, *La Vie et la mort de Marcel Gonstran* (Paris: Denoël, 1971).

— *L'Eau-de-mort guildive* (Paris: Denoël, 1973).

— 'Interview avec A. Brossat et D. Maragnès', in Alain Brossat and Daniel Maragnès (eds.), *Les Antilles dans l'impasse? Des intellectuels antillais s'expliquent* (Paris: Editions Caribéennes, 1981), pp. 30–36.

— *Frères volcans* (Montreuil: Editions La Brèche, 1983).

— *Une journée torride. Essais, nouvelles* (Montreuil: Editions La Brèche, 1991).

— 'Contre le misérabilisme en littérature', *Tranchées* (January 1993), pp. 67–68.

Price, Richard, and Sally Price, 'Shadow-Boxing in the Mangrove', *Cultural Anthropology*, 12.1 (1997), pp. 3–36.

Ridon, Jean-Xavier, 'Maryse Condé et le fantôme d'une communauté inopérante', in Christiane Albert (ed.), *Francophonie et identités culturelles* (Paris: Karthala, 1999), pp. 213–26.

Rosello, Mireille, '*Pluie et vent sur Télumée Miracle*', *Présence francophone*, 36 (1990), pp. 73–90.

— *Littérature et identité aux Antilles* (Paris: Karthala, 1992).

Roumain, Jacques, 'La poésie, arme de combat', *Cahiers d'Haïti*, II.4 (1944), pp. 39–42.

— *Gouverneurs de la rosée* (Paris: Editions Messidor, 1991); originally published by Les Editeurs Français Réunis, 1946.

Scharfman, Ronnie, 'Rewriting the Césaires: Daniel Maximin's Caribbean Discourse', in Maryse Condé (ed.), *L'héritage de Caliban* (Pointe-à-Pitre: Editions Jasor, 1992), pp. 233–45.

— 'Au sujet d'héroïnes péripatétiques et peu sympathiques', in Madeleine Cottenet-Hage and Lydie Moudileno (eds.), *Maryse Condé: une nomade inconvenante* (Pointe-à-Pitre: Ibis Rouge Editions, 2002), pp. 141–48.

Schwarz-Bart, Simone, *Pluie et vent sur Télumée Miracle* (Paris: Editions du Seuil, 1972).

— 'Interview accordé à R. Toumson', in GEREC (ed.), *Sur Pluie et vent sur Télumée Miracle de Simone Schwarz-Bart (Textes, Etudes et Documents, 2)* (Paris: Editions Caribéennes, 1979), pp. 15–22.

Sellin, Eric, 'Pastoralism and Nostalgia in Jacques Roumain's *Gouverneurs de la rosée*', in R. Antoine (ed.), *Carrefours de culture: mélanges offerts à J. Leiner* (Tübingen: Gunter Narr Verlag, 1993), pp. 473–80.

Serres, Michel ,'Le Christ noir', *Critique*, 29 (1973), pp. 3–25.

Suvélor, Roland, 'Vincent Placoly ou le parcours inachevé', *Tranchées* (January 1993), pp. 14–17.

Toumson, Roger, '*Pluie et vent sur Télumée Miracle*: une rêverie ency-clopédique: sa structure, son projet idéologique', in GEREC (ed.), *Sur Pluie et vent sur Télumée Miracle de Simone Schwarz-Bart (Textes, Etudes et Documents, 2)* (Paris: Editions Caribéennes, 1979), pp. 25–73.

van den Abbeele, Georges, 'Introduction', in Miami Theory Collective (ed.), *Community at Loose Ends* (Minneapolis: University of Minnesota Press, 1991), pp. i–xxi.

Zimra, Clarisse, 'Tracées césairiennes dans *L'Isolé soleil*', in J. Leiner (ed.), *L'Athanor d'un alchimiste: Colloque international sur l'œuvre d'Aimé Césaire* (Paris: Editions Caribéennes, 1987), pp. 347–67.

— 'Introduction' to Daniel Maximin, *Lone Sun*, trans C. Zimra

(Charlottesville and London: University Press of Virginia, 1989), pp. xi–lix.

— 'Daughters of Mayotte, Sons of Frantz: The Unrequited Self in Caribbean Literature', in Sam Haigh (ed.), *An Introduction to Caribbean Francophone Writing: Guadeloupe and Martinique* (Oxford: Berg, 1999), pp. 177–94.

Index